RICHA
A BROTHI

David Jenkins, born eleven years earlier than his brother Richard, left school in his early teens to join the police force, rising eventually to the rank of chief inspector. He is now retired from the police force and is a widower living in South Wales, where he has lived for much of his life.

With Richard's blessing and encouragement he began to assemble a life of the actor for which Richard Burton intended to write a personal introduction. Since his brother's death in 1984, David has continued to record both his own recollections and those of his family in order to present to the world the Richard they all knew.

RICHARD BURTON – A BROTHER REMEMBERED

David Jenkins
with Sue Rogers

ARROW

This edition published by Arrow Books Limited 1994

1 3 5 7 9 10 8 6 4 2

First published in the United Kingdom in 1993 by
Century
Random House UK Ltd, 20 Vauxhall Bridge Road,
London SW1V 2SA

Arrow Books Ltd
Random House UK Ltd, 20 Vauxhall Bridge Road,
London SW1V 2SA

Random House Australia (Pty) Limited
20 Alfred Street, Milsons Point, Sydney,
New South Wales 2061, Australia

Random House New Zealand Limited
18 Poland Road, Glenfield
Auckland 10, New Zealand

Random House South Africa (Pty) Limited
PO Box 337, Bergvlei, South Africa

Random House UK Limited Reg No 954009

A CIP catalogue record for this book
is available from the British Library

ISBN 0 09 925571 5

Printed and bound in Great Britain by
Cox & Wyman, Reading, Berks

Contents

To my dear sister Cis, queen of the Jenkins family, who died just before this book went to press.

Acknowledgements

Perhaps I ought to explain why I started writing in the first place. Initially I had no intention of writing for publication, despite Samuel Johnson's dictum 'No man but a blockhead ever wrote, except for money'. After I retired from full-time employment, I merely wanted to occupy my time writing about my family so that my grandchildren could read about us long after we had gone. We were a formidable family with seven boys (almost a pack of rugby forwards) and four girls. I felt a particular pleasure in writing about the individual characters. This was in 1981, some three years before Richard died.

Later, friends suggested I should write about Richard's life. Richard was aware of this project and spoke to me about it at his home in Haiti in December 1983, eight months before he died. He suggested that when I finished the book I should bring it to his villa at Céligny, near Geneva, so that he could read it and write an introduction. His sudden and untimely death ruled this out.

This book then, is the result of a ten-year project which reflects Richard Burton from a brother's perspective. I have not intended to write a detached comprehensive biography, but rather a memoir of a maverick character who never failed to surprise and delight his family.

I came to feel very strongly that no one, except recently Melvyn Bragg, had done justice to my legendary and charismatic brother. He was one of the greatest Shakespearian actors of his generation and without doubt one of the finest raconteurs in the world; he was also a man of great complexity of character, whose talents lay rooted very much in his Welsh origins, to which he was unflaggingly loyal. As a witness to his childhood, and as one who knew him well through the triumphs and turmoils of his unparalleled career, I have aimed at revealing the real Richard

Burton, who was sometimes misunderstood and misrepresented by those who hardly knew him at all.

I have endeavoured to describe in some detail both the large close family into which Richard was born and our way of life in Wales almost seventy years ago, as I believe that these had the greatest possible impact on Richard's subsequent development.

I would like to pay tribute to the following who have provided me with invaluable information and stories about Richard's life: my three sisters (Cis) Cecilia James, Hilda Owen, Cassie Jenkins; my brother Verdun Jenkins; my nieces Rhianon Trowell, Marian Mastroianni, Megan Owen and Siân Owen; and my great nephew Guy Masterson-Mastroianni who has contributed a special memory of his own. I am also grateful to the following: Jane Bekheit; Philip Burton; Sally Burton; the late Professor Nevill Coghill; Paul Daneman; Barbara Davies; Susie Denby (nee Preece); Meredith Evans; Christopher Fry; Sir John Gielgud; Robert (Tim) Hardy; Maggie Nichols; the late Sir Anthony Quayle; Ibo Kent St George; Andrew Sinclair; Mair Thomas; Brook Williams; the late Emlyn Williams; the Reverend Eric Williams and Rhydwen Williams.

In addition to those who kindly shared their recollections of my brother with me, I am also grateful to those authors whose books have thrown light on diverse aspects of Richard's life, amongst them Philip Burton, Fergus Cashin, Paul Ferris and Penny Junor; and of course Melvyn Bragg, whose comprehensive and meticulously researched *Rich* added greatly to my understanding of Richard's career, especially his films. For the background to *Cleopatra*, and *Boom!* I am indebted to Harry and Michael Medved's entertaining work, *The Hollywood Hall of Shame*.

I would like to thank Roderick Brown for his excellent editing and coordination in the final stages; Edie Conway and Dave Rogers for their hard work in typing and correcting the original manuscript; Andrea Henry for her cheerful attention to detail; and my agent Elspeth Cochrane and my publisher Mark Booth for having such faith in my long-cherished project.

Perhaps most important of all, I owe a special debt of gratitude to my daughter Sue who has painstakingly edited my work.

Sally Burton; *The Magic of Meredith Jones* by Richard Burton (pp47–49) is reproduced by kind permission of *The Sunday Times*, London and Sally Burton; *Meeting Mrs Jenkins* by Richard Burton (pp72–79) is reproduced by kind permission of Sally Burton; the extract from *The Last Time I Played Rugby* by Richard Burton (pp88–94) is reproduced by kind permission of *The Observer*, © *The Observer*, London, 4 October 1970; the piece by R.H. Case on Shakespeare's *Anthony and Cleopatra* (pp113–114) comes from the Arden Shakespeare edition of 1906; *The Trials of Travel With Liz* by Richard Burton (pp143–146) is reproduced by kind permission of *The Observer*, London; the extract from Gabriel Byrne's article on the making of *Wagner* (pp182–184), originally published in *Image*, is reproduced by kind permission of Gabriel Byrne/The Aquarius Literary Agency; extracts from an interview Richard gave to journalist David Lewin (pp186–187) are reproduced by kind permission of its author; the speech by the late Emlyn Williams (pp238–243) is reproduced by kind permission of his literary executors.

Photographic Acknowledgements, 1 *Swansea Evening Post*; 2, 4, 20, 23 The Jenkins family; 5 Susie Denby; 8, 11, 12, 21, 27 Rex Features; 13 Movie Portraits; 9 Harlech Television/Arfon Haines-Davies; 15 London Features International Ltd; 16 The Hulton-Deutsch Picture Library; 17 *The Taming of the Shrew* Production Company; 18 *The Daily Express*; 24 Valerie Douglas; 25 Verdun Jenkins; 26 Douglas Morrison/*The Daily Express*.

Every effort has been made to obtain permission to use material in copyright, but the author apologises to anyone whose material may have inadvertently been used without prior permission.
                                        David Jenkins, 1993.

Introduction

When we consider the appraisals, criticisms, reviews and biographies written about Richard Burton, we are reminded of the measure of the man and realise that his greatness has still not been adequately accounted for.

Some lose their way in the early beginnings; others fail in dealing with the towering presence and the voice; still others are obsessed with the legendary inebriate and lover.

As a chronicler of Burton, David Jenkins has many advantages. He is a brother, born into the same family of the same parents, often sharing the same bed and always the same table. As such he is equipped – and eager – to erase misconceptions; he is amply equipped to inform – things only a brother could know.

If he has any disadvantage, it is only the disadvantage of passionate brotherly affection. Unashamedly biased, he writes in the heat of genuine filial loyalty as warm as the blood in his veins.

David Jenkins has a fascinating story to tell; this is more than another biography. It is a testament of quiet pride in the career of an outstanding Welshman and a still more outstanding brother who had to bid farewell to family, friends and admirers the world over far too soon.

Rhydwen Williams: Poet and novelist; Crown Award for Poetry 1946 and 1964; Arts Council Award for Best Novel 1986 and 1989; Daniel Owen Award 1986; Fellowship Welsh Academy of Writers, 1989; Honorary MA (Open University); Honorary MA University of Wales.

Chapter One

The family from the valleys

The mountains have changed more than the village since we were
children. Once bare of trees, a vast free playground for us, they
are now thickly planted with conifers, gold Japanese spruce and
Sitkas with sharp blue-green needles. Where we ran and chased
one another, walkers and picnickers now dutifully observe the
paths of the Forestry Commission.

Our home was Pontrhydyfen (the name probably means
'Bridge over the Ford in the River Afan'). A small, untidy mining
village, it is pressed against rounded flanks of the mountains and
folded into the steep-sided Afan Valley, five miles north of the
smoking industrial steel town of Port Talbot in West Glamorgan,
South Wales. The village, all grey local stone, is completely
dwarfed by a four-arched bridge striding huge and high above it,
unimpeded by anything, even the presence of its only possible
rivals, the Chapels. This is the *Bont Fawr*, originally an aqueduct
built some two hundred years ago to take water to the growing
industrial areas to the south. Pontrhydyfen has been described as
bleak and sunless, and, true, the mountains do loom in a dour way
on overcast, dull days, but there is also a rugged, melancholy
beauty to the place often noted with surprise by visitors, and
absorbed – how far? – into the characters and temperaments of the
inhabitants.

Although Welsh was the first language of everyone in
Pontrhydyfen, children and teachers alike, lessons at the village
school were usually conducted in English. Nonetheless, Welsh
predominated in the playground, and when it did make itself
heard in the classroom from time to time, it was without the sense
of shame and official disapproval so powerfully conveyed in
Richard Llewellyn's classic novel of Welsh life, *How Green Was
My Valley*. Things are different now. Since 1954, there has been a
separate Welsh primary school in the village, drawing children

1

from a very wide catchment area, a reflection of the need to preserve our language and culture in a world dominated by conformity. Richard would have approved of that.

Another fundamental change in Pontrhydyfen, so typical of villages throughout the country, was the loss of the village shop, the old heart of the community. The Co-operative Stores was the scene of the traditional Friday shopping – Friday was pay day, and my mother received all the wage packets, so that, amongst other things, she could arrange for our rent to be paid. Carrying the fugitive scents of flour, polish and wood, the shop was where our mothers and older sisters exchanged news, gossip, speculation, recipes, cures, you name it.

The two sources of employment were the coal mines, both long closed: the local Oakwood colliery, and the Powell Dyffryn colliery a few miles north of the village. By the 1920s prospects were gloomy. Migration to towns in England to find better paid, more secure employment became common (four of my cousins left the area, for example, to become doctors or teachers) and together with the decrease in family size, it re-shaped the village: not so many children to run over the mountains even if they were allowed.

Poverty and hardship did not always predominate – certainly not for us younger children, free of the overwhelming sense of responsibility that oppressed our elders. We were only too aware that there were other families worse off than we were. Nevertheless, the more I reflect on his background the more unlikely it seems that Richard should have emerged and developed as he did.

My mother was first a mother at eighteen and was last a mother days before her death aged forty-three in 1927. Even by standards of the time, there were a lot of us. Had they all lived, Richard would have had as many siblings as Christ had disciples. As the youngest-but-one, Richard never knew what it was to lack a horde of loving older brothers and sisters. This was a family to be brought together on so many occasions important to the adult Richard; a family to be fretted about, written to, telephoned at all hours, day or night; a family to whom he was ceaselessly generous – all this stems, I believe, from the circumstances of his birth, from a life crowded with affection.

Richard Walter Jenkins, a miner, married Edith Thomas, then a barmaid, on Christmas Eve 1900; he was twenty-four, his bride seventeen. The first child, Tom, was born in 1901; a daughter who died in infancy was born in 1903; she was named Margaret Hannah. Cecilia – always Cis – came in 1905. A year later there was Ivor in 1906. Another daughter, also named Margaret Hannah, was born, and died very soon after birth, in 1908. Then three more boys: William in 1911, myself in 1914 and Verdun (named patriotically after the World War One battlefield in Northern France) in 1916. Hilda was next, born in 1918, Catherine (always Cassie) followed suit in 1921 and Edith (always Edie) in 1922. Richard himself came into the world in 1925, and the last of us, Graham, was born in 1927.

My father was a short, strongly-built man, with intelligent brown eyes, and a gentle manner. He was born at Efail Fach, a part of Pontrhydyfen where *his* father, Thomas, kept the mill. Large families prevailed then, but his only sibling was a sister, Jane. The contrast between his upbringing and that of the thirteen children he fathered must have been great indeed, and may partly account for the difficulty he had in coping with the responsibilities of parenthood, particularly after my mother's untimely death. He spent most of his working life in the mines, though later he become a plate-layer with the old Great Western Railway.

A one-line portrait: he was a miner and he drank. I would love to be able to contest the much-publicised accounts of my father's devotion to drink, but apart from stressing that they are exaggerated, I cannot do so. It seemed to me as I grew older that my father's main interest was alcohol, and I have memories which hurt me still of my mother, and later of my sister Cis, pleading with him to cut down on the drinking bouts, or to come straight home after collecting the unemployment benefit known as the 'dole'.

Watching these scenes, these arguments, these pleas, and feeling the sadness and exasperation that went with them, something akin to contempt for father grew in us. I certainly remember the shame and disgust his drunkenness made me feel, even as a young lad. Sometimes I thought he was plain silly, such as when, in his cups, he would sing to my mother or chatter inanely at her, mouthing exaggerated endearments. It is tempting to idealise my mother as the pure selfless one, devoted to children and home, and to condemn my father for his self-absorption and

3

..., and his humiliation of his family. She rarely, if ever,
...d her total subjugation to the family and devotion to
..., the idea of her doing something for her own pleasure was
...e alien to her.

The pub was the miner's solace, his escape from life in the pits.
My brief spell underground made me determined to get away.
Mining is hardly pleasant now, but was far worse then, with no
pithead baths, and instead of today's safety lamps candles whose
naked flame sometimes triggered off gas explosions. My father
was comparatively lucky the day his flame found a pocket of gas:
he survived, though he was blown unconscious, and suffered many
serious burns to his face, chest and legs, from which it took him
many weeks to recover.

There were times when my father would be overcome with
remorse, when he would make a solemn promise not to drink for a
month, and keep it. What a wonderful change in the atmosphere!
Instead of the whisperings and the anxious peerings through the
window, there would be noisy cheerfulness and sober singing. My
oldest sister's voice was particularly lovely – they used to say she had
a bell in every tooth. Richard as a toddler must surely have been
aware of, and affected by, these changes of atmosphere, even if the
exact cause was incomprehensible to one so young.

Still, however drunk he was, I do not remember him ever laying
a hand on any of us. He was never aggressive unless someone – a
friend, an acquaintance – deliberately challenged him when he
had been drinking.

There was also a lighter side to life with him. He was a
humorous man and a great story-teller, and we loved to sit and
hear him when he was sober and calm, delighting us with his wild
exaggerations. He would revel in holding a room with a highly
embellished anecdote. Little Richard would sit on his knee for
hours, absorbed.

Then there was father's sentimental side. He had a beautiful
tenor voice and loved to sing folk songs, Welsh and Irish. One of
his party pieces was to sing and dramatise the many verses of a
Welsh favourite, *Gelert The Dog*, about a medieval prince who
slays his dog in the mistaken belief that it has killed his child.
Whenever he performed this epic, my father could always reduce
my sisters to tears.

4

He could be carried away by sudden, sporadic enthusiasms. Once, when our financial situation was particularly bad, he came home with a semi-blind, toothless greyhound that could hardly stand, and attached to whose feeble leg was a piece of rafia string – not that there was the remotest possibility of its having the energy to escape. Father paused at the doorway, looked at my mother and the rest of us, and declared with theatrical flourish, 'Boys [he always said this] all your troubles are over.' We exchanged wry glances.

A favourite pastime was the study of horse-racing, in which he became quite an expert. It was nothing for him to spend a week at the Derby, family commitments thrown to the wind. On the rare occasions he won there was a grand spree, much to my mother's mortification.

My sister Hilda recalls that when my father was unemployed he would cheerfully volunteer to do household chores for her. This was a ploy; he needed a few shillings for his beer. When she paid him, he would always remind her that when he died there should be neither flowers nor mourning; all the family should celebrate with a good meal. Drink was not mentioned, however; even my father forbore to advocate alcohol for a funeral.

During the last part of his life, when the need for escape had perhaps subsided, my father mellowed considerably and drank a lot less. He became a contented old man, a quiet figure by the hearth. And he remained solidly Welsh always, even when the English language began to creep into village life. He would think us snobbish if we turned up speaking English.

My mother was seen by the rest of us as little less than an angel. She was born on 29 January 1882 at Llangyfelach, near Swansea, into a poor mining family – though one of her brothers later rose to be colliery manager, a coveted post. She was the youngest of five and was working as a barmaid at sixteen when she met my father.

She was a tall, beautiful woman, and her gentle maternalism extended to my father as well as to the rest of us. She was the guiding force for the entire family. I often overheard her telling neighbours that all she hoped for in life was that she would live long enough to rear her children. Her fear was not groundless – it was not unusual for women to die before they were fifty, especially if they had borne many children.

5

She felt a deep distress at not being able to pay the bills or the ten shilling rent. I can remember my frustration when my father would walk to Cwmavon, where the Unemployment Exchange was, to collect his weekly dole money – one pound ten shillings. You could buy a lot of food for this money, but he, as I say, would spend some of it in the pubs on his way home. I know I was only a child, but I was well aware of my mother's alarm and tenseness, constantly looking out through the kitchen window to see if there was any sign of him coming up the road. Eleven, twelve, one o'clock would strike, and there was still no sign. Eventually, after an eternity of waiting, he would turn up after closing time, having spent a good deal of the precious dole money on drink.

We all worried about mother, but for some reason she confided in me. She suffered immense agony of mind and I was conscious of it the whole time. She could not bear to go to the stores or landlord herself to explain that funds were short, and would ask one of us to go instead. We disliked it, but would not dream of refusing her.

As may be imagined, my mother had a deep dread of alcohol and would talk to us, often at length, about the evils of drink. We were deeply affected and our attitude, even as adults, was shaped by her words. As a young police constable I caused a sensation in Barry Dock Police Station when I admitted that I had never been in a public house. This at the advanced age of twenty-two, and in South Wales!

For many years, indeed, there was an unspoken agreement among us children that no one would drink in our native village. It was of paramount importance to preserve the image that our mother presented to the world.

And what of the children of this match? We were – are – a tough, sturdy, outgoing bunch. The introverted, more reflective side inherited or absorbed from our mother was present in some, Richard among them, more than others; but to all appearances we were extrovert and self-reliant.

Tom was strong, kindly, fatherly, with a wry sense of humour. Of Cis, I need only say that she was a second mother not only to Richard but to us all. She had my mother's selflessness, but with greater spirit and a keen sense of justice. Perhaps even in those

6

days a daughter could express her feelings less inhibitedly than a wife.

Ivor was physically the biggest and strongest, and he slotted in to the role of natural leader, particularly after our mother's death. Nicknamed 'King Farouk' or 'Ivor Stern' by Hilda, he ruled the household with the proverbial firm hand.

All the boys but Will had been given two Christian names; he carefully noted the omission, and later added his own to become William Denver. My mother called him the 'Happy Wanderer' – he was the roamer of the family, leaving the mine as soon as he could to join the army. I remember he used to wear seven waistcoats as a boy – all at once! – and was inevitably known as 'Will Waistcoat'.

I shared Will's desire to escape the drudgery of the pits and joined the Metropolitan Police Force in October 1934, later returning to Wales. I always had a strong desire to improve my lot and sweated over the police promotion exams. My interest in the police service had been roused one day when the local police officer was standing outside our home, and my father said to me in Welsh, 'Do you realise that the local policeman will be able to retire when he is forty-five years old on half pension or after thirty years with a full pension?' This stuck in my mind, and I made up my mind there and then to join the police service. I was not going to bury myself working hard in the coal mine down in the bowels of the earth with *no pension*.

Verdun left the mine to become a fitter technician in the Port Talbot steel works, and in his spare time worked at his other talents – horticulturist, artist, singer, compère, entertainer and comic. When Richard visited us in Wales during the last twelve years of his life, bringing Susan, then later Sally, he made a point of placing his wife opposite Verdun during dinner. The ploy never failed; no matter how nervous the newcomer, she was immediately put at ease by Verdun's manner.

Hilda is the only one of us who has spent her whole life in Pontrhydyfen. She was the oldest girl at home when our mother died. Her irresistible sense of fun was tempered but never dimmed by tragedy and premature responsibility; resilience carried her through.

Cassie was an open, attractive child, always popular with Ivor because she was so honest and rarely initiated any mischief, though she was inclined to follow the others' lead. She was the only one of the girls to work outside the home for much of her adult life, as a nurse.

Edie, a year younger, was reserved and unassuming, quite different from the other two. Only five when our mother died, she suffered deeply. The three girls clung together for mutual support and formed a bond which lasted a lifetime. Edie, unlike the others, was never strong and as a young adult developed heart trouble. She died at forty-four after an unsuccessful operation. It is curious that, apart from the two baby girls and Ivor, who had a tragic accident in his sixties, the only ones to die prematurely were the two named after our parents, Edie and Richard.

Richard was born in 1925, and then there was Graham, the last born and still regarded affectionately as the baby of the family. Villagers used to recall my mother's initial despair when she found, a year after Richard's birth, that she was pregnant again. 'Another mouth to feed. God almighty.' And she broke under the strain; the baby was motherless at five days old, but mercifully there was a big brother – Tom – and his wife to take him in. Graham grew and thrived with them in neighbouring Cwmavon. Tom, thought by many to be his father, nurtured him with care and ensured that, like Richard, he would not follow his older brothers down the mine. Ability and charm have always co-existed in Graham, the most like Richard in appearance and mannerism. He moved up steadily in the public relations field and became manager of the Afan Lido in Port Talbot, later settling for a time with the BBC Sports Department.

The chapel was the core of our social and spiritual lives. *Our* chapel – there were three in our small village – was Bethel, the Welsh Baptist. There we would go for the morning and evening services, and for Sunday School in the afternoon. We never questioned it – it was an accepted part of our lives.

Sermons, today relatively tame affairs, were then delivered with a sense of the dramatic worthy of any actor. The minister's voice would at first be perfectly modulated and well controlled. Then slowly, deliberately, the full repertoire of his oratory would be revealed. At the height of his delivery he would ask a question as if he expected a response from the congregation. Then, with theatrical fervour, he would repeat the question with greater emphasis. Sometimes it seemed that his penetrating look and his finger were directed specifically at me. The effect was devastating. I could not have stood or spoken if my life had depended on it! Then suddenly, to my great relief, he would lower his powerful voice almost to a whisper and answer the question himself. The preacher often punctuated his sermon by recalling the names of four or five Welsh literary giants, afterwards repeating in English, 'wonderful company, wonderful company!' Thus he allowed himself a breathing space before continuing with the flow of rhetoric.

In summer, we would all swelter in our 'Sunday best', and the longer the minister preached, the hotter he became, until huge beads of perspiration dripped onto his collar. Eventually he would take his large pocket handkerchief and wipe his brow. It was a masterful performance.

My mother was the chapel-goer. I cannot recall my father ever attending, though he was not irreligious; he believed in the teachings of the Chapel and was an avid Bible- reader. To everyone's astonishment, seven ministers of religion turned up for his funeral!

Easter Monday, as everywhere in Wales, heralded spring with the *Gymanfa Ganu* – a major annual singing festival for which chapels of the same denomination would join together. Rehearsals of the programme would begin months ahead and a near-professional performance would draw tears of emotion from the congregation – all active participators, of course – and, afterwards, deep sighs of relief from the young reciters and singers.

More important still for children was the Whitsun Festival – another explosion òf song and jubilation. Chapels of every denomination would assemble outside the local school for singing, after which we all marched through the village with great pomp and pride. Then we would return to the chapel vestry for a high tea, an event in itself. Immediately afterwards we would retire to our respective fields. Members of Jerusalem Chapel would assemble in one field north of the chapel, and members of my chapel would meet in a field on the other side of the village and

9

play games: three-legged races, sprinting, dancing and scrambling for sweets thrown from a box.

Again there were months of preparation – my mother would bend devotedly over the sewing machine, to complete my sisters' traditional white dresses and the sailor-suits for us boys. It was of paramount importance that the sun should shine on the great day, and anxiety banished sleep for nights beforehand.

The first of our houses, where eleven of the thirteen children were born, was in a small stone terrace at the end of the *Bont Fawr*. There were twelve houses (ten of them long since demolished as unfit for human habitation) and I can still remember all the families who lived there – like us, they were miners' children. We had two rooms downstairs and two bedrooms; I shared one with three of my brothers, and my three sisters shared the other with my parents. Our oldest brother Tom married and left home for neighbouring Cwmavon when we were very young; our oldest sister Cis used to lodge with the Handfords, a family of drapers, for whom she worked as a housemaid, in Taibach, a suburb of Port Talbot five miles away to the south. She later married and settled there.

There we were, like the proverbial sardines in a tin. As the family out-grew the house, my mother busied herself with arrangements to move to a bigger one. We were fortunate now in having both father and Ivor in full-time employment, so we could afford the new rent of ten shillings a week – and eventually, in 1924, off we went, to number 2 Dan y Bont (the name means 'under the bridge'), the house where Richard would be born. This was like a mansion by comparison – it had three storeys and there were *three* bedrooms, two large and one small. My parents, and later, baby Richard, had one large room to themselves – we rarely entered – and two beds in the other housed the three girls and the three boys respectively. Ivor had the luxury of the small room to himself.

Downstairs there were two reception rooms and the kitchen. We could afford to furnish only one, the parlour, maintained in a remarkably pristine condition – doubtless because it was rarely used – with a polished table, chest of drawers, chair and settee, and a few family photos. The unfurnished room we used for

10

boxing and other games. The one blessing known to a miner's family – free coal – was stored in an underground room, under the front room. Finally, there was a gloomy nondescript room below the kitchen, where the workers of the family would bath when they got home, filthy, from work and where mother did all our washing by hand.

Family life centred around the kitchen, my mother's domain. There were two wooden tables, one round for the children, one square for our parents and the older ones – at fourteen, the school-leaving age, we moved up to the square table and were considered grown up. There was barely room for us all to eat together, though with much effort, this was achieved on Sundays.

Then and the rest of the week mother ensured that there was food in the pantry. We all had enormous appetites; but the children, at least, never went hungry. I remember well the delicious, traditional Welsh stews she used to make; and the tarts, pastry rolled out on a flat plate – she made three of those every day. Occasionally in summer, mother made up picnics which we ate on the mountain sides. Our joy sprang less from the picnic basket than from the supreme pleasure of having her to ourselves in the open, away from the pressures of home, which weighed so heavily on her.

Our entertainments and pleasures were simple. Mostly, of course, we children played outside: pavement games; the rugby ground for the boys; roaming on the mountains, setting up 'camp' with tents made of sugarbags; river-swimming. . . I can hardly doubt that more responsibility fell to the girls, though tasks were divided and allotted in the typical way – girls in the kitchen; boys fetching coal, chopping wood.

Winter evenings were spent in the kitchen, where it was warm; we might not have had the parlour at all. We took *John Bull* weekly, and in my eagerness to learn to spell I used to plague my sister Hilda to give me dictation tests from it. I also insisted on testing my three sisters until they were sick of the sight of *John Bull*. Father loved his treat, the *News of the World* on Sunday, and would regale us by reading out descriptions of the most brutal murders he could find.

There was no wireless set at home, so on days when there was an international rugby match we would troop up to the landlord's quarters at The Miners' Arms to listen to the match, though never in a thousand years would we be allowed in the bar!

I have tried, in these brief paragraphs, to call up those images of a Welsh childhood which are most relevant to understanding Richard's background. Many details have to be left out, but I hope that the essentials are there: a close, loving family, aware of, but not truly menaced by poverty; full of incidental joys and enthusiasms; facing its difficulties (drink) and its tragedies (death) with some unyielding sense of being together. If anything was given to Richard, it was that feeling of belonging.

Chapter Two

Richard's first years

So Richard was born at 2 Dan-y-Bont, Pontrhydyfen, on 10 November 1925. When it was first made known to a film-going public that he had been born at this address, a number of people claimed that his birthplace was a much smaller terraced house in Station Road; was he therefore trying to lay claim to superior origins? The family have always found this idea amusing. Far from playing down his humble background, if anything he over-emphasised it, causing us to remind him that there were, after all, people far worse off than we had ever been.

Richard was born in a bleak winter – 1925 was a cold year. It was the eve of Armistice Day, when the glow of patriotic pride felt for the fallen of a war only seven years gone and the ceremony of Remembrance would hold off, just briefly, the painful realities of falling pay, massive unemployment, hunger, and the dreaded tuberculosis. This was the area with the highest mortality rate in the country.

What were the chances, then, for this baby, twelfth in a struggling mining family? A solid, robust twelve pounds infant, he was welcomed – another boy after nine years and three girls, and a healthy one at that. The girls doted on him and cossetted him; in fact we all made a great fuss of him. As a baby he was carried around almost continuously on my mother's body. It was the custom then for mothers to tuck babies into a large shawl which they then wrapped carefully round themselves, so that the baby was safely held in the folds of material against the bosom. The last baby to be breastfed freely, he used to bite the breast wickedly from time to time and was smacked – the only instance of corporal punishment I can recall from of our childhood. On other occasions my mother would show her displeasure by putting him down, but there was invariably someone ready to pick him up again. We all found him irresistible and no doubt were inclined to spoil him, as

13

far as a child can be spoilt when he is the twelfth born and there are still nine other mouths in the house to feed.

My father used to smoke an old clay pipe which he had bought from Port Talbot market for a penny. I found its smell repulsive, but as a toddler Richard loved to observe him carefully, and whenever he had a chance would pick up this old clay pipe and pretend to smoke it. He had a delighted audience before he was even two.

He was not an angelic child. At any opportunity he would get up to mischief and I suppose we encouraged it. He was physically attractive and loved to show off, and might have been heading for precociousness. But tragedy intervened and his life was turned upside down.

Our mother had borne for many years, virtually single-handed, the burden of family responsibility, sometimes going without food to provide for her children. Because of the pressures of her life, she had grown physically and emotionally weaker; by the time baby Graham was born, in late October 1927, she was seriously run down. We sensed that all was not well, but mother had had so many babies before, and had always returned to her place, centre stage in the household – usually the kitchen – after her brief withdrawal to the bedroom, so we were not seriously alarmed at first.

Then, on the morning of 31 October, there was suddenly a frightening atmosphere in the house. I can remember the confused, fearful feelings I had, unable to understand exactly what was going on, certain only of the magnitude of the ill-defined disaster. The doctor and midwife, my father and Cis (married and now with a home elsewhere) were rushing about the house in a state of confused preoccupation.

I was the only child in the house that morning. About nine o'clock my father came falteringly down the stairs and I realised with mounting horror that he was saying to me, '*Mae dy fam wedi marw.*' Your mother has died.

Our mother had been everything to us. Her death was the end of our world, and I do not think I have ever fully recovered from that day. Gradually the house filled with people until by the evening it was packed – this was the Welsh custom of filling all spaces after a death, of bringing endless plates of food, of listening to the

14

bereaved going over the events; all therapeutic perhaps. But our spirit was broken.

Richard, mercifully, had been taken off by Verdun for the morning for a piggyback ride on the mountain side, so he was spared the initial panic and anguish, so terrifying to a small child. All of us were kept safely out of the way of the funeral; we were cushioned, over-protected perhaps, from the immediate reality of our mother's death.

Reality it was, however, and although at first there was a constant flow of helpers, aunts and neighbours and cousins – it seemed the whole village was rallying round – we had to find some way of coping.

One thing was certain: the two youngest children could not stay at home with the rest of the family. So Tom and his wife Cassie took Graham to their home in neighbouring Cwmavon, a few miles south on the road to Port Talbot, and Cis and husband Elfed took Richard with them to Taibach, a northern suburb of Port Talbot itself. Cis said later that she had hoped from the beginning that she could have Richard, since she had always been half in love with him and sensed that the feeling was mutual. It was. Richard's adoration of his big sister was probably the one thing that enabled him to cope with such a traumatic transition. His mother had suddenly vanished; his father and brothers and sisters were still floundering in their own grief, and he was being uprooted from his Welsh home to a quite separate community, one which was mostly English-speaking, where even his sister's husband spoke Welsh only rarely. He needed Cis, as well as the rest of us, and from the first, he was to be a welcome regular visitor to his old home.

Life in Pontrhydyfen had to continue. My father was too shaken by his loss to assume full responsibility, so it was Ivor, now twenty-one, who came to the rescue, postponing his marriage to do so; he took command of us – even my father was somewhat in awe of him. Hilda, at ten, took up the traditional role of the oldest girl-at-home and did the daily chores and much of the shopping.

Ivor worked in the mine. He was strong, tough and bristling with confidence. He discovered that my mother had left debts of three hundred pounds. It was she who had always handled the finances: my father was concerned only if there was no money for his beer, so he probably knew nothing of this debt. It now became a matter of honour to repay the three hundred pounds and thereby remove the stigma from the family.

Clearing it was to take years – formative years in which the principle of staying in credit was instilled into us. Many have stuck to it for a lifetime; even Richard was obsessive about never borrowing. So the weekly pay packets brought home by Will and myself were routinely handed to Ivor each Friday. Hilda was responsible for seeing that all the groceries were correctly recorded in the Co-op book, which Ivor meticulously inspected every evening.

Still, Hilda was fearless enough, if her need was great, to think up all manner of schemes to outwit him. She had never owned a watch, but had noticed that there was a brand new display of ladies' watches in the Co-op, and dearly wanted one for herself. The cost? A prohibitive eight shillings and sixpence. The arrangement with a sympathetic aunt working there was that no entry would be made in the Co-op book as long as Hilda paid the weekly sum of one shilling. She managed this for six weeks and then was rushed to hospital with acute appendicitis – and two weeks left to run. Cassie was to take over the payments. Double calamity – there was no money, so Cassie, with sinking heart, was forced to explain all to Ivor. Questioned in her hospital bed, Hilda had to confess that for six weeks she had added sixpence to the cost of the Sunday joint, threepence to the laverbread and threepence to the eggs, thus clearing one shilling for the watch. My father, Cassie and Edie had been involved in the scheme. Ivor, appalled, immediately confiscated the watch and returned it to the Co-op, lecturing Hilda on the evils of her devious and extravagant ways.

About twenty years later the family were all staying at Richard and Sybil's Geneva home. Hilda held the floor one night relating the episode of the watch. Ivor grew visibly more and more uncomfortable as it unfolded – Richard, it seemed, had never heard it before. He was a great stirrer, and loved to see Ivor in a tight corner. He had a pretty shrewd idea of how the family had been ruled in his infancy, and of how Ivor's cautious approach – to put it politely – had remained throughout his adult life. (Questioned once in a television interview about his brother, Richard declared that if Ivor had a mouthful of ulcers, he would not part with one of them.) The day after Hilda's recitation, Ivor marched off to a classy Geneva jeweller's and bought his sister a brand new gold watch.

Perhaps Ivor's conscience over the watch incident was the more pricked because of his own treasure-trove which he used to keep in the airing cupboard, under a pile of shirts. Hilda and Cassie knew of its existence quite early but did not let on. Rulers, it seemed, had their own special exemption laws. Despite his tyrannical ways, I believe he cared deeply about the family, though his occasional heavy-handedness made him very unpopular with Hilda, Edith and Verdun from time to time. My father was a figure of reduced status, pottering about the house when he was there, not greatly missed when he was not. He seemed to accept that Ivor was in charge, and never quibbled about his dictates.

Whatever the shortcomings of the old home and its motherless régime, Richard loved to visit it whenever he could. Away in Taibach he pined for Pontrhydyfen for some years, though I am sure he would have opted to stay with his sister had he been forced to choose between the two family homes. The links between Taibach and Pontrhydyfen were unbreakable, but in maintaining them, Cis was leading an almost impossible life. Just married (to Elfed, a young miner whom she had met through Chapel while working for the draper in Taibach), as well as trying to fulfil the traditional role of the miner's wife, she had the full-time care of her little brother and a great weight of worry over the rest of her family, five miles down the valley. In a valiant attempt to meet the needs of all (except perhaps herself) she struggled to keep both homes going. Every week, and at first even more often, she would take Richard back to the family home and set about putting it in order. She said later that she used to look about her in despair when she arrived, not knowing how or where to begin. I find myself thinking, chastened, that my own recollections of the discipline and the tricks played are all very well, but Cis saw the basics: mounds of unwashed clothes, dirty floors and a poorly-stocked larder.

She used to start by cleaning up, Richard trailing along after her, and then make some food to supply the family for at least a little while after she had gone. The washing she would take back to

Taibach on the village bus – twopence each way. More than once she missed it and had to walk all the way, half carrying her little brother and dragging the laundry bag.

And when she got home there was no real relief. Her marriage was still new, and the partners had to adjust not only to each other but to the physical and emotional pressures which sprang from that motherless home down the road. Elfed worried that his young wife was wearing herself into the ground and exhorted her to do less, but it was impossible for her to comply. So she found a compromise: she continued as before, but without telling her husband. The laundry basket would be carefully hidden at a neighbour's house until Elfed had gone to the pit, then she and Richard would go to collect it. Thus the washing and the whole painstaking cycle continued.

Richard was openly bewildered by it all. It seemed to him that they were complicating their lives for no reason. Over and over he would say to his sister in Welsh, 'Why can't we all go and live in Pontrhydyfen? Then you won't have to go back and fore and work so hard.' Cis would soothe him and explain as best she could. But deep down his dream was also hers, and she saw it as the solution to many of their problems.

Eventually, but without much hope, she gathered enough courage to discuss such a move with Elfed. To her astonishment and delight, he agreed. We could not contain our delight and Ivor and the boys began working away at the house, preparing two rooms for the separate use of Cis, Elfed and Richard. Then there was a hitch.

Elfed's mother and others in his family expressed their doubts that such an arrangement could possibly work. How could any marriage survive in such cramped conditions? Elfed thought hard about the whole thing, and finally decided against it. With hindsight, it probably was the best decision, but we were bitterly disappointed at the time.

'I cried for a fortnight,' recalls Cis, 'and Richard cried with me.'

However Richard bounced back cheerfully, secure in his sister's love – and so the old pattern continued. It has been said that he was such a miserable and homesick little boy at first that he ran away. Cis remembers differently. The three of them, out shopping, were peering into a shop window when suddenly she

18

realised with horror that he had vanished. 'We searched every-where,' she says. 'We were frantic.' Finally they found him at the house of Elfed's sister, his Auntie Margaret Ann – happily munching away at something, pleased with his prank and showing scant remorse for the worry he had caused.

Richard loved sleeping at Pontrhydyfen. 'When he stayed overnight he would sleep in our bed,' remembers Hilda, 'two of us girls at the top and Richard with the other one at the bottom.'

During the day the young Richard adored the rugged freedom of Pontrhydyfen, and he thrived in it – running wildly over the mountains with the other boys, learning all about the gang mentality and the mechanics of jungle survival. Here he learnt to punch and fight and defend himself, winning the praise of 'Dadi Ni' his father, now mellowing himself but delighting in the reflected glory of sons, even very small ones, who knew how to win a brawl.

Chapter Three

Schoolboy and draper's assistant

A few short months after our mother's death and Richard's move to Taibach, Cis became pregnant. Elfed had said that a boy would be nice; 'a playmate for Richie', but the baby was a girl. Marian was born in November 1928. Richard, now just three, effectively had a younger sister. Partly because of his nature, partly because he was a veteran of family life and sharing, he took Marian's arrival in his stride. He would play for hours at the back of the house while Cis worked in the kitchen and attended to the baby – always with an eye out for him.

Three years later – Christmas Eve, 1931 – a second daughter, Rhianon, was born. Richard was six and most indignant at the timing of the thing. 'What's this baby coming, and we wanted to go and see Father Christmas?' he protested to Cis.

Apart from the brief periods after the births of her daughters, Cis continued as before to support her brothers and sisters as well as husband and children. She used to do the washing for the lot, including starched collars for Ivor. At the time of Rhianon's birth, Elfed's mother did the collars. Ivor, noticing a drop in standard, promptly sent them back. Cis, being Cis, shrugged her shoulders and did the lot again. Then at night there was endless sewing – piles of it. Her daughters have a vivid memory of her nodding off at the hearth, needles in hand, energy reserves depleted, compelled, at least temporarily, to give in to exhaustion.

Meanwhile, Richard was a lively, highly mischievous child finding his own friends outside the immediate confines of the James home. His particular friend there was his cousin Dillwyn Dummer. Dillwyn lived nearby, and Richie and Dill, as they were known, made an irrepressible team who would defend each other to the last. There was a patch of waste ground behind their primary school known as 'The Marsh', where schoolboy scores were settled. If anyone picked a quarrel with Dillwyn he would nominate Richard, so much stronger and more robust, to fight on his behalf. Richie relished the chance to fight, developing an assertiveness which was to remain with him.

There used to be a boxing instructor in Inkerman Row (the street directly behind Cis's house in Caradoc Street) who coached the local boys. Still a skilful boxer himself, he was greatly admired by the boys; when they fought, Richard and the others would put his lessons into practice. A circle would be chalked out for the ring and the whole matter was treated with great seriousness. The winner would be presented with a pair of cast-off pram wheels, on which to go hurtling down the hill. With no money for toys, it was the age of improvisation.

The part of Taibach where Mam James (Elfed's mother) lived, known as 'The Side', was the northern edge of Port Talbot, its monotonous rows of terraces leaning against the bare mountain. As the boys grew, the 'Side' gangs became more sophisticated in their conflicts – or was it just more violent? One lad, Leonard Nettle, the biggest and toughest of their gang, was the best fighter and was appointed as leader. There were often fifteen boys on each side; the fights would take place, deadly earnest, on the mountain. It was commonplace for them to emerge with black eyes, deep cuts, even the occasional broken arm, but they rarely consulted a doctor. Tom Hawkings, the local ambulance man, had a soft spot for the boys and regularly tended their wounds.

Tree-climbing was a popular and less aggressive pursuit. Richard, at about eight, fell somewhat sensationally out of a tall tree and was rushed to hospital, where coincidentally he was found to have acute appendicitis. The nurses made a great fuss of him; he lapped it up with little show of discomfort.

The close bond between Richie and Dillwyn extended way beyond the 'Marsh' and the gang warfare. They adopted each other's families as their own. They became members of a new, breakaway Chapel at the same time. Then there were the visits to Uncle Ben, one of the James clan who had broken his back in the mine and was crippled from the waist down. Richard and Dillwyn used to help him while away the hours with games of Monopoly – a dull assignment for most active boys, but apparently they enjoyed it. They frequently stayed in each other's houses and

21

made a point of sharing a bed when one of them had measles or chicken pox so that the other would be sure to catch it all the sooner and they could miss school together. They revelled in all sorts of tricks: charioting down the 'Side' in Dillwyn's pram, with a fine disregard for the wall at the bottom; untying the girls' plaits with glee; dangling dead mice in front of Mam James and stealing carrots from her garden. If either of them faced a ticking off, Richard would be selected to face the whip of Mam James's tongue. He was probably aware that she was mostly bark and very little bite, and that she had a soft spot for him; and so he invariably won her round by turning on the charm and telling her the most outrageous lies.

Mam James and Richard developed an understanding, and on one occasion were found sipping a quiet glass of ale together in her kitchen. This in the home of one who reserved her most fierce attacks for those who indulged in such a wasteful activity as drinking alcohol – the ruination of mankind and the degradation of the soul.

Some years later Leonard Nettle, who looked much bigger than his age, was regularly delegated to march into the 'Jug and Bottle' at the Talbot Arms to get a flagon of beer – one was all they could afford between the lot of them. They would celebrate the success of the exploit by having a secret drink together, always allowing plenty of time for their breath to lose the incriminating evidence before they dared to go home.

Len Nettle was a useful friend in many ways. The boys all enjoyed a visit to the local cinema, properly called the Picture-dome, but commonly known as the 'Cach' (Welsh for shit) because it was such a dive. If you came from the 'Side' you were likely to be banned, but if you knew Leonard you had no problem, because nobody could keep him out. Richie and Dillwyn naturally made a point of being in the right camp.

So began Richard's first exposure to the screen – loving Westerns, loathing anything soppy. Still showing silent films, the Cach resounded with jeers and boos and the rustle of sherbet papers as the owner patrolled constantly in a vain effort to quieten the rowdy customers.

Dillwyn and Richard were soon to move in different directions. Dillwyn said he was always conscious that Richard was the bright one. It was Richard who sat and passed the scholarship exam – the passport to grammar school and the coveted 'bright future'. He in turn was to envy Dillwyn's early entry to the world of wages and relative freedom. His old playmate left school at fourteen, and worked as a baker's roundsman for the Co-op – earning the princely sum of five shillings a week.

By the standards of the 'Side', where money was scarce and quality of life poor, Richard was relatively privileged, and often inspired envy. He had a bicycle, for instance, which he gladly shared, and which made him feel, he said, 'a prince of the valley'.

Chapel ritual was as important in Taibach as it had been in Pontrhydyfen; the James family, including the three children, used to go three times on Sunday. Richard was keener than the girls, less likely to play truant. Marian recalls that her conscience must have been gnawing at her, because the first time she opted out of chapel and headed for Porthcawl, she was sick most of the day. Richard delighted in pointing the moral finger.

Elfed and Cis were devout members of the Gibeon Chapel. During Richard's childhood there was a split in the congregation between the supporters and opponents of the minister Dr Caerau Rees, who had somewhat radical views on certain issues. One of these issues was his own salary; he was convinced that he needed a rise, and the congregation, which included those with the power to grant the extra money, could not reach an agreement over it.

Richard's interest was roused by the whole affair, and he pestered Cis and Elfed to tell him the full story. They always resisted. But he was intrigued by the divide, and the minister's sermons now held increased fascination for him. The gossip among the opponents would return, true village-style, to the ears of Dr Rees himself, thus providing him with fresh ammunition and the impulse to denounce the objectors in his next sermon. From the pulpit he thundered that they only came out at night like a colony of 'blackpats' (cockroaches) to expound their views with venom. They should have the courage, he declared, to approach him directly.

Richard, always captivated by a strong personality, was greatly impressed and listened with rapt attention. When the family – Cis, Elfed, Mam James and company – met at home after chapel for a cup of tea, the dramatic sermon and the meeting afterwards were the chief topics of conversation. Elfed's father, a deacon at the chapel, used to encourage Richard to give a re-run of the discourse, always in Welsh. This he did with relish, mimicking the minister perfectly and thumping the table for greater emphasis. Dr Rees, told about this later, was astonished that his sermons had actually got through to such a young mind. I believe that it is more likely that Richard used them, unwittingly, as an early exercise in dramatic skills, looking more to the form than the content.

Soon this practice of taking the stage at home and repeating the sermon became a weekly ritual as predictable as Sunday tea. And when he went back to Pontrhydyfen the performance would be given once more, with additional dramatic gestures. He used to begin, for instance, by gravely asking his three sisters to bow their heads in reverence. They did so with great solemnity. Richard did the same and prayed, with wicked dignity, in Welsh.

Then followed the sermon itself. He would exploit the techniques of crescendo and diminuendo to the full, and gesticulated freely with both hands, something he came to abhor when he was on the stage. My sisters could hardly contain themselves as he gradually worked himself up to a frenzy. Finally they dissolved into fits of giggles. Richard peered at them disapprovingly before joining in, delightedly, himself.

I have always been convinced that those early observations of pulpit drama were the beginnings of Richard's leanings towards the stage. He used to tell his sisters that he intended to become a preacher when he grew up. He clearly reasoned that if he could hold a roomful so well as a child – he was still only ten – how much more ably would he hold a chapel congregation as an adult. Little did he know how far along that particular line he was to progress.

The eventual outcome of the division in the Taibach chapel was that the incorrigible Dr Rees and his band of followers, including the entire James family, left the Gibeon chapel and built another which they aptly called *Noddfa* ('Refuge'). Harmony was restored. Richard meanwhile continued with his mock sermons, but enjoyed other types of performance as well. He loved to play about on the old organ in Cis's home, though he never had formal music lessons. Moreover on Sundays, ten minutes before the service and by careful arrangement with the Minister's wife, he

24

used to play the organ in the new chapel, with panache if not total accuracy, singing sister Cis's favourite hymn as she walked down the aisle. Later he learnt the Latin words of 'Ave Maria' and gave regular solos to the family.

Richard's love of mimicry, so merciless and so accurate, extended beyond the chapel. Mrs Jackson, a neighbour in Caradoc Street, was a victim of it because her unfamiliar Gloucestershire accent was a challenge to Richard's talent. Then there was always the family – the differences between us provided him with endless raw material. I had formed a habit of pointing my finger and gesticulating wildly when in discussion with Richard. He would observe the mannerisms more closely than the logic of the argument, then reply to me in the same style.

Richard remained an expert mimic all his life. I well remember the time when he was playing in Shakespeare at the Old Vic in London in the early 1950s. He was not very well known then, neither was he well dressed: he often wore scruffy grey flannels and sweater to match. One day, he took a walk around the docks in London's East End, and was admiring a ship when he was approached by a cockney, who said to him, 'What ship are you on mate?' Richard promptly replied in a perfect cockney accent and named the ship that stood in front of him. He carried on talking and convinced his listener he was a cockney.

At home with Cis, his favourite meal was bacon and laverbread, the 'Welsh caviar', with rice pudding to follow. Seafood was quite a feature of Welsh life when Richard was a child. The cockle women would go from street to street, carrying three baskets of cockles and laverbread on their heads to sell on the doorstep. Long after he had become famous he would always send for two pounds of laverbread whenever there was a special occasion to celebrate.

On the whole Richard was fond of his little niece-sisters. He and Marian were the ones who had their noses in a book, more often than not, when Rhianon pestered them to play. 'Just let me finish this chapter,' Richard would mutter resignedly before joining in the game.

Many of their recollections of Richard are humorous. Rich, about eleven, when asked what he wanted for Christmas, announced confidently, 'I want a swinging tit.' Cis and Elfed looked at him in disbelief. 'You want what?' 'The Swinging Tit,' repeated Richard innocently while the girls giggled. 'A great game.' He promised to show them all the object of their incredulity in the toy-shop window the following Saturday.

So the entire family trooped off to the toyshop where Richard triumphantly hailed his heart's desire in the centre-piece of the window display; a board laden with skittles and an ill-defined object on a string – presumably the swinging tit itself, with which to knock the skittles over. They never did find out the real name and dared not draw attention to the error; it remained a long- time favourite in the James family, whatever its proper title.

Marian and Rhianon vividly recall Richard's generosity – on occasions he would give away his last penny. Local beggars came to know him as a soft touch. He often gave them a shilling and sometimes a half-crown. Elfed was once so incensed that he roared after the beggar and delivered a lecture on the immorality of taking such large amounts from a small boy. Richard remained nonchalant.

Richard could be moody though; sometimes he was un-believably gentle, caring and considerate; sometimes scathing, impatient, cruel. He would, say the sisters, have made a terrible teacher. In his big brother role, he had to help them with their homework. 'Can you just explain that to me Rich?' 'No! I've said it once already!'

One evening Marian asked him to help her do some preparation for the 'scholarship' exam, as the hurdle of the eleven plus was known. Richard, by then safely installed at the grammar school and a superior thirteen-year-old, gave the required explanation with his customary roughness, adding sceptically, 'So you think you're going to pass the scholarship, do you?' Marian, wounded, convinced herself she would never pass – and did not even sit for the exam. She might be forgiven for holding it against him, but she does not, not any more at least.

This sophisticated grammar school boy act held little sway with Cis, who was more concerned with whether he washed behind his ears. The same boy who treated Marian with such scorn was unceremoniously boxed up the stairs with a scrubbing-brush when he refused to have a bath after a game of rugby.

He would insist on playing rugby in his school clothes, so of course he got into a terrible mess. He loathed wearing his green peaked school cap, which he shoved to one side, or, more often, stuffed in his pocket, and stubbornly refused to respond to his teachers' exhortations to wear it decently ('for the good name of the school') in the street.

At home there were further rows when Richard got home late –eleven or eleven thirty, way past youth club closing time. 'Talking with Mered,' [Meredith Jones the teacher] he always explained when he eventually appeared. Elfed and Cis knew it was true, but were not the less angry for it.

Then there was the local librarian. During the war Richard loved to help him fire-watch for incendiary bombs whenever he had a chance. More long talks about literature and history; more inspiration and fascination. Richard was drawn to such people as if to a magnet. The library was Richard's main source of reading matter – there were few books at home. Just before he died he told me that he had been given, around this time, a modest four-volume encyclopaedia which he devoured eagerly and repeatedly, as if it were a gripping novel. Absorbed in doing his homework or reading, he would stubbornly refuse to go down to the cellars with everyone else when the siren sounded.

By the time Richard was attending the Grammar School, I was a junior police officer in my twenties in Llantwit Major, a little town near the coast, thirty miles south-east of Pontrhydyfen. Every week I would call on my rest day at my sister's house in Taibach. I used to look forward to seeing Richard marching jauntily home from school, rugby boots slung over his shoulder. He was always pleased to see me, and was a willing audience to my tales of police life, attracted by the manly glamour of the police force, and even more so by the idea of earning money. How welcome then were the occasional half-crowns I used to spare him out of my wages! For a while he seriously considered becoming a police cadet, and though I was flattered by this plan at the time, it soon became clear to me that he showed a lot of promise at school, and that we all needed to encourage him to stay there.

27

But whatever we thought about the prospects open to Richard there was that question of money; no small matter. It was November 1941. Richard, nearly sixteen, was due to sit the School Certificate exam the following summer. No one doubted that he would do well, but with two young children, the approaching financial strain of Christmas and, most significantly, Elfed out of work, keeping Richard at school was undeniably difficult. Many of his friends, including Dillwyn, had been at work for some time. To stay on at school was very much the exception rather than the rule for Taibach children. The family agonised over the decision. There was a plan for those of us in work to club together to help – it was Elfed's idea, I believe – but we could not raise enough to be really useful.

It has been said that Richard was taken out of school because the whole James family resented Cis and Elfed's having been burdened with him at all. In fact we all acknowledged that Elfed had made a willing sacrifice in taking him in, that it was no easy task for a lowly-paid miner with two children of his own – and Elfed was as reluctant as anyone to ask Richard to leave school.

Leave he did, however, at the end of the Christmas term. His disappointment and despondency were great, but, with everyone else, he tried to make the best of it. Elfed's father had found him a job at the Taibach Co-op as a draper's assistant, stressing that there was a great future in it for him. We all strove to believe it, but we were not totally convinced. On the other hand, none of the family had a clear understanding of what Richard's future might actually be. Many people have declared, with hindsight, that they could see there and then that Richard had the makings of a star. I do not believe a word of it. We all agreed that he was bright, that he had what we called 'a future'; but never once did we dream of his rise to fame.

Richard, then, grudgingly took up his post in the Co-op's outfitters department, for thirty shillings a week. As his former teacher, Meredith Jones, quipped too many times, 'He was not cut out for this kind of work.' Richard himself said, many years later, 'I was the most maladroit person. Even now I can barely light a cigarette without burning my nose.' He always confided in us that he dreaded to think what the men would look like when he had measured them up for their suits. He said that he had

28

to control an urge to run off and live wild instead of accepting straight-jacket of the daily grind. He confessed to Hilda that he hated it.

Not only Richard but the entire community, indeed the country, was living under a cloud at the time. The war was in its third year; there were shortages of virtually everything and working-class families suffered great hardship. Standard clothing was being issued, and my brother 'Jenkins the Co-op' was responsible for selling it under the coupon system. His generosity, or careless disregard of the system, or both, nearly cost him the job. He told us that many of his customers made all sorts of excuses when they were short of coupons, and he invariably accepted their hard-luck stories. He had no anxieties about the manager's wrath when the coupons were checked; he was totally carefree about the whole thing.

Cis, however, was not. She worried deeply about him and his future and knew that if he lost the job his prospects would be gloomy indeed.

There was also Richard's moroseness; his black moods when he came home. He no longer warmed his feet good-naturedly on the tank as he did when doing his homework – he now went out in search of the street gangs of his childhood who were hanging around in the streets, in the dance halls, in Berni's ice-cream parlour. Because of his size and his acquired toughness, he fitted in easily with the older crowd and had no trouble discarding his previous image of the conscientious schoolboy. He smoked and drank with brash self-assurance; he exploited his good looks and revelled in the interest of the most sought-after of the girls. And he was impossible to live with.

When I first visited my sister's home after Richard had left school, then went to see him at the Co-op, where he was almost defiant, I was very distressed. I remember feeling particularly helpless because I did not have the means to do anything about the fact that my little brother, of whom we were all so proud – first of us to reach grammar school – was serving behind the counter. We all felt the same. But one man had more status, more 'push' than we did – his former teacher, Meredith Jones, who was equally appalled when he walked into the Co-op one day and saw Richard.

'What can I do about it?' Richard said to him, hopelessly. '*Do*

29

ed Meredith. 'Get you back to school, boy. But if you
o help you, you've got to help yourself!'

th Jones had a certain amount of influence with the
on authority, and he was Secretary of the Port Talbot
Youth Committee. But there had to be a good reason for Richard,
only two years away from National Service, to return to school.
He had to demonstrate that he was worth something.

There was one obvious way – perhaps the only way – to do that.
Philip Burton, Richard's English teacher at school, and a part-
time broadcaster, had already recognised Richard's acting ability.
He had just written a radio documentary called *Venture –
Adventure*, an account of the effect on South Wales boys of the Air
Training Corps. Richard was one of nine boys to be given a part in
January 1942, ironically just after he had left school. Meredith
Jones was now forming a drama section of the Taibach Youth
Club. He urged Richard to divert his energies away from the
streets, pubs and dance halls, and into this new drama project.
Richard saw the possibilities at once. Once again he had a sense of
purpose, and his mood altered accordingly. We were all struck by
the difference in him.

The Youth Club was a very serious concern, with no room for
those only interested in the social side. Before you could do any
dancing, or even sitting around and talking, you had to take part in
one of the activities, drama being the central one. From seven to
nine p.m. you would be hard at work in the drama group or
whatever, then the 'social' followed between nine and ten. The
older generation used to call the club a den of iniquity – with little
justification, according to its former members. Certainly for
Richard, drama was the main attraction. His interest in girls rarely
equalled theirs in him – confident in his own appeal, he was very
nonchalant about his many admirers. Cis says she used to be a
mother-confessor to the girls, who would turn up at the house to
wait for him, drinking endless cups of tea while they poured out
their feelings. Eventually Richard would appear in the passage-
way, stamping his boots, and, to Cis's discomfort, would march
straight past them without a word.

'Don't you dare walk straight past them like that,' she
admonished him. 'Fancy coming in and hardly showing you've
seen them.' He would look at her, all innocence. 'Well,' he'd say,

'I didn't ask them to come. If they're daft enough to hang around for me . . .' which was true. Richard could often be heard singing:

'There were seven pretty girls at the Secondary School,
And the prettiest of all was in form Two A,
Every night after dark we would take them to the park,
Oh! you can't marry seven pretty girls.'

The one girl he saw quite a lot of, to the envy of many including younger brother Graham, was called Catherine Dolan. Catherine remembers Richard as a very sexy young man, but it was never serious, she says, and anyway he was more interested in rugby.

One perhaps more important romantic episode in Richard's life came to light only recently. During his schooldays he became very friendly with Susie Preece. Susie must have had some acting ability, though she was quite unaware of it. She remembers the time when Philip Burton was selecting his cast for the school production of *The Apple Cart* by George Bernard Shaw. Richard was to play the American ambassador. Susie, to her surprise, was also sent for. Even when she was asked to read a passage from the play she was puzzled. Recalling the incident she says that Burton was so meticulous in his casting, and Richard so obviously talented, that she did not think of herself as in the same league.

During Richard's time at the Co-op, he got to know Susie Preece's mother, who was a regular customer. She often used to leave Susie's sister, Gwen, in his care while she did the rest of her shopping. Richard already had something of a reputation as a womaniser – 'But my sister was quite safe with him,' Susie recalls, 'since she was only four at the time!'

Richard always spoke to Mrs Preece in Welsh; he was charming to her and she came to like him very much. After a few months in the job, he sent her a message to the effect that new white shirts had just arrived and were to be sold at the bargain price of two shillings and sixpence each – cheap even for the early 1940s. There was a sale on, he announced eagerly when she came in. Duly impressed, she immediately bought a shirt each for her husband and son. At the back of her mind was the hint of suspicion that Richie in his enthusiasm and eagerness to please had 'invented' the bargain price. But she thought no more of it until several weeks later when she discovered by chance that she was indeed

31

favoured – there had been no sale on, and the official price of the shirts was considerably higher than Richie's two and sixpence. As always he showed a fine disregard for the consequences of his bluff, and we never discovered whether there were any. Once again he demonstrated his happy-go-lucky attitude to the job – and something more; he wanted to impress the mother of the beautiful and sought-after Susie.

Having shrewdly made a hit with Mrs Preece, it was through her that Richard made his first date with Susie. By this time he was back in school and his old enthusiasm for life re-established. He behaved, Susie says, as though he had never left. With infinite care and politeness he enquired of Mrs Preece if he could take her daughter to the Regent Cinema in Taibach. Permission was duly granted – such a charming young man, after all. Susie herself was more cautious, and agreed to go only on the strict condition there was to be 'no hanky-panky'. Richard promised to behave impeccably, and kept his word.

Shortly afterwards Richard asked for another date; this time the meeting-place was to be outside the Chapel of Ease Cemetery, a favourite rendezvous of his. Susie had a feeling he would not turn up, so she sent her friend Enid ahead to check. Only when she established that he was indeed there waiting for her did she venture to the spot herself.

Richard and Susie's intermittent courtship continued through his early months at Oxford. Home for Christmas vacation, he met her at the YMCA dance hall in Port Talbot, and took her home, again the chivalrous suitor. They arranged again to meet at the Chapel of Ease on Boxing Night. Best friend Enid was again in tow as chaperone-cum-scout, then when her job of confirming Richard's attendance was done, she made herself scarce. Richard was becoming increasingly passionate. 'Well, he tried his nonsense with me,' Susie recalls matter-of-factly. 'But I wasn't having any of it.'

A few days later Richard was sitting in Sami's, the local Italian café, tucking into an ice-cream, when he spotted Susie's young sister Gwen. Was Susie at home? he enquired politely. Hearing that she was, he polished off his ice-cream and was at the door within minutes, charming Mrs Preece as usual. Susie, washing her hair, could hear his unmistakable voice floating up the stairs. They made another date, this time for the Regent Cinema in Taibach, and sat through the film little dreaming that he would one day be up there on the screen.

'Yes, I really loved Richard,' Susie said wistfully, more than forty years later. 'He had so much chemistry, and such charisma, such charm. How could anyone not fall for him? And as for conversation – he could keep you spellbound. We used to climb the same mountain, the Mynydd Emroch, that he and P. H. Burton used to climb together for Richard to practise his breathing and throwing Shakespeare's lines across the valley with his powerful voice.'

Many years later, when Richard was married to another Susie – Susan Hunt – the pair met again at Hilda's house. She was thrilled when he asked about her mother, who had become a great fan of his. He presented Susie with a copy of his little book *A Christmas Story* for her mother, inscribed thus:

I Mrs Preece. Diolch yn fawr iawn.
Rwyn dy garu di o hyd. Cofiwch y Co-op?
Cariad
Richard

To Mrs Preece,
Thank you very much. I love you always.
Remember the Co-op?
Love,
Richard

Richard loved women; he loved learning and drama; and he had a third great love, one to whom he was unbendingly faithful. Richard, like most Welshmen, was devoted to rugby. He had three Welsh trials as a schoolboy but never got his cap for Wales, and has often said that, given the choice at the time, he would have sacrificed his acting career to play for Wales. That would have been his ultimate passport to heaven.

He always loved talking about the great characters and international players of the past, particularly of his old club Aberavon. Richard later wrote several published articles about his love for rugby, so typical of Richard with their untrammelled enthusiasm; the love of a finely-honed anecdote; the drama and vitality of the game; the almost too exuberant use of words, adjectives especially, to tell the tale.

33

In the piece that follows, which Richard wrote in the 1970s in celebration of a much-loved rugby club, the use of imagery is especially dramatic. Perhaps only he could describe the town 'planning' of working-class Wales as 'a kind of geometrical Euclidian nightmare'. I think the piece is very evocative of his youth:

Aberavon

Show me a sheet of newspaper with the word Aberavon on it and I will pick it out at a casual glance. Aberavon is when I was a boy! There I played on the Athletic grounds and there I watched on countless Saturdays the legendary immortals of my childhood and fancy. And the names Ned Jenkins and T. O. James, Mog Hopkins and Randall Lewis, Miah Macgrath and Sid Williams, Arthur Bassett and Walter Vickery, sing with a bell in every tooth, not necessarily in that order, and the roll-call is long and of course my brother Ivor (who I regret to say defected to Neath for a season or two, but we got him back). Indeed so much did I want to be an Aberavon player that I once asked my brother-in-law, the late Dai Phillips, if he could get me a game for them. He was secretary of the Club and a member of the Big Five. 'One of the warm-up games,' I explained hurriedly, 'at the beginning of the season against second-class teams.' I was nervous and justly so. 'Dai John' was known as no lover of fools, and was as brusque as a tank when the occasion arose. The occasion had arisen. 'First of all there are no second-class teams in Wales, and you wouldn't last ten minutes.' That was that. I'd played for Aberavon, of course, but only as a schoolboy. Oddly enough Dai John was one of the selectors then too, but now I was twenty-eight, world famous and despite the fact that I was working very hard, he was certainly right. He might have softened it a bit though, I thought at the time. Like saying, 'Get into trim for a couple of months and we'll see about next season.'

One of the mysteries about Aberavon which I have never satisfactorily explained to myself is that though my entire family support Aberavon to a man – to a woman I may say – we are a large family. Why did we support Aberavon, I repeat, when we were all born in Neath?* We had great respect for the latter, but our hearts belong to Aberavon. Distance to the two grounds is no explanation. Our house was almost – to a couple of hundred yards – equidistant from both the Talbot Athletic Ground and the Gnoll. And actually, indeed, the buses for Neath stopped outside the door while those for Aberavon were a quarter of a mile away.

I lived and breathed the game. An idyllic Saturday was as follows. Get up at dawn, pick up the newspapers from Mrs Dangerfield's and deliver them. Meanwhile collecting most of the newspapers I had delivered during the week. Porridge for breakfast. Deliver old newspapers to my Auntie Edith Evans's Fish and Chip shop. Eye the potatoes in the same chip-shop. Total earnings about two and seven pence ha'penny. Sixpence for me and the rest for my sister. Rush off to the Plough, change into rugby togs and play a game for the school. Win, home and a bath. Lunch (dinner) and then the slow walk to the ground (by this time I was living in Taibach) starting off with my brother-in-law Elfed and his father, and the crowd of adults slowly swelling – I never as I remember, went with other boys but always with grown-ups – as the concourse of steadies converged and swelled from other streets. Leave them just before arrival at the ground to poach in over the railway line to Dyffryn Yards, slide down the siding behind the standing stand. In fact I don't think I've ever paid to watch Aberavon. As a schoolboy, I sneaked in and as an adult I was always a VIP and was a guest of the club. The conversation before the appearance of the teams: 'I hope that dull devil Harry Jones isn't playing. Last week against Llanelli he turned inside when all he had to do was sling it out to Randall. Good God, he had enough men outside him to have scored in Groes.' 'Willy Barham looks very pretty in the loose but is he pushing his weight in the scrum?' 'Gifted, very gifted, lovely sidestep, lovely dummy, neat kicker, but let's face it boys, he's not a killer. Too bloody nice off and on the field.' 'He ought to have a couple of liveners before the game, a half bottle of whiskey would work wonders.' 'We'll have to watch it today. No walkover.' Ned will see them off today

* Here, Richard means we were born within the boundaries of Neath Borough Council.

though. And then the roar of the crowd as the teams trotted out onto the turf. Make it a needle match and pack the ground. The tossing of the coin. The referee's whistle. And the Wizards would join battle. Then win. Home for tea. Replay the game in the street under the gas lamps with Tommy Mainwaring and Trevor George and Dillwyn Dummer, with newspapers folded over twice and tied around with string as a football making a cylinder amazingly handy, if you'll pardon the pun, and it would last a long time, a couple of weeks perhaps, and also useful for dropping goals, taking penalties, converting and punting. Amazingly, you could play full fifteen a side games, or ten aside, in an ordinary street. For goal kicks there was the nearest blank wall with the 'H' drawn out on it. I wonder if anybody in this affluent society plays rugby like that nowadays. Then home for supper, and a read afterwards. And so to bed.

There were moments of vast comic relief. I remember an Aberavon wing who had been continually harassed all season. Suddenly snatching up a butterfly's chance, and with a couple of changes of direction turned the whole defence to stone and scored an impossible try. The crowd roared. He trotted impassively back to the half way line with slow deliberation, lowered his knicks and showed his taut, muscular posterior to the *crachach* [snobs] in the grandstand, in all its hirsute glory.

And of course, there is the great day when we beat Cardiff at home, to a full house. Cardiff, in their heyday, were reckoned to be the best club team in rugby, and could have represented Wales without too much demur.

But with drizzle on the slates, and the smoke coming down from the chimneys, and hard and rough games against Swansea and Abertillery and Bridgend and Newbridge and Maesteg, and the higgledy-piggledy streets and crescents and closes, which seen from the top of the mountain is a kind of geometrical Euclidian nightmare. To that town, Aberavon, and its rugby team, I pledge my continuing allegiance. Until death and after.

* * * * *

Richard's 'continuing allegiance' to rugby, and to Aberavon, never diminished. Together with his constant need for news of Wales,

and even the *taste* of Wales – how he longed for the dishes of his
youth when he could have had the most exotic meals in the world!
– it is an indication of how strongly embedded in the adult Burton
was the young Richard from the valleys.

Chapter Four

The return to school

While Richard, the firebrand, the young Lothario, the actor in embryo, still languished in the Co-op, Meredith Jones, with his customary fire and determination, intended his youth club to make a name for itself. He selected a part-time instructor of the drama group, one Leo Lloyd, and very soon asked him to enter the Youth Eisteddfod – the first of its kind. Richard was one of the seven youngsters selected for the production of *The Bishop's Candlesticks*. He threw himself into it and the drama group in general, and as his sense of purpose grew, he became less of a tearaway.

Most evenings he was to be found at the Taibach Youth Club, either rehearsing or deeply involved in one of the discussion groups. He also began to develop a passionate interest in Shakespeare and in Welsh literature; Meredith Jones's inspiration was having its effect. Still enjoying the relative independence of a wage earner, Richard no longer had the time or the inclination to loaf around the streets.

The day of the Eisteddfod arrived, and, as everyone had anticipated, the club won first prize. Richard also came second in English reading, third in English recitation and second in the singing solo.

Philip Burton, the English master, could hardly fail to hear of his former pupil's success. He, meanwhile, had been continuing to produce radio plays in which his pupils were often involved. How ironic that Richard, tied to the Co-op, had to be excluded.

Still, things were beginning to move behind the scenes. Not only Meredith Jones, but a more influential figure, County Councillor Llewellyn Heycock (who lived less than two hundred yards away from Cis and Elfed) was working towards Richard's reinstatement, with the backing of Philip Burton, the headmaster, and the family.

Richard was overjoyed when they succeeded. Cis remembers the afternoon he flew into the house and up the stairs in search of her.

'I've got good news for you! I'm going back to school!'

So, finally, and against all the odds, Richard Jenkins was back at Port Talbot Secondary School in September, 1942. His return caused a sensation in both classroom and staff-room. The boys were wary, the girls greatly impressed, and the staff's response was mixed. Because he had missed so much schooling he was put back a year, but in a way he was too mature, too brimming with self-assurance. There were inevitable clashes, and rugby field and playground served as outlets for his frustration, for his difficulties in conforming. He was notorious as a 'dirty' player on the rugby field. There was a certain ambivalence about Richard. On the one hand he was extremely generous of spirit and would go out of his way to help a friend or an underdog. On the other, the pranks of his childhood evolved into more sophisticated acts of bother at school, and his vindictiveness could be boundless.

Richard now knew he had to make the most of his chances, which meant making a real impression on Philip Burton. In November came the school's drama production, *Gallows Glorious*, about John Brown the American abolitionist. Richard came back to school after most of the casting had been done, so he had to content himself with a small part. But he played it with such verve and excess that he drove his producer to distraction and provoked all kinds of accusations about upsetting the balance. Nonetheless, Philip Burton was well aware of his pupil's talent and continued to take a keen interest in him. He was much impressed by Richard's determination and the way he rose to a challenge; when presented with a test piece he would practise it laboriously for weeks on end, perfecting every detail, finally delivering it triumphantly to his teacher.

Richard's confidence was mounting. My regular visits to Cis's house continued, and he loved to boast about how he mastered the various subjects. He knew, of course, that he had long overtaken me academically. 'History, Dai?' he would say, roughly. 'It's just a matter of dates. Must be a bit like your law swotting – know the dates and the rest fits in.' I was suitably impressed, as I was supposed to be.

Meanwhile the financial problems at Caradoc Street had not been resolved.

Finally Philip Burton decided to try to come to the rescue. For some time he had been brooding over what he later called his 'Pygmalion Complex' – the strong need to nurture and develop a young mind with the goal of preparation for an acting career. He was a perfectionist himself and particularly approved of those who followed the same conscientious line. He was looking, now, to Richard. He offered to sponsor him and to ask his landlady in Connaught Street (about ten minutes' walk from Caradoc Street) to give the boy a room. It so happened that a man who had occupied the other room at his digs had just been called up, so the room was free. Mrs Smith readily agreed.

Philip Burton recalled about thirty years later – I am not sure how accurately – that Richard had been pathetically keen to leave home, to move on, already driven by the flame of ambition. I suppose it was probably at least partly true. He said to Richard, 'They'll never let you go, you know.' He was certainly right in predicting that. I did not see that there was any great dilemma though. To me, the matter was quite straightforward: here was a wonderful offer to remove the fear of struggle and uncertainty from Richard's life and to give him a golden opportunity. He would still be close to his sister/mother and her family, and to us all. It sounded like an ideal arrangement. To Cis, however, it was far from ideal. It involved parting with her beloved brother/son, handing him to the care of another before he had reached maturity. And how was she to know for certain that it would be entirely to his benefit? Cis has said, many many times, that in a sense she has always regretted agreeing to the arrangement.

But agree, in the end, she did. Philip Burton's idea developed to the stage where he thought full adoption would be the best scheme. However, there was a snag. Full adoption was not possible because Burton was just twenty days short of the legal requirement of being twenty-one years older than his prospective adoptee – the former was then thirty-eight, Richard eighteen. So the plan was that he should become Richard's guardian instead. The appropriate solicitor's document was drawn up and my father was approached for his signature. He promptly refused. He may not have been the great leader or initiator in the family, but he had firm ideas on certain issues, and one of them was that he was not going to be party to the signing away of any of his children.

When I next called at Cis's house, she carefully explained the situation to me: I was to be asked to sign the document. Once again, perhaps partly influenced by the straightforwardness of my police training, I did not see a conflict. The act of transferring guardianship was understandably difficult, psychologically, for my father, particularly as he had never actually taken responsibility for the care of his youngest sons. But there were no such emotional blocks for me.

I went along to Connaught Street, where Philip Burton was waiting for me. It was 17 December 1943. I had met him several times before, and had always found him exceptionally courteous and charming.

I suppose on that occasion he had reason to win me round, and to make a fine impression! Once again he stressed that Richard had a future at school, and that he hoped to give him every assistance academically and, if that was what he wanted, on the stage. These expressions were now sounding very familiar to our working-class, non-academic ears. I decided that we could have every confidence in Philip Burton and I was proud and happy to sign the guardianship papers.

From then on Philip Burton became Richard's guardian, guide and personal tutor. Not for some years, however, did Richard change his name from Jenkins to Burton by deed-poll.

When the two were interviewed together after Richard's rise to fame, Philip Burton was asked about the 'adoption'. 'He didn't adopt me,' Richard interrupted, 'I adopted him.' And Philip, on reflection, agreed – there was something, he said, very stubborn about Richard once he had made up his mind he was going to be an actor. Burton ostensibly tried to talk him out of it – but only to put his pupil's determination to the test.

'Right,' he declared to his charge when he had moved himself and his few belongings to the neat terraced house in Connaught Street. 'If you're going to be an actor you've got to change your voice and your speech.' The voice was rough, or so Philip Burton said; the accent was strong Port Talbot. The years of discipline began.

Richard slept in a small upstairs room; the downstairs front room, or parlour, was given to teacher and pupil for evening study. Richard, willing captive though he was, used to call it a room of terror. At school all day, he would start again at four in the afternoon in this little room and they would be at it until ten at night, often much later.

'Ferocious discipline, it was,' said Richard: hour upon hour of drilling the vowels over and over and over. Richard remembered it vividly throughout his life. It was nearly all done, he said, through poetry, which suited him anyway – much easier to learn than prose. And as Philip Burton always reminded him: 'Sense must come first, and the voice, if you have it, will follow.'

Thus did the sculptor chip off the rough edges and begin to shape a new Richard.

The demands of wartime police duties meant that I saw less of Richard now. But I used to talk to him on my own, sometimes during his visits to Cis's home, sometimes when he came to see me in Llantwit Major and explained to me the workings of the regime. Of course, I knew he always loved to embellish and exaggerate. But I am sure there was a real strict régime in that house: Philip Burton was very much in charge. He abhorred smoking and drinking, so Richard used to go off for a quiet smoke in the outside toilet. If Miss Audrey Smith, the landlady's daughter, spotted Philip coming back, she would nip out sharply to warn him.

Drinking at home, even in the outside toilet, was impossible, but Richard used to go to the pub now and again at lunchtime from the sixth form, deliberately invoking the wrath of his guardian who was likely as not to be teaching him in the afternoons. He would be sent home at once, and stalked off defiantly. According to his peers, he got into enough trouble at school to be expelled three times over – but he never was.

For all its strictness, the house in Connaught Street managed to be remarkably homely. Philip, who had been lodging there for over twenty years, was warm-hearted as well as firm, and the landlady, Mrs Smith, was as motherly as Richard would allow her to be.

Miss Smith recalled recently the time when Richard and Mr Burton had had one of their rows. Richard had stayed out all night and Philip waited up for him until the small hours. Miss Smith let him in, much relieved, at eight next morning, bedraggled and rather sorry for himself. Asked where he had been, he announced gloomily that someone had stolen his coat from the YMCA and that he had gone to lie down and meditate in the Chapel of Ease Cemetery. We shall never know if his story was true!

Despite this new, all-absorbing life, Richard was as devoted as ever to Cis and her family, and went back regularly to his old home. In fact, Cis and her daughters have somewhat painful memories of Richard's time at Connaught Street. He would turn up at Cis's home, complaining about the rules and regulations at his new one. He had, for instance, to clean all the shoes regularly and there was no getting out of it. Cis, indignant when she heard of this, told him he should have said he did not know how to do it; but clean the shoes he did. He would often come back home to Cis, and invariably, Philip used to come looking for him. He would tell Cis ruefully, 'His heart isn't in Connaught Street, I know.' She could not deny it, any more than Richard could. He had many positive feelings towards his guardian, but close filial affection was not among them.

Aptly enough, during the term in which the guardianship papers were signed and Richard moved to Philip Burton's house, the school's drama production was George Bernard Shaw's *Pygmalion*. Burton confidently cast Richard in the role of Professor Higgins. The Welsh accent, of course, still prevailed, and Emlyn Williams could not resist teasing Richard, for years afterwards, about the incongruity of that first major part.

Richard's acting in the play, performed at school and at the YMCA, was well received by the *Port Talbot Guardian*: 'As the Professor he displayed dramatic talent that made him a dominating personality and brought out all that was best in the acting of his opposite number, Dilys Jones, as the London Flower Girl.'

For us, his family, it was a great occasion, and not surprisingly we were bursting with pride. I remember that Richard, nearly eighteen, had a small beard, and that I was much affected by this – it is always something of a shock to be confronted by the maturing of a much younger sibling. But, more significantly, this was the first time I had seen my brother on the stage, and I was greatly impressed. We all were. We noted the greater polish in his delivery, the fact that he had already mastered the art of keeping still and of avoiding the wild gesticulating of which he had previously been so fond. No doubt much of this, if not all, was due to Philip Burton. Things certainly seemed to have moved a long way from the mock sermon entertainment by the fireside. But we still thought in terms of the here and now, the realities of forging a career and earning a living, with no real expectation of a dramatic future for Richard.

After the performance, we joined Philip, Richard and the rest of the cast for a party. Philip was increasingly optimistic about Richard's future. He later confessed that a year or two earlier, all he knew for sure was that the boy had strong looks and a strong personality. Since then he had become increasingly excited by Richard's quite unusual talent, combined with a special feeling for poetry and language. The process of acquiring acting technique was painful and difficult. 'But he learnt,' said Philip, 'with astonishing thoroughness.' Richard in turn admitted that despite their differences, Philip had become a kind of a god in his eyes.

Back in the classroom, he had recovered the lost ground with relative ease and matriculated in English literature and maths – his best subjects – as well as English language, Welsh, history, geography and chemistry. He was on the road which could well lead to higher education, and that was still a sure way out of the confines, geographical and commercial, of the valleys.

Then Philip Burton spotted the following advertisement in the *Western Mail* dated 21 August 1943:

Emlyn Williams wants Welsh actors

Mr Emlyn Williams is looking for several Welsh actors and actresses for small parts in his new play which will open in the autumn. Types wanted vary from young people to character actors and actresses. A Welsh boy actor is also required. Boy applicants must be fourteen years by December 1, but are expected to look younger. Those who think they can fill these roles should write within seven days to Mr Williams at 15, Pelham Crescent, London SW7, giving age, qualifications and enclosing a recent photograph.

Seventeen-year-old Richard was urged to apply, and so went to audition at the Prince of Wales Theatre, Cardiff. There were literally queues of other nervous hopefuls and their mothers, teachers and sponsors. The piece, not surprisingly, had had a stunning response from those now waiting to see the great Emlyn Williams, the living trademark of contemporary Welsh drama.

He himself remembers 'a boy of seventeen, of startling beauty, and a quiet intelligence. He looked as very special human beings tend to look at that age – he looked. . . . imperishable.'

As it turned out, Richard was too old for the part which had been advertised, but he was given another. This role – in *The Druid's Rest* – was his first job in the professional theatre; and it was at this point that he changed his name to Burton.

Richard himself looked back at that period in a radio interview:

I'm not quite sure why I wanted to be an actor. But I think that originally I was striving in some way to acquire an education of almost any kind, though one doesn't think of acting as an education in the ordinary sense of the word. Nevertheless, it was possible to go to the Royal Academy of Dramatic Art on a scholarship, and acquire a knowledge of the world at least, and spend two years in London. The other side was, I think, that I thought that I might be able to act well enough to make a living out of it.'

Emlyn Williams, then, set that 'living' in motion. Spotted and nurtured himself by a schoolteacher, Miss Sarah Cooke, he paved the way for other young Welsh hopefuls and created a real alternative to the chapel pulpits for the dramatically minded.

Ironically, in the light of Richard's later drinking bouts, *The Druid's Rest* was set in a pub; Richard played one of the innkeeper's sons. In the play Williams affectionately mocks the tendency of the Welsh to allow their imagination to triumph over commonsense: the innkeeper and local policeman become convinced a dangerous murderer is in their midst. The 'murderer' turns out to be a harmless literary Welshman who enjoys a pint.

Gladys Henson, Richard's stage mother, remembers him at rehearsals 'always talking about rugby – or dozing off.' She warned him he would have to treat rehearsals seriously if he wanted to make the grade. 'Oh, you know me, Glad,' he retorted cheerfully, 'I go my own way.'

Despite such tendancies, Emlyn Williams was impressed, not least by Richard's 'tremendous reserves of natural timing'. The part was small, but Richard played it, Williams says, 'with assurance, as if he had been in the theatre for years.'

The play went on tour and eventually came to Cardiff. Richard appeared on a Welsh stage as a professional for the first time, and was duly hailed as 'accomplished' by the critic of the *South Wales Evening Post*.

All the family went up on the train and we sat in the front rows. Even my father was there. We all met Emlyn Williams for the first time and, predictably, we were impressed. He was a celebrity to us; but not a patronising one – not even when he told Richard afterwards that his father was a 'little pippin'.

During the Welsh run of the play, Richard bought his first real presents for Cis and Ma Smith – inexpensive little prints of the *Mona Lisa*, which they both treasured. Cis still has hers. He was beginning to enjoy the fruits of his new career – already his earnings of ten pounds a week were way above those of his brothers and friends back home, who were mostly in the mines.

In the spring of 1944 the cast of *The Druid's Rest* gave Richard a small farewell party before he joined the RAF. Philip Burton was there. The play had not been a resounding success, but for Richard it was a beginning – a foot on the ladder.

Richard never forgot those who had given so much and worked so hard to offer him the once-in-a-lifetime chance denied many other precocious, talented valley lads. He was well aware of the extent to which certain local people had made his rise possible, by their advocacy of his potential.

How much he valued these efforts is made clear in his own adult reminiscences. Much has been written about Richard, but comparatively little has been said about the man who Richard himself believed to have changed the course of his life. Meredith Jones acted as his mentor, and was also an orator, guide, philosopher, counsel and a supreme virtuoso in the art of conversation. The following article by Richard is his response to an invitation by the *Sunday Times* to write about the man who groomed him for stardom. In it, he puts his enthusiasm for excesses of description and sometimes over-larded imagery to affectionate and heart-felt good use.

The Magic of Meredith Jones

Meredith Jones was a schoolteacher, a recognisable spiritual descendant of Geraldus Cambrensis and Shakespeare's Fluellen – passionate, fluent, something of a scholar, mock-belligerent, roughly gentle, of remarkable vitality and afraid of nobody. He was the concentrated essence of a kind of bi-lingual South Walian, unknown perhaps over the border, who speaks the alien English tongue with a loving care and octosyllabically too! No short word for them if a longer one will do – men of brilliantly active vocabularies who love an audience.

In the more suspicious and austere North of the Principality, we South Walians are described with an amused tolerance as *Sioni Hoys*, a rough translation of which would perhaps be 'Johnny Shouts' – makers of great flaming gestures for the love of it, who turn all things, from rugby football to a walk over the Brombil to T. S. Eliot, into powerful drama in the telling of it.

I remember Meredith Jones talking, for instance, of *The Love Song of J. Alfred Prufrock* and holding us all, a group of young boys, spellbound as he unfolded with conscious looks of wonder the marvellous courage of the man Eliot to write the poem *Prufrock* at the time that he did. 'No, if I should die boys think only this of me or Sassoon and Owen and Thomas with their beautiful bitterness but I have measured out my life with coffee spoons. What a gesture gentlemen.' Meredith would in the high flow of his talk, describe anybody of whatever age or sex as 'Gentlemen', as if at a council meeting. 'What quiet bravery, and who's to say, who will argue with me, who will deny that Prufrock's slow death was not the more terrible?'

His stage was an elementary council school, leaky, and many years condemned, with buckets and bucket-boys at the ready for the ever-threatening rain. He worked hard. All day long he taught eleven-plus boys the rudiments of arithmetic and English to prepare them for entrance into the Local Grammar School and at night he presided in the same school over a Youth Club. And always he talked and couldn't bear to stop.

At night when the club was shut he would invariably say, 'Walk home with me boys,' and delightedly we would; for what we all knew was that some lecture to be delivered would be only half completed by the time of our arrival at his house, which would mean a further half-hour of talk while he offered to walk us back home. A further walk even might be necessary while he talked and talked. His subjects were legion.

'Consider the tax on the brain, gentlemen, of the great mathematician pondering in his chill chambers at Cambridge the incontrovertible fact that there is no square root of a minus quantity. Let us examine the mystery of numbers, let us involve ourselves with him, let me explain.' And he would. And astonishingly we potential corner boys and billiard markers would catch a glimpse of the glory of man from Meredith's play with the assumption that two and two makes four.

He had a trick too, of reducing the most august and Olympian figures to the familiar, the known and the nudge-able:

'Honest and ugly old Van [Van Gogh], boys, smouldering like slag, painting in the high sun until it burned his brain. Put your hat on, Van, they told him, put your hat on.'

His manner was such as perhaps a few adults could tolerate, and his seemingly deliberate dismissal of facts, dates and figures as trivial was perhaps maddening to the more educated. He defended the local habit of exaggeration which approached sometimes very near mendacity, as if it were a virtue. He would argue that it was the unconscious and poetic shaping of a story that sometimes distorted its more prosaic accuracy, and how relieved were the secret liars and stretchers of fact.

Indeed his description of Truth as a shadowy wing-three-quarter running for ever down a ghostly touchline was an acting tour de force. 'Nobody will ever catch him,' he would say, 'And he never will go in to touch.' Great artists, philosophers and poets eternally corner flagging will never get their arms around the legs of truth. He would actually do the run in small, playing all the parts himself – the majestic philosopher, the mad artist, the wild crying poet, and Truth royal, immutable, faintly effeminate and untouchable. It was a remarkable performance.

His impact on me was decisive but not immediate. It was

cumulative, not a blinding moment of revelation. I felt with him my mind broadened with every step I took. I couldn't believe this week that I was so ignorant last week, or this year that I wondered for twelve months in the darkness that was last year. He taught me to love the English language without actually talking about the English language. He taught me to be a reader without actually being much of a reader himself. I became, indeed, an under-the-bedclothes-with-a-torch-reader, bequeathing to myself, no doubt, a legacy of bad eyesight in my middle age, while Meredith, because he was too busy, became a past master at the art of 'glancing–through'. He had glanced through everything, and could elaborate on it and was extremely difficult to fault.

Since I left Meredith Jones's circle I have enjoyed the talk of many pretty talkers; notably the gifts of the gab of falling actors, at large in the nearest pub, and unpublished writers, bitter among the gas-rings and the dirty dishes, and Oxford undergraduates who rarely took firsts. They were thruppenny thinkers all, dealers in warped platitudes and twisted clichés, but none had the huge personality of this man, or possessed the dark-eyed insolence to take on an opponent in the opponent's special subject and destroy him with a fire of improbable and, to the specialist, infuriating irrelevancies. To his death, and lamentably he is dead now, I never saw him matched.

My debt to this man, and my devotion to his memory, are, I hope, apparent in this article. Without him I would have missed a large slice of life – I would not have gone to a great university and I would probably not have become an actor. I would not have had the courage to answer an advertisement and I would never have gone to London except possibly in a leeked red beret and with an enclosure ticket for Twickenham. I would, I suspect in some unpleasant job, have become morose, suspicious, bitter and impossible to live with. I might even have become a politician.

* * * * *

Having released into a headier atmosphere one such as my brother, Meredith Jones would have had little to be sorry about.

Chapter Five

Oxford student and Air Force cadet

Luck and good fortune have frequently played their part in Richard's life: this moment was no exception. Being wrenched from the first tantalising achievements of an acting career – if career is not too strong a term at this point – to take part in statutory defence training might well have snuffed the candle of his achievement before the wick was truly lit. Fortunately the government had set up a scheme whereby cadets from the Armed Forces could go to university on a special wartime six-month course; Richard won a place at Exeter College, Oxford and arrived there in April 1944.

The scheme combined academic courses with rigorous RAF training. Richard, not surprisingly, chose to read English. His tutor at Exeter College was Nevill Coghill, Merton Professor of English, whose opinions of Richard, published later, were unequivocal: 'This boy is a genius and will be a great actor. He is outstandingly handsome and robust, very masculine and with deep inward fire, and extremely reserved.'

I am left wondering what masculinity and inward fire had to do with scholarship and learning, but there it is. Richard had a knack of inspiring such comments.

Richard himself remarked years later that at the time, the Welsh, and especially the South Welsh, were an academic tribe and were inundating the Oxford colleges – Exeter being, after Jesus, that with the strongest traditional links with Wales. Not to appear to be Welsh in these circumstances was his explanation for his name-change! It seems to me that he needed to justify his action – that his conscience was not quite easy over it.

He revelled in the beauty of his new surroundings. 'I fell in love with it,' he said more than thirty years later, 'and have remained in love with it. If I get the chance, I go back there. It had, and still has, a curious almost mystic impact on me.'

There was much for him to fall in love with at the ancient university which had remained outside the achievements of even the great Philip Burton. Its Gothic quadrangles, medieval lanes. Classical libraries, constantly shifting vistas of pinnacles and crockets; gargoyles and gables made the heart of Oxford a vision of antique scholarship that was not illusory. The contrast between this and the dour, back-to-back bleakness of Taibach and Port Talbot was almost bewildering. Exeter College itself, facing Trinity College across the aptly-named Broad Street, was founded in 1314, and its ranged quadrangles, mainly seventeenth and nineteenth-century work, were dominated by a Victorian Gothic chapel, its walls alive with costly marbles and carvings, that was about as far removed from the Valleys' vision of Chapel as can be imagined.

Nonetheless, to me, and to the rest of the family, free of Richard's mystical proclivities, his main interest at the time appeared to be drink. He boasted to Ma Smith that he had learnt to put away vast quantities of beer. To Cis he was more reticent, fearful of upsetting her. She visited him once or twice, and was awestruck by the beauty of the colleges, but while she was there, one of the students muttered something about a pint. 'What?' said Cis, genuinely appalled. 'Beer? In a place like this?'

'Well, we do have the occasional drink,' Richard admitted cautiously.

The bravado, the accounts of himself as 'Beer Burton', he reserved for the rest of us. I remember his boastful anecdotes during that Christmas vacation when he returned to South Wales. He was proud of maintaining that he could put away two pints faster than any other undergraduate. Confident that this was just a phase, that he would come through it and mature, I refused to let it worry me. I might have been more concerned if I had been through such a phase myself – twelve years older and with the memories of my father's drinking, and my mother's and sister's misery still vivid, I was a hesitant drinker. At the time, I thought that Richard was indulging in the typical excesses of youth and freedom – neither Cis nor Elfed touched alcohol, and the entire James family were vocal in their criticism of any spending on drink, so he did have traces to kick over.

As for my father, Richard had asked me if I would pass on to him the news of his Oxford scholarship. My father's reply, in

51

Welsh, was true to character. 'Davy bach, it would have been far better if by some stroke of genius he had achieved the highest accolade in the land by winning his cap for Wales in the field of rugby at Cardiff Arms Park; and in that happy and glorious event, at the end of his day he would have gone to heaven with great composure, and hand in hand with the Archangel Gabriel.' It was, I suppose, predictable. There was little point in trying to reason with him.

Richard was determined to make his mark in the acting world of the university: after all, not everyone there, however talented or privileged, could claim to have acted professionally. So shortly after his arrival at Oxford, he approached Professor Coghill about a part in Shakespeare's *Measure for Measure* – then being rehearsed by the Oxford University Dramatic Society under Coghill's direction – or rather, a substitute body, since OUDS itself was bankrupt and temporarily suspended.

Richard went to Coghill's room and offered to recite to him. He chose a conventional piece – Hamlet's soliloquy 'To be or not to be. . . .' He told me afterwards that the professor, clearly impressed, had said: 'Well, there's very little I can teach you.'

But to Richard's dismay, the play was fully cast. Determined to make his mark, and aware that time was short – his six months at Oxford would soon be over – he eventually persuaded Coghill to let him understudy the leading role, that of Angelo. He used to call rehearsals early before Hallam Fordham, the leading man, had arrived. Hallam, affected by his understudy's almost desperate eagerness, later suggested that Richard played in half the performances.

There are conflicting reports of what followed. Richard insisted that the pressure he had brought upon Hallam precipitated a nervous breakdown in the latter. 'One forgets one's youthful ruthlessness,' he said thirty years later. 'I wouldn't dream of doing that now.'

Nevill Coghill's recollections are less dramatic. He says that Fordham, an RAF officer, was posted away from Oxford before the play's first performance. 'When I cast him for Angelo, he warned me that he expected shortly to be posted elsewhere, and I was on tenterhooks for fear that he would be taken from me – until Richard appeared, so that my king was guarded by an ace. In due course Hallam was posted away, and Richard stepped effortlessly into the part.'

The one certainty is that Richard took the part, and correctly saw it as the unalloyed golden opportunity. He told me later that he was ruthless in his determination to succeed. He must have felt his six brothers and four sisters tugging at his sleeve and saying, 'Now is the time to go out there and show your mettle.'

We were not there in person, but we had a pretty good idea that there was a chance for Richard to impress those with influence – and power.

He took the production very seriously. Musing over the difficulty of pronouncing 'Ha!' in one speech, he decided to thump the cloister wall to heighten the effect. During one performance a piece of the age-old wall came away. 'Half blinded, I stumbled off,' said Richard; Coghill's account was calmer.

But whether or not the impact on the wall was minimal, the impression on the audience was anything but. Night after night, Richard had a standing ovation. Nevill Coghill was so impressed that he invited Hugh 'Binkie' Beaumont to come down from London and see him act.

Beaumont was then managing director of H. M. Tennent Ltd, the company which had presented *The Druid's Rest*, and was one of the most influential theatre managers in London. Now he was coming to Oxford specifically to see my young brother on the stage. Directly after the performance he invited Richard to come and see him in London as soon as he had finished his RAF service. Richard was jubilant.

By this time, Richard had met Dylan Thomas. On one occasion, they were in a bar together during Richard's spell at Oxford, and he was enjoying one of Thomas's anecdotes. Another member of the audience was called out to be told that his child had been stillborn. Dylan apparently made a cruel joke that they were 'a stillborn little couple, anyway'. Richard, then nineteen, later recalled that he felt 'immensely superior to ordinary beings and immensely cruel.'

The mature Richard definitely had a poor opinion of his younger self, acting talent and tenacity apart. Certainly contradiction permeated his life: the roughness and thoughtfulness towards the characters of the 'Side'; the cruelty and tenderness to

53

his young niece-sisters; the disrespect and reverence for his teachers, particularly his tutor-guardian; the contempt and chivalry towards girls. The one person to whom he was always consistent was his adored Cis, 'more of a mother than any mother could have been.'

This characteristic ambivalence was especially marked during Richard's full-time RAF service which began in the autumn of 1944.

From the beginning Richard was prepared to be bored and frustrated. Just at the time when he was really beginning to make an impact on the theatrical world, he was swept away to the RAF. Not that he was ever really part of the war. Because there was a superfluity of air crew, the Oxford cadets were classified as 'Pilot-navigator-bomb-aimers' instead of being assessed and divided into pilots and navigators. They were sent initially to Torquay for training and aptitude tests. There, Richard was in the same group as a Jewish East Londoner called Mick Misell, who was to become famous as actor Warren Mitchell. After an early brush over a remark of Richard's about Jewish control of the theatre, they became firm friends. Mitchell remembers the time at Torquay – Richard apparently started a Welsh Male Voice choir, though there were few Welsh male voices in the place.

More memorable than the singing, though, was the drinking. And when they were sent to Canada the drinking increased, despite heavy restrictions on alcohol sales.

There are a number of remarkable parallels between Richard and Dylan Thomas. A study of their respective letters, for example, reveals that they each wrote, very carefully, the kind of letters that were expected – withholding the darker side which in both cases involved long and degrading drinking sessions, and affairs, some of them unsavoury, with women.

Richard sent affectionate, humorous letters and postcards from Canada to Cis and the family. This is what he felt they would want and he was right, of course. The wryness, the aimiability, the rueful, self-deprecating humour, the attention to detail pertinent to the family are all typical of the way Richard, charming but a little selective, would give us what we wanted to hear about the

wide-eyed boy making good. This letter, from Manitoba, is dated
10 June 1945.

Dear All,

I've just completed a three-day trip by rail across half of Canada. When
in Montreal two days ago I sent you a postcard – has it arrived yet?

Sleeping in the train was a nightmare of sweating arms and legs, crossed
over each other in all manner of fantastic postures. I am at present lying
on an RAF bed, and even that feels like heaven compared with the train
journey.

I'm due to begin training on Monday, and am I dreading the work? I am
rapidly developing a Canadian accent – very good too; I dare say I could
pass for a genuine Canadian anywhere – outside Canada – Shanghai or
somewhere.

Winnipeg is only thirty miles away. We're allowed to visit it every ten
days interval for forty-eight hours. Money is very easy to spend over here
– fortunately however I'm the 'saving' type, as you know! Shall probably
return to England bursting with money, smiling toothlessly as I give
money away right, left and centre. [Note 'toothlessly']

Dic bach would have gone stark staring mad if he'd lived in the last
town I lived in. It was the centre of a 'dry' state. A 'dry' state is one in
which the drinking and buying of beer and liquor is prohibited by law.
Poor old Dick – he must be getting on – staggering happily into his 80's.

Hector is back again – Did I tell you he's been cut again?

Well, he has. Also I have been suffering for a week with a painful
abcess on my left jaw. I've christened him Samuel (He is not, under any
circumstances to be called Sammy). One more lump and I shall begin to
think my centre of gravity has changed.

From now on I shall drop you a line every ten days. It would be
advisable if you started writing soon otherwise I shall be home when I get
your letter. (I'm getting a little confused, I feel.)

I am writing this with a fountain pen I have acquired. It cost me four
dollars – it's really quite cheap – equivalent of an English pound note – in
case you're a little rusty.

Goodbye for now. I wish I had been there for the Gymanfa Ganu [a
song festival]. Was it the usual J. Jenkins success? I'm sure he was
entertaining. 'Nawr te! Codwch ar eich traed – un o donnau prydferth
Joseph Parry.' ['Now then! Will you please stand on your feet – one of Dr
Joseph Parry's beautiful tunes.']

Yours ever,

Richie

'Dic bach' was our father – I doubt whether Richard wrote to him directly, and certainly it was unlikely that my father wrote to him. It was typical of Richard that he should shift the focus of his own dismay over the 'dry state' on to our father. In reality, he made sure he did not go without alcohol himself, even temporarily. As a smokescreen, he would stay at a Home Hospitality Centre run by a woman known as Aunt Sally. She was a strict law-abiding churchwoman; Richard felt that by staying at her house he would be above suspicion, and sneaked out at night to drink illicitly.

Richard was fond of recalling that Aunt Sally, catching him once in the early hours, made an impassioned speech on damnation and the flesh. When she had finished, he paused theatrically. 'Aunt Sally,' he declared, 'an old doctor friend once told me that if you want immortality, you must find it in the gutter.' Then he left.

The 'Hector' of this letter was one of the boils on his face which often plagued Richard. Despite his good looks and his awareness of them, he was always ready to laugh at the flaws in his appearance and – unconsciously? – turned them to good effect, even making a humorous tale out of the episode when he had been upon the mountains with a girlfriend, only to have passion replaced by pain when she unintentionally squeezed a boil on his bottom.

Another letter home from Canada, sent from Portage la Prairie, is dated 4 July 1945.

Dear Everybody,

I've just received a spate of your letters – three or four of them. One of them – one, by the way, which I am going to frame, containing a short note from Elfed! When I saw this phenomenon I said to myself, 'Oh Lord, mighty in battle, great in wisdom, Father of thought, explain this to me – Elfed, I shouted, has written!' If he writes again I shall become a gibbering idiot. That's a fact.

Well, I've bought three pairs of stockings – one of them is a pair of fishnet stockings. I don't know who is going to wear them. I am not sending any until I acquire sufficient money to fill a box up with all the good things of earth.

I don't think that bananas will stand the long journey but I will send *one* as a trial. If it arrives o.k. I'll send more.

A woman is getting pure silk stockings for you from Minneapolis. She is also, I hope, going to send Rhian fach [little Rhian] a parcel. I don't know what's to be in it. I know she's going to try waxing bananas to see if they endure the journey.

I was disappointed to find that Carys [a cousin of Marian and Rhianon] failed the examination, but I expect she'll pass next time.

At present I'm dressed in the most extravagant suit of clothes you ever saw. White socks, grey tweed trousers, a velvet coat and a blue-check shirt. They all belong to the son of the house, at which I'm staying. He's just my size! Oh boy!

I'm going to write a short letter to Mam and Dad James [Elfed's parents] this afternoon, if I find time. I am on a forty-eight hour pass. We get them every ten days as I probably told you before.

I have received a letter from Mam James. She told me that if there is no one here I can talk Welsh to, I must talk to myself. I am very healthy now – Samuel died a premature death. Hector too, is slowly declining. Ah well. He has been a good and faithful servant, but all good things must come to an end.

Give my love to everybody. Must close now and write to P.H.B. He's all by himself I hear. He told me that he saw you Cis. Said how nice you were. (Be careful Elfed.)

Yours ever,

Richie

P.H.B. is, of course, Philip Burton.

Richard's postcards to Rhianon were straightforward and fraternal, with many references to promised presents: 'tons of ice cream, chocolate and wonderful little gadgets'. He knew his words would conjure up Utopian visions for the girls in war-starved Wales, where everything was still rationed, and ice cream and chocolate were as remote as gold bars.

By the end of August he was on a hitch-hiking trip with Dai Maesteg (Dai Maesteg was the nickname of an RAF chum, Maesteg being a town to the north of Bridgend. I never knew his real name.) round Canada and the United States ending up in New York. A postcard duly arrived from Niagara in early September:

Dear Rhian,

Here I am at the famous falls, only 700 miles from New York.* Will reach New York tomorrow with a bit of luck. I have also travelled two thousand miles from Winnipeg. Dai Maesteg is with me. We are hitch-hiking.

Richie

* He was exaggerating. The distance is only 400 miles.

57

What he did *not* say was that he and Dai Maesteg had only two dollars between them when they set off. Nonetheless, with the stamp of respectability provided by their Air Force uniforms they had no trouble getting lifts. From Buffalo to new York they were driven by a woman going shopping. 'I thought this was the most American thing that every happened,' Richard told me later. 'That a woman should drive four hundred miles to shop.'

They spent their first night in New York camped on the steps of the main post office, and then managed to get into a fraternity home of Columbia University, since it was vacation time. Their RAF uniforms continued to help, and so did their Welshness; in bars they were given drinks and food in exchange for singing in their native tongue. They also managed to get complimentary tickets to a Toscanini concert and to the musical *Oklahoma!* and one old lady was so impressed by their singing that she made them a present of fourteen dollars. They went back to camp in Canada very pleased with themselves.

Richard was careful and meticulous in all his letters. He took considerable pride in his letter writing, and a lot of thought was invested in the creation of an apparently effortless end product.

Much later, he turned this conscientiousness into a joke. Writing to me in 1972 he announced: 'Arcanely enough (my vocabulary is so immense that I try to make everybody, force everybody to look up at least one word in my letters otherwise the buggers won't remember that I've written!) . . .' Richard, reading it over before posting it, crossed out the bit about his vocabulary being immense.

The caring family boy of the letters home may have been one reality, but the punch-ups and drinking sessions represented another. Mick Misell recalls that Richard was one of the wildest of the conscripts in Canada and that one night he really had a go at one of the sergeants. His motive? Apparently Richard was incensed by the sergeant's attempt to hide his Welshness under an American accent.

Such behaviour was not confined to Canada. I remember thinking at the time that it was just as well he never actually fought in the war or he would surely not have emerged alive.

As a brother, and an older one at that, I was taken into his confidence more than Cis and her family, and I concluded that he was as mad as a hatter. But at least it was some consolation to me that his devotion to literature, and especially Shakespeare, continued unabated. When he was not working or involved in a spree of some kind he used to bury himself in the Bard's complete works. He was really hooked.

Before embarking on a new job around this time, Philip Burton went to Cardiff to discuss the post with his predecessor. Richard, back in Britain, went along too – and they paid a visit to the small police station in Llantwit Major where I was based.

I still remember the impact Richard's appearance had on me. He was not in uniform this time, but carefully clad in a brand new sports jacket with pressed grey trousers. Philip Burton must have taken him to Savile Row, I thought, my mind inevitably rolling back to the dreary days at the Co-op drapery.

Suitably impressed, and almost, but not quite, in awe of my young brother, I played the attentive host and took them both along to see St Donat's Castle, a great medieval fortress on the nearby coast, and the small and beautiful adjoining church. Richard was, I noted, every inch the young gentleman. Moreover any police chargeroom coarseness in my manner instantly vanished in the company of 'the Burtons'. They were both all courtesy and charm, and if anything remained of the old animosity between the two of them, they certainly succeeded in hiding it from me.

After his brief spell at Oxford, Richard was heard to speak with a decidedly cultivated accent when he came home – this was not uncommon in those who had been 'away to England' and always frowned upon. Anxious that Richard should not be viewed as a snob, Hilda was quick to remind him he was not at Oxford now.

Her mild rebuke brought Richard down to earth very quickly, and he soon demonstrated that he had not lost his Welsh accent. He was cautious for a long time afterwards, until the years away from Wales and his acting career gradually effected their own changes in his voice.

Hilda recalls another incident when Richard came to Pontrhydyfen to see her in January 1945, dressed in his RAF uniform. She noticed a huge tear in his trousers, and he, product of the age and used to the attentions of his sisters, promptly asked her if she would repair it for him.

'How did this happen then?' asked Hilda. 'Oh,' said Richard with characteristic casualness, 'Mick Misell and I picked up a few chickens on the way down.' 'What have you done with them?' asked Hilda. 'We sold them because we were short of money,' Richard admitted without much sign of guilt. 'You ought to be ashamed of yourselves,' said the forthright Hilda.

He made another visit in his RAF uniform late one night to Cis and her family. It was mid-winter, cold and bleak. Elfed was working nights, so Cis and her two daughters decided to cheer themselves up by going to bed together and swapping pyjamas.

They were all tucked up and giggling away when the doorbell went. Richard and Philip Burton had decided to make a surprise visit. There were few people they would have got up for that night, remembers Cis. As it was, they all trooped excitedly downstairs and stayed there talking until the small hours.

It is doubtful whether Richard would have confessed very many of his Air Force antics to the family. The worst of them, according to Mick Misell, took place in Norfolk, in the winter of 1945/46, after the group's return from Canada. Apparently there had been some kind of unofficial directive that the boys at Richard's rural station should be more or less left to themselves. It was not the wisest way of handling this group who had been trained and who had been to Canada and back, but who had not really participated in the war at all.

In November 1945 Richard celebrated his twentieth birthday by getting hopelessly drunk with a group of wild Irish friends. They decided to demonstrate the technique of putting a fist through a window without getting the slightest scratch. 'It was all quite innocent,' Richard said later. 'But we did smash 179 windows and we got seven days jankers.'

Around this time, Mick Misell told Richard he could get him posted to London because of a useful contact in the Air Ministry. But Richard preferred to stay on in Norfolk, intending to play some rugby, translate a novel from Welsh into English, and go on studying Shakespeare.

The last stretch of conscription seemed interminable. Not surprisingly, Richard was increasingly impatient with the whole thing and felt that it had served little useful purpose, apart from giving him time to read and enjoy himself.

Robert (known to friends as Tim) Hardy's account fits into this background – he and Richard were already friends having met at Oxford, and he was in Norfolk during that frustrating period of marking time until demobilisation. He later recalled vivid images of Richard in a pub with 'the usual clutch of followers, all listening to him.' It seems there was a powerful, almost frenzied aura of excitement – it was a rootless time when Richard and his fellow conscripts were dangerously free of military discipline.

The RAF gave generous leave, however, as Richard and his peers were virtually an embarrassment still, with little to occupy them. Philip helped Richard to get radio parts – by this time he had left teaching for a full-time post with the BBC, acting as a producer in Wales, and during the summer of 1946 they spent a glorious week seeing plays in Stratford. Richard was captivated by the production of Marlowe's *Dr Faustus*, which starred Hugh Griffith as Mephistopheles. Afterwards, intoxicated by the power of the drama, he worked on speeches from it with Philip, and began to talk of playing Faustus himself one day. (He did, of course, but not at Stratford.)

His fascination with the part of Faustus can be seen, with hindsight, as an eerie forerunner of his own life:

'Why, this is Hell, nor am I out of it;
Thinks't thou that I, who saw the face of
God, And tasted the eternal joys of heaven
Am not tormented with ten thousand Hells,
In being deprived of everlasting bliss – oh Faustus,
leave those frivolous demands which strike a terror
to my fainting soul.'

The following winter Richard celebrated his twenty-first birth-day with less violence than his twentieth had seen, but still, I gather, with vast amounts of beer.

There must have been two celebrations, for Cis recalls that she and Elfed were invited by Philip Burton to a birthday dinner in Cardiff – an occasion still further removed from window-bashing days. Cis remembers the event as one tinged with sadness. It felt wrong, both to Richard and to her, that she should be a guest on such an occasion. She was not ungrateful or unhappy to be asked, but she was painfully aware that her home was no longer Richard's, and never would be again. It was a time of change in another sense, too: when Richard attained his majority on 10 November 1946, he was no longer Philip Burton's ward.

When demobilisation finally came, servicemen who had taken the university short course had the option of returning to continue their studies to degree level. Robert Hardy did; Mick Misell and Richard did not. Richard's plan, in fact, was to return to Oxford after a couple of years, when he would have a better chance of winning a blue for rugby. He had been warned that competition from the colonials would be high in the post-war period.

Chapter Six

Sybil and early stardom

Richard never went back to Oxford. He remembered the cocktail-party tones of his pre-conscription tempters: 'If you want to be a professional, dear, you come and see us. We'll arrange it for you.'

He decided to take up 'Binkie' Beaumont's invitation and went to see him in London with high hopes. He was not disappointed; almost immediately he was signed up, with a contract with Tennent's for five hundred pounds a year. 'Bloody marvellous!' said Richard. 'Ten pounds a week whether I work or not.'

Richard was secure – financially, professionally, practically. He had his contract, which led to several West End stage performances; he had Philip Burton, still very much his protector and guide; he had Emlyn Williams, now closely involved in London Films Productions; and he had Daphne Rye. She was Tennent's casting director who had auditioned him for *The Druid's Rest*. Again there are echoes of Dylan Thomas. Dylan was constantly being helped and supported by friends and admirers, among whom Margaret Taylor stands out, buying, for instance, an Oxfordshire cottage and later the famous Laugharne Boat House for him.

Richard did not have (nor did he need) such a benefactress, but Daphne Rye, a caring and perceptive woman, offered him rooms at the top of her house in Pelham Crescent at the very moment when he was looking for somewhere to live in London. It was a bonus that Emlyn Williams and his wife were just up the road. And one of Richard's first roles in London, a minor one it has to be said, was in a production of Daphne's at the Lyric Theatre: *Castle Anna* by Elizabeth Bowen and John Perry, which opened in February 1948. He also understudied the lead and looked, at one point, like taking it over; a repeat of the Oxford *Measure For Measure*. This time, unfortunately, it did not happen, though apparently many where convinced he would be better than the leading man in the part.

Soon afterwards, however, during the summer of 1948, Richard was on tour in a play called *Dark Summer* when Emlyn Williams got in touch with him. His message was startling – come for a screen test! The film was *The Last Days Of Dolwyn*, inspired by the sacrifice of a Welsh village which was to be flooded to provide a reservoir for an English city. Emlyn Williams wanted Richard for the part of Gareth, the young hero of the story; indeed he had written the part for him. Others, more influential than the author, needed convincing: it was primarily for the producers Alexander Korda and Anatole de Grunwald that Williams arranged the test. After all, who could be certain that an actor only just making his mark on stage could seduce the camera? Richard arrived just in time for the test, and got the part; back on tour with *Dark Summer*, he received a telegram from Emlyn Williams: 'You have won the scholarship' – a telling quote, of course, from the latter's play *The Corn Is Green*.

Richard was understandably thrilled, but – and this aspect of him always infuriated us as a family – he did not get round to replying. He was so totally disorganised and unbusinesslike, despite the best of intentions and frequent promises to mend his ways. When he was older and his career was more established, he always had someone to look after his contracts, his finances, his mail: our brother Ivor; lawyers; secretaries. . . but at this early stage, he had no one. And I think he needed someone, even then.

Fortunately Emlyn Williams already knew Richard and was confident that the absence of a response did not signify indifference to the offer. So on the first day's filming he greeted Richard with feigned surprise – since he hadn't bothered to reply, how were they to know he had accepted the part?

Richard, as always, apologised and re-affirmed his enthusiasm for making the film. But that carelessness, which so often had hurtful consequences, was already ingrained in his character, and he seemed powerless to change it, if indeed he really wanted to. It was almost as if Richard, always the little brother to all of us, and mothered by Cis with a dedication that his own mother could not have matched, was unable to grow up and take full adult responsibility for himself.

Furthermore, Richard was not happy without a woman – another characteristic which was to stay with him all his life, and one closely linked to his reluctance to face life alone. Of course he had a lot of appeal for women; this was apparent from his school days. There had been a number of girl friends, notably Catherine Dolan, Susie Preece and Eleanor Summerfield, a lively actress he knew from RAF days, to whom he almost became engaged. And now, there was Sybil.

Sybil Williams was a vivacious eighteen-year-old drama student who just managed to get a small part in *The Last Days Of Dolwyn*. Richard, prodded by Emlyn Williams one day during a break in the filming, introduced himself. Emlyn had privately decided that Richard was dabbling too deeply in the world of night clubs and one-night stands. So he was delighted when Richard and Sybil immediately responded well to each other. She was charmed by him, and he was impressed by her as well as attracted.

So although he had plenty of good-looking women to choose from, Sybil had the added bonus of a striking personality: she was intelligent; a thinker. And, not unimportant, she was Welsh. Born in Tylorstown in the Rhondda Valley, she was the daughter of a pit manager and thus from a more privileged background than we were. There were nonetheless some remarkable similarities in the early lives of Richard and Sybil. Her mother had died when she was a child, and she too had been brought up by an older sister; moreover she had taken part in drama productions at school, and she also worked for a time as a shop assistant. Sybil's great ambition had been to become an actress, and when she was seventeen she won a place at the London Academy of Music and Drama.

When the filming of *Dolwyn* was over, Richard and Sybil discovered, perhaps to the surprise of both and certainly to Richard's, that they did not want to part. He brought her home to see the family – and more importantly, for us to see her. We were all impressed. She had a lovely smile, and a winning sense of humour. I remember her sighing and saying that all the Jenkins boys had slim ankles, and how she envied that!

Very soon afterwards the wedding date was fixed – 5 February, 1949, at Kensington Registry Office. It was to be a quiet, informal occasion with just a few friends. No member of the family attended the wedding. We did not really know about it till it was a *fait accompli* – he informed Cis shortly after the ceremony.

The wedding clashed with a rugby international between Wales and Scotland. Every self-respecting Welshman who could not be at Murrayfield would be glued to his wireless set for the afternoon. Richard was no exception. Perhaps it was as well that Sybil was involved in the stage play *Harvey* and had to go off after the midday reception for the Saturday matinée performance. She came back to find Richard in a grim state of post-alcohol despair because Wales had lost the match: hardly the most romantic start to a marriage.

But Sybil was remarkably resilient and could cope from the start with Richard's moods. Sybil realised early in their marriage that her own acting career would have to take second place. She did not seem to mind – her devotion to Richard was greater than her professional ambitions.

Richard continued his pursuit of experience, success and fame. Then an unexpected setback occurred. Early in 1949, he was given a part in Terence Rattigan's play *Adventure Story* in which he was to work with Paul Scofield. It was a historical drama about Alexander the Great. Scofield, slightly older, definitely more experienced, was to be Alexander – an imperial, conquering, questing character well suited to his intelligence and maturity, and Richard had the important supporting role of Alexander's older friend Hephaestion. It would be a splashy part, and in the West End, too: plenty of opportunities to attract all the kinds of attention he sought; it was a part to increase any young actor's standing. Yet it never happened. Shortly after rehearsals began, Richard was replaced by Robert Fleming. He was bitterly disappointed.

As so often in Richard's life, there are conflicting accounts of this episode. Some of the cast felt that Richard lost the part because he was too striking to be effective in a minor role – a perverse compliment. The producer, Peter Glenville (later to direct Richard in *Becket* and *The Comedians*) claimed that he was too young – he was twenty-three and looked it – to play Scofield's senior. 'I was supposed to play Paul Scofield's older friend,' commented Richard wryly, 'but how can anyone . . . he looks a hundred and eight to begin with.'

The gap, however, was quickly filled. Christopher Fry had written a new play, *The Lady's Not For Burning*. It was a demanding one, both for players and audience. Set in late medieval England, it was a verse drama – not usually the stuff of box-office success – recounting the entwined fates of a soldier of fortune, tired of the awfulness of life, and an alluring witch ironically full of will to live, despite the sentence of death hanging over her. As a contrast to the complexities and paradoxes of adult life, Fry had written two young characters, a boy ('Mayor's Clerk'), and a girl, Alison, who, untainted by what happens around them, fall in love and elope. Daphne Rye had been instrumental in getting the play staged: appropriately, John Gielgud, one of the very few actors with the cachet to draw audiences to 'difficult' pieces, was to be both director and star. Richard auditioned for the boy's part. Now part of theatre history, the *Lady*'s success was initially far from assured. On a preliminary provincial tour, reaction was cool and attendances were low. The West End however was a different story entirely. Critics admired it; more surprisingly, audiences came for a year, fully prepared to work hard to appreciate the elegant wordy games of logic played upon them by a superb cast; a *succes d'estime* began coining it. The *Lady* was hot. This was, of course, delightful for Richard.

Christopher Fry gave me his own recollections of events, in a letter in the autumn of 1985:

> John Gielgud was playing in St John Rankin's *The Return of the Prodigal* which was about to finish its short run at the Globe Theatre, and he had already held the first reading of *The Lady's Not For Burning*, due to follow at the Globe after a preliminary tour. At the end of the reading he said he felt that the actress and actor cast for the parts of Alison and the Mayor's Clerk weren't quite right, but he had possible replacements, a young actor and young actress, who would read for me the next evening after the performance of *The Return of the Prodigal*. I went to the theatre the next night with Pamela Brown [who was to play the witch] and we stood in the wings while the young couple – the girl was Claire Bloom – gave their audition. Richard was clearly nervous. I think he had just been dropped from the rehearsing cast of Rattigan's *Adventure Story* and now he sat on a chair on the stage, his feet crooked round the chair-legs, not making a great job of the reading.
>
> 'The girl's all right,' Pam whispered to me, 'but I don't think the boy will do.'
>
> Luckily, Gielgud told Richard to talk with me about the part, and to

come back the next day for a second reading. That was the unpromising start to a performance that was to electrify audiences until he left *The Lady* in January 1950.

Sir John Gielgud also remembers *The Lady* well – and Richard's part in it:

> He arrived at the first rehearsal and just walked into the part; I never had to tell him anything except to stop yawning when it was lunchtime, because he was anxious to get away. But he had the most wonderful instinct, immediately. And there was this scene, which has been talked about a lot, in which he had to scrub the floor in the second act while Pamela Brown and I were playing a love scene, sort of across him.

Quite a joke was made of this floor scrubbing episode; Richard effectively stole the scene, making it impossible not to focus on him rather than on the main characters.

Richard's films in the late 1940s and the first year of the 1950s were fine for the time, but in contrast to later achievements, appear small-scale and provincial. The British film industry was still producing quite a number of pictures then, but many were cheap programme fillers. Richard's were certainly better than that, but I suppose they were also-rans after the particular thrill, for us, of his debut in a Welsh subject.

The first, *Now Barabbas Was A Robber*, saw Richard playing an Irish criminal in a prison story – adequate, not without its moments, but not a classic. That was in 1949. *Waterfront*, released in 1950, was a comparatively gritty piece highlighting the woes of unemployment amongst Mersey seafolk and their kin, and featured the redoubtable Robert Newton. It packed a genuine emotional punch and was the more brave for appearing in a world that seemed to want froth; and the next one, *The Woman With No Name*, was precisely that. Richard, adding to his repertoire of nationalities, starred as a Norwegian airman who marries an amnesia victim in bigamous circumstances. It was typical of that genre of love stories beset with thrillingly romantic problems, and I cannot really believe that Richard felt right in such a part.

Finally from this period there was *Green Grow The Rushes*, most notable for being backed financially by the industry's union. Richard had good company – Roger Livesey and Honor

Blackman – but it was not a great hit. In these years, it was the stage rather than the cinema which made the better use of Richard's talents.

In January 1950, Richard moved to The Lyric, Hammersmith, to appear in *The Boy With A Cart*, again by Christopher Fry. *The Boy With A Cart* was based on the legend of Cuthman, the shepherd boy who is 'called' from Cornwall to build a church in a Sussex village. He takes his old mother right across the south of England in a home-made wheelbarrow to answer the call. Richard, and the seventy-two year old Mary Jerrold who played his mother, made the play – just one act – both credible and very moving. Christopher Fry recalled Richard's contribution to the play:

> Again there was the great economy and truth that had made the other performance [in *The Lady's Not For Burning*] so memorable. Stillness and restraint were things he was master of. At this time he took less easily in performance to excitement, high spirits or rhetoric and I think this was still true of his Prince Hal and Henry V at Stratford [1951] as I remember them. Gielgud, directing *The Boy With A Cart*, had to work quite hard with him to produce the high spirits of Cuthman's first speech ('This is the morning to take the air,' etc.) but when he found his way, his performance shone.
>
> When my wife and I went backstage after a performance of *The Boy with a Cart* towards the end of its run, Richard told me that he and Diana Graves (who was playing Mrs Fipps) had a plan to do *A Phoenix Too Frequent* at the Dolphin Theatre, Brighton, (then a try-out theatre for H. M. Tennent's, now, alas, no longer there) for a week or two of performances for the fun of it, and asked if I would direct it. I said I would if we could get Jessie Evans to play Doto, which is what happened, and we had a very happy time rehearsing it and putting it on. Richard was great fun to work with – always in good humour, and the source of some brilliantly comic anecdotes to lighten the way.

Though not in the same league as his previous Fry play, this new play was very important because it marked Richard's first real leading stage role in London and under the direction of a theatrical genius, too. It meant that he would be noticed – his part dominated the play. Richard's performance in *The Boy With A Cart* greatly impressed the critics. Harold Hobson of the *Sunday Times* declared that he had 'brought his own cathedral with him'.

Paul Daneman, understudy for Richard's part, generously echoed the critics' enthusiasm:

He arrived, I remember clearly, on the first day, to read it, and it's very good poetry; some of Christopher Fry's best work. And the part of Cuthman is almost a solo part, with a chorus and one or two other characters. And he read it magically – we all sat there and there was this wonderful voice and this extraordinary feeling for poetry. Richard knew – oh, always knew, whether by instinct or whether Philip Burton had taught him – he knew that speaking verse was a matter of sense rather than slavishly following iambic pentameters and things like that. He just had a natural feel for verse, and a beautiful, beautiful voice. So he read it well. Well that was fine.

We rehearsed for a long time – in those days we had about six weeks to rehearse a play. And Richard had learnt it, bit by bit, but never did anything. He never did anything at all. Now in those days, actors did lots of things. You know, we were really – or most of us – trained in the old school. And we tended to act and characterise. Richard did nothing. And we all started to say to each other – when is he going to do something? When is something going to happen? and this went right through the six weeks and right up to the dress rehearsal; he still wasn't doing anything.

And I remember on the first night Richard came on and did exactly nothing . . . exactly what he'd done at the first reading. And we all thought – oh, well, that's it. Goodnight. And when the curtain fell, there was huge applause and people started to come round and everybody said – 'My God, that boy! That boy is wonderful. He is the most wonderful. . . .' and this went on all night. People talked and talked about Richard. It was the next day that Hobson said – 'this boy has a cathedral in his eyes', or whatever it was. And it was true. He had this extraordinary thing of stillness and simplicity, which takes most actors a lifetime to learn. And he did it absolutely right from the beginning.'

For Richard it was another milestone: one of the influential actors who came to see him at the Lyric was Anthony Quayle, on the lookout for someone to play in his 1951 'Festival of Britain' season at Stratford. It was to be a season of some significance, as part of a laudable attempt to reinvigorate British self esteem, at a low ebb after years of hardship and rationing. More than any other Stratford season, this one would remind the nation of its proud history. The parts Quayle needed to fill were Prince Hal in *Henry IV* and then King Henry in *Henry V*: reputation-making parts. He offered them to Richard, who immediately accepted.

Richard said later that he felt that Anthony Quayle was 'taking

Richard in the early 80s taking a nostalgic look at the 'Bont Fawr', the bridge which gave the village of Pontrhydyfen its name.

Left: The only photograph of Richard's parents, Richard and Edith, taken on their wedding day, Christmas Eve 1900.

Below: Port Talbot Secondary Grammar School rugby team – Richard Jenkins (Burton) second row, sixth from left. He later had three international rugby trials.

Right: Susie
Preece, gifted
schoolgirl ten-
nis-player, with
whom Richard
had an early
romance.

Below right:
Cecilia James,
to whom this
book is dedi-
cated – 'no
ordinary
woman'.

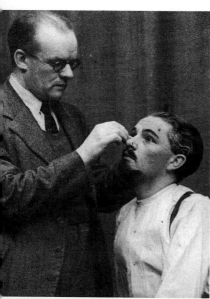

Left: Philip Burton applying Richard's make-up for *Pygmalion* at the Port Talbot Secondary Grammar School.

Below: Richard as an RAF cadet in 1944 – second row fifth from left.

Right: Richard in *My Cousin Rachel*, his first Hollywood film, 1952. (Rex Features)

Above: Richard in *Hamlet,* 1954. Eight former Hamlets went backstage at the Old Vic to congratulate him.

Right: Richard as King Henry V, one of his great Shakespearean achievements on stage, in the 1950s.

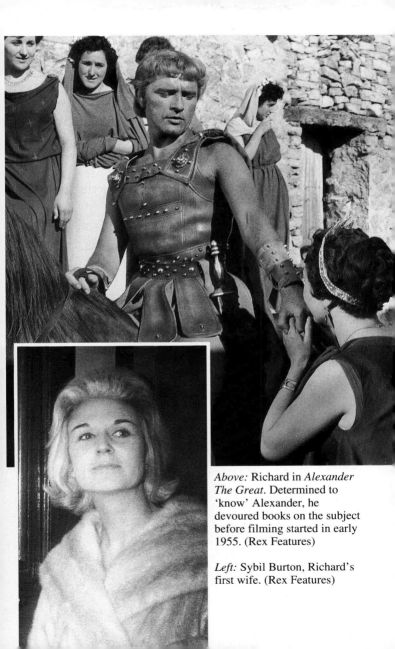

Above: Richard in *Alexander The Great*. Determined to 'know' Alexander, he devoured books on the subject before filming started in early 1955. (Rex Features)

Left: Sybil Burton, Richard's first wife. (Rex Features)

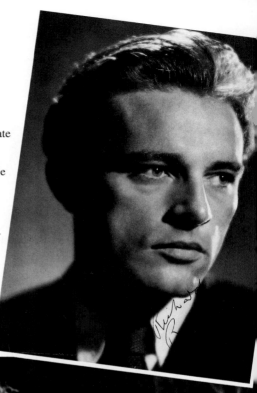

Right: Richard in the late
50s, his career – and
charisma – well estab-
lished. (Courtesy Movie
Portraits)

Below: In *Camelot*,
New York, 1960. For
Richard and his co-star
Julie Andrews
Camelot was a magi-
cal triumph. Richard
was rewarded with
the New York Drama
Critics' Award for
the best musical
performance.

a big chance' on him. But Quayle was more confident. 'I thought that there was no question that he could not do it triumphantly and that he was going to be a great, huge, thumping star. It was perfectly obvious.'

Richard enrolled both Philip Burton and Tim Hardy to help him refine, intensify and seize as his the great part that had been offered him. When he saw *Henry V* on stage, Phil wrote in his diary, 'there's no doubt about R.'s greatness. I feel proud, humble, and awed by God's mysterious ways.' I remember clearly my own impressions of Richard playing Prince Hal. I was aware from the start of his magnetic effect on the audience, and like everyone there, I was fascinated by his whole performance. He really played the part as if he had been groomed for it all his life. He had this quiet natural flair – this innate ability. I was riveted, and not in the least surprised by the critics' eulogies. Kenneth Tynan's perception of Richard as Hal shrewdly caught the qualities of latent life and vitality that gave much strength to silence: 'Burton is a still brimming pool, running disturbingly deep . . . he commands repose and can make silence garrulous. . . For all his bold chivalry this watchful Celt seems surely to have strayed from a wayside pulpit [How apt *that* was!] . . . In battle, Burton's voice cuts urgent and keen – always likeable, always inaccessible.'

Richard was ready to play Prince Hal and King Henry V, because he too was a young pretender, filled with wildness and reckless disregard but who hid within himself the power to focus all attention on him, to dominate through force of presence, to be brighter than those around him. It was his moment, and he knew how to take it.

Humphrey Bogart saw Richard play Prince Hal at Stratford, and accosted him backstage. 'You're wasting your time on the stage,' he said. 'Go to the States and I'll look after you there.'

This was one of many instances of temptation that Richard would have to face. There was further contact with Bogart – he visited Richard and Sybil at the house they had rented near Stratford. Carving the meat at his host's table, Bogart repeated his offer. Not long after this, of course, Richard did actually go to Hollywood – but more of that at the right moment.

The Stratford season confirmed what the two Christopher Fry plays had first intimated to the world. Richard was a star, not just

71

in the ordinary sense of being a recognised name, one to spell large on posters – he was far more than that. He was unarguably brighter than those around him. He had qualities defined by words that have lost their potency through application to blander lights – charisma; intensity and a mesmerising, seductive presence. I think he knew this more than most – the question was, what to do with it? There was the promise of Shakespearian triumphs to come: that would appeal to the orator and the lover of language in him so carefully nurtured by Philip Burton. But the practical application of being a star was stardom: glamour, wealth, profligacy, excitement, adulation. That was found further West than Warwickshire – in New York and Hollywood. Richard had had an infecting encounter with the more lucrative side of glitter, when, before the 1951 Stratford season began, he had been on his first professional trip to the United States, taking Sybil with him. *The Lady's Not For Burning* transferred to Broadway; it performed commendably, and Richard was noticed by a new set of critics. Richard in turn noticed, I think, the wealth, the easy affluence of the East Coast unhindered by such tiresome conceits as rationing. I can only guess at how this affected him – but I am sure it did, especially as it may have also been the occasion of his first trip to Hollywood.

According to Richard, it was on this visit to America with *The Lady's Not For Burning* that he went across to California and met Elizabeth Taylor for the first time – though I suspect that that happened a year or two later. He wrote about it in the mid-1960s – when the romance between them was at its strongest – in a piece entitled *Meeting Mrs Jenkins*. He clearly delighted in creating this (no doubt embellished) account of their first meeting; then closed the piece by bringing it up to date, giving it a coda describing his then life with Elizabeth: 'Paris, photographers, restaurants'. I have included this later section at this point, because it puts the ironic flavour of the Hollywood episode, so shrewdly viewed with hindsight, into a proper context.

Meeting Mrs Jenkins

The house in California – it was in the Bel Air district of Los

Angeles, I think – looked as if it had been flung by a giant hand against the side of a hill and had stuck.

From the main living room, master bedroom, guest bedrooms, dining room, kitchen level, the house jutted and dropped one floor to a 'playroom'.

The 'playroom' was not for children.

It was complete with bar and barman, hot-dog simmerer, king-sized double-doored two-toned refrigerator, drugstore hotplates, big-game trophies on the walls (the host was a big-game hunter who acted in his spare time) and huge, deep, low divans and easy chairs – villainously uncomfortable for men, but marvellously made for cute little women who could tuck their little legs away and blazingly efface their cute little pretty pouting little personalities in niches of the vast furniture and make like cute little pussycats.

Below the 'playroom' the house again jutted and dropped to the swimming pool, the showers, and the changing rooms.

It was my first time in California and my first visit to a swank house. There were quite a lot of people in and round the pool, all suntanned and all drinking the Sunday morning liveners – Bloody Marys, boiler-makers, highballs, iced beer. I knew some of the people and was introduced to the others. Wet, brown arms reached out of the pool and shook my hand. The people were all friendly, and they called me Dick immediately. I asked if they would please call me Richard – Dick, I said, made me feel like a symbol of some kind. They laughed, some of them. It was, of course, Sunday morning and I was nervous.

I was enjoying this small social triumph, but then a girl sitting on the other side of the pool lowered her book, took off her sunglasses and looked at me. She was so extraordinarily beautiful that I nearly laughed out loud. I didn't, of course, which was just as well. The girl was not, and quite clearly was not going to be, laughing back. I had an idea that, finding nothing of interest, she was looking right through me and was examining the texture of the wall behind. If there was a flaw in the sandstone, I knew she'd find it and probe it right to the pith. I fancied that if she chose so, the house would eventually collapse.

I smiled at her and, after a long moment just as I felt my own smile turning into a cross-eyed grimace, she stared slightly and smiled back. There was little friendliness in the smile. A new ice cube formed of its own accord in my Scotch-on-the-rocks.

She sipped some beer and went back to her book. I affected to become social with others but out of the corner of my mind – while I played for the others the part of a poor miner's son who was puzzled, but delighted by the attention these lovely people paid to him – I had her under close observation. She was, I decided, the most astonishingly self-contained, pulchritudinous, remote, removed, inaccessible woman I had ever seen. She spoke to no one. She looked at no one. She steadily kept on reading her book. Was she merely sullen? I wondered. I thought not. There was no trace of sulkiness in the divine face. She was a Mona Lisa type, I thought. In my business everyone is a type. She is older than the deck chair on which she sits, I thought headily, and she is famine, fire, destruction and plague, she is the dark lady of the sonnets, the only true begetter. She is a secret wrapped in an enigma inside a mystery, I thought, with a mental man-to-man nod to Churchill. Her breasts were apocalyptic, they would topple empires down before they withered. Indeed, her body was a miracle of construction and the work of an engineer of genius. It needed nothing except itself. It was true art, I thought, executed in terms of itself. It was smitten by its own passion. I used to think things like that. I was not long down from Oxford and Walter Pater was still talked of and I read the art reviews in the quality weeklies without much caring about the art itself, and it was a Sunday morning in Bel Air, and I was nervous, and there was the Scotch-on-the-rocks.

Like Miniver Cheevy I kept on drinking and, in the heady flow of the attention I was getting, told story after story as the afternoon boozed slowly on. I went in swimming one or twice. So did she, but, lamentably, always after I'd come out. She swam easily and gracefully as an Englishwoman would and not with the masculine drive and kick of most American girls. She was unquestionably gorgeous. I can think of no other word to describe a combination of plenitude, frugality, abundance, tightness. She was lavish. She was a dark unyielding largesse. She was, in short, too bloody much and not only that, she was totally ignoring me. I became frustrated almost to screaming when I had finished a well-received and humorous story about the death of my grandfather and found that she was turned away in deep conversation with

74

another woman. I think I tried to eavesdrop but was stayed by words like Tony and Janet and Marion and Sammy. She was not, obviously, talking about me.

Eventually, with half-seas-ed cunning and with all the non-chalance of a traffic jam, I worked my way to her side of the pool. She was describing – in words not normally written – what she thought of a producer at MGM. This was my first encounter with freedom of speech in the USA, and it took my breath away. My brain throbbed; I almost sobered up. I was profoundly shocked. It was ripe stuff. I checked her again. There was no question about it. She was female. In America the women apparently had not only got the vote – they'd got the words to go with it.

I was also somewhat puzzled and disturbed by the half-look she gave me as she uttered the enormities. Was she deliberately trying to shock me? Those huge violet-blue eyes (the biggest I've ever seen, outside those who have glandular trouble – thyroid, et cetera) had an odd glint in them. You couldn't describe it as a twinkle . . . Searchlights cannot twinkle, they turn on and off and probe the heavens and so on.

Still I couldn't be left out. I had to join in and say something. I didn't reckon on the Scotch though. . . . I didn't reckon that it had warped my judgment and my sense of timing, my choice of occasion. With all the studied frenzy of Dutch courage I waded into the depths of those perilous eyes.

In my best chiffon-and-cut-glass Oxford accent I said: 'You have a remarkable command of Olde Englishe.'

There was a pause in which I realised with brilliant clarity the relativity of time. Aeons passed, civilisations came and went, brave men and cowards died in battles not yet fought, while those cosmic headlights examined my flawed personality. Every pock-mark on my face became a crater of the moon. I reached up with a casual hand to cover up the right-cheeked evidence of my acne'd youth. Halfway up I realised my hand was just as ugly as my face and decided to leave the bloody thing and die instead. But while contemplating the various ways of suicide and having sensibly decided, since I had a good start, to drink myself to death, I was saved by her voice which said, 'Don't you use words like that at the Old Vic?'

'They do,' I said, 'but *I* don't. I come from a family and an attitude that believe such words are an indication of weakness in vocabulary and emptiness of mind. . . . Despite Jones's writing that in times of acute shared agony and fear, as in trench warfare, obscenities repeated in certain patterns can at times become almost liturgical, almost poetic. . . . I ran out of gas.

There was another pause; more empires fell, captains and kings and counsellors arrived and departed. She said three four letter words. These were, I think, 'Well! Well! Well!'

Somebody laughed uneasily. The girl had turned away. I had been dismissed. I felt as lonely as a muezzin, as a reluctant piano lesson on a Saturday afternoon, as the Last Post played on a cracked bugle.

I went home and somebody asked, when I told them where I'd been, what was she like. 'Dark. Dark. Dark. Dark. She probably,' I said, 'shaves.' To nobody in particular, I observed that the human body is eighty per cent water.

It wasn't until five years later that I saw her again, across a restaurant – I can't remember which restaurant or indeed which country or continent. I think she waved at me. I think I scowled back – particularly at her new husband. She had the impertinence to look happy, even radiant. I had liked him a great deal, but now he'd married this girl I write of, and he hadn't even had the grace to ask me to be in *Around The World In Eighty Days*. I was the only actor in the world who hadn't been asked – with a promise of a small Cézanne – to act in that film. I still liked him and though I bitterly resented her obvious happiness and though I muttered mysteriously to myself words like 'bucolic' and 'bovine content', I believe that I forced a smile at them through my clenched teeth as I left.

The years have gone by – seven or eight. It's Sunday in Paris in early winter. There is a persistent drizzle of cold grey rain. This pleases us. It means we can walk to Fouquet's and not ride in the car because the poor little notorious couple will not be bothered by paparazzi. Their cameras do not like rain. She is excited at the thought of this tiny expedition – Fouquet's is one block away from our hotel. She glows. I am excited too. I glow. 'Is the dress all right?' she asks.

'Whenas in silks my Julia goes,' I say. 'Then, then, methinks, how sweetly flows the liquefaction of her clothes!'

'Richard,' she says, 'I'll methink you right across the liquefaction of your face if you don't give me a straight answer. It is all right?'

'Lovely,' I say. 'And don't shout and bawl at me like that,' I say, 'or you'll be a partner to the shortest marriage since my Great-Aunt Mary Jane Loughor dropped dead just as she was signing the marriage certificate in the chapel vestry.'

We went down in the elevator. I tipped the concierge a wink – the only kind of tip I really enjoy giving. We walked along the Rue de Berri to the Champs Élysées. We turned right, towards the Arc de Triomphe – the cold rain had swept the great street empty of people. Almost. There was a man and a greyhound. A Fiat car squelched through the wet. We were alone in a street in a city where all but us and the man with the greyhound and the man in the Fiat had died in a vast silent painless war that had come in the night.

'Alone, alone, all, all alone,' I sang, 'alone on a wide, wide sea! And never a saint. . . .' The Fiat screamed into a U-turn. The man parked it ahead of us. He leaped out of his car and started towards us. He was thirty-five years old; his hairline receded; he was wearing a short raincoat and pointed shoes and three cameras. And I had known him all, already know him all. I'd known him in Rome and London and Paris and Geneva. Had known him at airports and railway stations – I'd known him shout insults in Italian and French and English and German. I had not liked him. He was running towards us. He was unique because he was alone. I'd known him before only in numbers, running with with the pack, elbowing, screaming, frantic. I'd known him, with old-fashioned gallantry, call my wife a whore and me a gigolo and my friends pimps. I had not liked him.

'When,' I said, 'when the world is over, when the oceans and the graves deliver up their dead and this planet has gone screaming back to seething gas and we stand alone in an endless multitude for the final severe searching before the Supreme Judge, the last thing we'll see,' I said, warming to my speech, 'is one of these blokes trying to take a photograph of it all and asking the Great Mathematician to cheat his look a little to the left.'

'Now, Richard, don't start that rubbish, don't say things like that,' she said. 'Don't get into one of your death moods, we'll have it for the rest of the day. Trouble with the Welsh is,' she said, 'that they think everybody's Welsh, even Death.'

We had stopped.

'Why not? He's a local man,' I said. 'He's a very distinguished feller. We must be prepared for him and courteous when he comes.'

'Don't,' she said quickly. 'Don't make fun. You can't talk your way out of the fear of death.'

'You want a bet?'

'Don't, please don't talk about it.'

'Good God. It's the most absorbing subject and has been since the first man died.'

'And don't you die on me,' she said. 'I couldn't bear it again.'

'Don't you die on me either.' We stared at each other.

Her brilliant eyes had dimmed. The violet in them had turned dark – almost to blackness. They looked like water over coal, like black macadam in the rain under street lamps at night.

An emotion compounded of – who knows what? – of fear and love and pride and beauty and self-pity seized us both by the throat and shook us like a dog. The man crouched three feet away from us, backing as we walked, clicking and clicking. I feinted a kick at the photographer's left knee. As he dropped his camera I backhanded him across the face. He was off balance and fell quickly onto his back. Equally quickly he was up and clicking and clicking and cursing in a sweet courteous stream in three languages. I cursed back in four. The Welsh language is little known to paparazzi.

We entered Fouquet's. My wife was silent and bright with fury. I ordered a drink. 'Why did you do that? Why do you have to spoil the day?'

'I had to do something,' I said. 'I was terrified that I was going to cry and I can't abide weeping in a man.'

'Go back and apologize,' she said.

I went downstairs.

I came back.

'Did you?' she asked.

'Yes.'

'How did he take it?'

'Like a proper little gentleman,' I said. 'He belted me right across the chops.'

She laughed.

I licked the tender, slightly shredded flesh beside my molars, and I cursed some more.

'Stop that!'

'What's the matter,' I said, 'didn't you use words like that in Culver City?'

Her lower jaw hideously receding, her upper front teeth vilely bucking, and in a very highfaluting, nauseous English accent, she said:

'Yes, of course, *they* did but *I* didn't – I come from a race and family that believe the use of such words to be an indication of weakness in vocabulary and intellectual emptiness. . . .'

She smiled at me and patted my hand. I made a plaintive woofing noise and she smiled again.

The ice cubes in my Scotch-on-the-rocks melted and sank without trace.

* * * * *

Richard does not mention Sybil in this story because she was no longer his wife when he wrote it. But I suspect that the inflated importance given to that first meeting of Richard and Elizabeth has all the distortion of hindsight. Not that he was the loyal and devoted husband of Sybil with never a glance at other women – this would be out of character and Sybil knew it. Perhaps it was part of the attraction – after all for many years she was the chosen one and well aware of that, however many flirtations and affairs may have taken place on the sidelines.

As Richard moved out of the social norm as we understood it, and into the very different theatrical and film worlds, we became aware that he was now living by a different set of rules. They would not have done for us, but they seemed oddly apt in the artificial stage and studio set-up. Luckily Sybil was sufficiently initiated to be able to cope with it – had she not been an actress, she probably could not have married him at all.

There is a fundamental insecurity behind the facade of many actors – certainly there was for Richard. On the surface he was strong, confident, masterly; underneath he was a boy who suddenly found himself needing to impress a rootless world of men

79

and women whose lives were absorbed in role play – on the stage and off.

Chapter Seven

World fame

After the 1951 Stratford season, Richard was off to America again; this time to play the male lead on Broadway in Jean Anouilh's *Legend of Lovers*, which opened there in December 1951. A retelling of the classical Greek legend of Orpheus and Eurydice, it was historical, philosophical, complex: that combination had worked in London for Christopher Fry. It was less successful now; the run was short. The play served its purpose, however – Richard was well regarded by the critics. And again, he had an opportunity to look at what America might offer a bright young man. Then it was back to London for another play, *Montserrat*, adapted by Lilian Hellman, which opened in April 1952. This was more recent history – Venezuela, 1812; the struggle for independence from Spain. Richard played an idealistic officer unable to betray a revolutionary leader, despite a group of six hostages being killed. A relentless piece about the most searing kinds of moral dilemma, it too had a very short run, at the Lyric, Hammersmith. As with the Anouilh play, *Montserrat* gave Richard good reviews, but by now, I suspect, he wanted more than just appreciation in a vehicle that left the public cold.

And at this opportune moment, Hollywood became seriously interested in him. Alexander Korda, to whom Richard was bound by a contract dating from the *Dolwyn* days, now proposed to loan Richard to Darryl Zanuck, head of Twentieth Century Fox. Having been responsible for *The Grapes Of Wrath, How Green Was My Valley* and *All About Eve*, Zanuck, *de facto* ruler of his studio since 1935, was one of the most potent forces in Hollywood; certainly he was one of the most affluent, and willing to pay astronomical sums for talent. From the resultant deal for three films, Richard would take home £80,000. At that time, a car cost £275; a seat in the flicks to see the results of Richard's labours would set you back two shillings and nine pence; and I earned five pounds a week, not at all a bad wage in 1952.

Korda apparently sent Richard off with a party of his usual extravagant proportions; alcohol was not conspicuous by its absence. Richard was however perturbed by the absence of something else – the script of whatever film it was that he was now chained to. Still, this lack did not stop him from enjoying himself and treating Hollywood to a full-throttle rendition of a Welsh Shakespearian genius with an eye for the ladies. And soon the script materialised – *My Cousin Rachel*, from the bestseller by Daphne du Maurier. Everyone involved intended that it should repeat the financial and critical success of another du Maurier project with a sensual, intense British actor – *Rebecca*, with Laurence Olivier.

Olivia de Haviland played the title role of Rachel. She had been a major star for fifteen years and her previous two films had been *The Snake Pit* and *The Heiress*, for which she had won her second Oscar. When it opened, many critics derided what was a moody, brooding woman's picture set in a Cornwall entirely recreated on a Los Angeles back lot; but its intended audience found it satisfactory, and Hollywood rewarded Richard with an Oscar nomination for best supporting actor.

In October 1952 my brothers and I travelled up to Cardiff for the film's Welsh premiere at the Capitol Cinema. It was to be an event of local pride, complete with the fusty trappings of local dignitaries including the Lord Mayor. We were agog. Richard on stage in London or Stratford was one thing; Richard projected on a giant screen twenty feet high surrounded by all the storytelling artifice Hollywood had at its disposal was altogether something else. Our family pride knew no bounds and we wanted to tell the world, or at least all South Wales, which amounted to the same thing, that it was our brother, up there on the screen, taking his place with the stars – good, bad or indifferent but always magical – of our trips to the tiny, shabby cinemas of our childhood days.

This was no tiny, second-rate suburban picture-house, but the grandest, most opulent cinema around – the term picture palace seemed very appropriate to me. Tom, the oldest and most traditional of us, alternated between wonder at Richard's fame and indignation at the moral tone of the story – Richard was Philip Ashley who fell madly in love with his foster father's widow – and more especially at those screen kisses. 'Kissing that actress

82

with all those people watching,' Tom muttered, trying to come to terms with it all.

After the film, everyone was invited to a champagne buffet given by the cinema. We all thought it was quite magnificent, the sort of thing that had no precedent in Pontrhydyfen. Suddenly the manager of the cinema, Bill Hall, astonished everyone by announcing that Richard Burton had arrived in person, straight from Hollywood. There were gasps all round when Richard, in full make-up and authentic nineteenth-century costume, made his entrance. It took several moments for the realisation to sink in. This was Graham, who then bore an uncanny resemblance to Richard, gamely impersonating our brother. The audience loved it, and the local press had a godsend of a story.

Olivia de Haviland told a Hollywood writer how she felt about Richard: 'I shudder to think of the fame awaiting this young man. There isn't another leading man like him – he's the greatest in a decade. I would like to do a stage play with him.' Naturally we had known of Miss de Haviland as a true star for some time – was she not in *Gone With The Wind*, the most successful film ever? – and to have Rich praised by such a luminary increased our pride further, if that were possible.

Shortly after we returned home, my father read a piece in the paper describing Richard's vast earnings. When Richard next visited him, Dadi Ni asked, 'Is it true, Rich, they've paid you 50,000 dollars for twelve weeks work in that Holywell?'

Richard looked at him solemnly. 'No it's not,' he said. 'They paid me 150,000.'

My father in turn regarded his son over his Woolworth's spectacles, with one lens missing and one of the arms held together with a piece of string.

'What for?' he asked, genuinely puzzled.

For once, Richard was nonplussed. He grew fond of telling this story later, and always said, 'I couldn't explain it then, and I still don't understand it.'

Even if Richard could not understand it, Darryl Zanuck could. Richard worked in rapid succession on two more films, both released in 1953. The first, *The Desert Rats*, was as much a man's picture as *My Cousin Rachel* had been for women. Telling the story of a group of soldiers valiantly defending Tobruk against the suave and menacing Rommel of James Mason, *The Desert Rats* was rewarding financially, had a trouble-free set (Richard told me it was made in only three weeks), was easy to enjoy, and became what it had singlemindedly set out to be – a mainstream commercial hit. One of its lesser stars was Robert Newton, by then declining spectacularly into the final stages of alcoholism. Richard apparently warned him that too much drinking would kill him, a lesson as hard for Newton to learn then as it would prove for others in the future.

Almost immediately after this, Richard became wrapped up in *The Robe*. One of Zanuck's much-touted aphorisms was 'When you get a sex story in biblical garb, you can open your own mint'. It had certainly worked for *Samson and Delilah* four years earlier. In fact, *The Robe* was not so overtly sexual; it was to be reverential, heroic, intelligent, moving and grand – and of all its qualities, grandeur was to be the most important. This film was a determined attempt by Hollywood to counter the growing menace of television, which in the early 1950s was making serious inroads into film revenues. To counter that affect, something literally bigger than television was called for. *The Robe* was to be filmed in Cinemascope, a wide screen format that would occupy more of the viewer's field of vision than previous screen rations. Religious epics afforded many opportunities for extravagant displays that only Cinemascope could allow – sweeping panoramas, vast crowd scenes and so on.

The plot revolved around a Roman tribune, Marcellus, the official who had organised the execution of Christ, and who was subsequently so affected by his actions that he became a convert to Christianity, finally dying a martyr for his new-found faith. It was a costly picture, and one which took an age to film. By all accounts Richard enjoyed working with his two co-stars, Victor Mature and Jean Simmons, for rather different reasons, and opportunities for parties, drinking and madcap hi-jinks were limitless. Nevertheless the film dragged on, the focus of more attention than any other that year – not just Twentieth Century Fox depended on its striking a chord with huge audiences. The rest of the industry was very much aware that Cinemascope could be either a fillip to a tired medium, or a key element in its accelerated demise.

Fortunately, *The Robe* was a hit. Reviewers had mixed things to say about it, but the essential thing was that audiences bought both this film and its dramatic new format in a very big way, ensuring a long line of widescreen epics. British reviewers had their own views when it opened here in 1953, but we in the family thought it was marvellous, Tom, Hilda and Cassie especially. I saw it on the widest screen I have ever encountered, and was more impressed than ever by Richard's screen presence, a kind of quiet, resonant dignity in which his great on-screen professionalism shone through.

In 1953 Richard returned to the London stage. As this involved turning down a seven-picture deal with Zanuck, some might have thought this a foolhardy gesture, but I think it was much more than that. Richard had a commitment to play *Hamlet* at the Old Vic and he intended to honour it. The money must surely have tempted him – Richard had a hard-nosed appreciation not only of what money could do for you, but also of what its lack could do to you – but his sense of honour and loyalty was always a strong one. In addition, *Hamlet* was *Hamlet*. There is I think something of the character of Hamlet in Richard's interpretation of Hal: a musing, thoughtful introspection and an awareness of being set apart by destiny to try to fulfil a particular role, no matter what the cost. But Hamlet was obviously a more mature part than Hal, one of the few great characters in the history of theatre that test the mettle of all who essay them. There were terrifyingly good precedents for Richard's Hamlet: John Gielgud, to name but one.

Richard came home to Wales for a week in 1953, just before rehearsals began in earnest, and we were all thrilled to see him, not as an alien celebrity but as our brother – and as our brother he stayed in Hilda's home. Famous he certainly was – *My Cousin Rachel* and The *Desert Rats* had already played to appreciative audiences in Britain, though of course *The Robe* was still a short while off from general release. Meanwhile *Hamlet* reunited Richard with several colleagues from the past including Claire Bloom, from *The Lady's Not For Burning*, as Ophelia and Robert Hardy, from Oxford.

Hamlet was first performed in Edinburgh in August 1953 as part of that city's festival; reviewers, if not exactly damning with faint praise, were only mildly enraptured. In London it fared rather better. Richard had not been totally at peace with his interpretation in Scotland. Philip Burton went north to discuss and advise – Richard still had an appreciation of the considerable learning and intuition that Phil could bring to any analysis of his playing. Whatever the imput from Philip and others, Richard felt more at one with his personal Hamlet by the time of the Old Vic opening. Still there was some dissent voiced by critics: the performance lacked finesse in some opinions, it lacked emotion in others. What it did not lack was an audience; *Hamlet* was a smash in box office terms.

The critics may have been divided, but some at least found much to praise. I remember one paper commenting, 'This young Welshman can be said to have come through the ordeal with a flourish denied to many of his famous predecessors.' I later discovered that eight of those predecessors, eight former Hamlets, had gone backstage at the Old Vic to offer their sincere congratulations: John Gielgud; Paul Scofield; Alec Clunes; Michael Redgrave; Alec Guinness; Ernest Milton; Esme Percy, and Robert Helpmann, who saw Richard's interpretation three times.

It was not only in taking on *Hamlet* so early in life that made Richard unorthodox when it came to Shakespeare. When Michael Benthall, his Old Vic *Hamlet* director, asked him (when in *The Druid's Rest*) which part he most wanted to play, Michael had expected Richard to say Romeo. Richard was unhesitating. 'Thersites', he said. Thersites was the scurrilous Grecian in *Troilus and Cressida* – not the obvious answer for a young, mesmeric leading man. Richard had gone on to talk of playing Hamlet: he always felt that an actor should not approach the play analytically or he would be paralysed by this work 'so full of quotations'; he should instead concentrate on the text, and what the producer had to say.

Richard had certainly been awestruck when asked to play Hamlet. Fortunately Katherine Hepburn had been with Michael in New York the day he rang Richard in Hollywood to offer him the part. Richard simply could not speak. As occasionally happened at all stages of his career, he was overwhelmed. Miss

Hepburn, a great admirer of his, realised what was happening and snatched the receiver from Benthall.

'Look here,' she said, 'You're to play Hamlet'. And she promptly hung up leaving Richard no time to protest.

Richard considered that the two media of the stage and screen were so diametrically opposed that they could not help each other. Yet he was irresistibly drawn to both. He began to declare to his family and friends that the ideal life of an actor consisted in alternating between the two worlds. Personally I felt that the stage was Richard's natural environment. In all but his best films he was more detached from his audience and from the role itself – because, I am sure, he had less faith in the medium. On the stage it was different, and especially when playing Shakespeare he was totally immersed. It was his world.

One of Richard's strongest memories of his early stage career was of Winston Churchill's unexpected appearance in the audience after over a hundred performances of *Hamlet* when the play was beginning to lose momentum and attendance was falling. Richard had always admired Churchill and that night, he said, 'I acted above myself. There is no orchestra pit at the Old Vic and Churchill was sitting in the front stalls, so I was acting almost in his lap.'

Churchill knew the part by heart and spoke Richard's lines along with him in a fierce mutter that would have exasperated Richard had it come from anyone else. 'But *Hamlet*', Richard commented, 'is a four and a half hour play, in the full version. It has to be cut. And whenever we came to a cut and the old man lost his place he'd get a bit annoyed.'

After the performance, Richard was in his dressing room when there was a sharp knock at the door. He opened it.

'My Lord Hamlet,' said Churchill gravely, 'May I use your lavatory?'

Years later when *The Valiant Years* was at the planning stage at the BBC, Churchill was approached for the necessary approval to have an actor portray him. 'Get that boy from the Old Vic,' he barked. Richard was delighted. It was a challenge, he declared, 'to convey the old man's greatness without melodrama, to try to give the essence of him without mimicry.'

Offstage, Richard had another world; one which pulled at his heart and to which he longed sometimes to return – the world of rugby. In his Twickenham piece for Cliff Morgan, written in 1970 to commemorate the centenary of the English Rugby Union, he eruditely, passionately and wittily expressed both his continuing passion for the game, and his sadness at being parted from it by the demands of these who now paid his personal piper. Unusually robust for an elegy, these are the relevant passages:

I'll tell you about the last match I ever played in.

I had played the game representatively from the age of ten until those who employed me in my profession, which is that of an actor, insisted that I was a bad insurance risk against certain dread teams in dead-end valleys who would have little respect, no respect, or outright disrespect for what I was pleased to call my face. What if I were unfortunate enough to be on the deck in the middle of a loose maul . . . they murmured in dollar accents? Since my face was already internationally known and since I was paid, perhaps overpaid, vast sums of money for its ravaged presentation they, the money men, expressed a desire to keep it that way. Apart from wanting to preserve my natural beauty, it would affect continuity, they said, if my nose was straight on Friday in the medium shot and was bent towards my left ear on Monday for the close-up. Millions of panting fans from Tokyo to Tonmawr would be puzzled, they said. So to this day there is a clause in my contract that forbids me from flying my own plane, skiing and playing the game of rugby football, the inference being that it would be all right to wrestle with a Bengal tiger 5,000 miles away, but not to play against, shall we say, Pontypool at home. I decided that they had some valid arguments after my last game.

It was played against a village whose name is known only to its inhabitants and crippled masochists drooling quietly in kitchen corners, a mining village with all the natural beauty of the valleys of the moon, and just as welcoming, with a team composed almost entirely of miners. I hadn't played for four or five years but was fairly fit, I thought, and the opposition was bottom of the third class and reasonably beatable. Except, of course, on their home ground. I should have thought of that. I should have called to mind that this was the kind of team where, towards the end of the match, you kept your bus ticking over near the touch-line in case you won and had to run for your life.

I wasn't particularly nervous before the match until I was disguised with a skull-cap and everyone had been sworn to secrecy. I heard a voice from the other team asking, '*Ble ma'r blydi film star'ma?*' (Where's the bloody film star here?) as we were running on to the field. My cover, as they say in spy stories, was already blown and trouble was to be my shadow, (there was none from the sun since there was no sun – it was said in fact that the sun hadn't shone there since 1929) and the end of my career the shadow of my shadow for the next eighty minutes or so. It was a mistaken game for me to play. I survived it with nothing broken except my spirit, the attitude of the opposition being unquestion-ably summed up in simple words like, 'Never mind the bloody ball, where's the bloody actor?' Words easily understood by all.

Among other things I was playing Hamlet at that time at the 'Old Vic', but for the next few performances after that match I was compelled to play him as if he were Richard the Third. The punishment I took had been innocently compounded by a paragraph in a book of reminiscence by Bleddyn Williams, with whom I had played on and off (mostly, off) in the RAF. On page 37 of this volume* Mr Williams is kind enough to suggest that I had distinct possibilities as a player were it not for the lure of tinsel and paint and money and fame and so on. Incidentally, one of the curious phenomena of my library is that when you take Bleddyn's autobiography from the shelves it automatically opens at the very page mentioned above. Friends have often remarked on this and wondered afresh at the wizardry of the Welsh. It is in fact the only notice I have ever kept.

Anyway this little snippet from the great Bleddyn's book was widely publicised and some years later by the time I played that last game had entered into the uncertain realms of folk legend and was deeply embedded in the subconscious of the sub-Welshmen I submitted myself to that cruel afternoon. They weren't playing with chips on their shoulders, they were simply sceptical about page 37.

I didn't realise that I was there to prove anything until too late.

* The Centenary celebration album.

89

And I couldn't. And didn't. I mean prove anything. And I am still a bit testy about it. Though I was working like a dog at the 'Old Vic' playing Hamlet, Coriolanus, 'Caliban The Bastard' in *King John* and 'Toby Belch', it wasn't the right kind of training for these great knotted gnarled things from the burning bowels of the earth.

In my teens I had lived precariously on the lip of first rugby by virtue of knowing every trick in the canon, evil and otherwise, by being a bad, bad loser, but chiefly, and perhaps only because I was very nippy off the mark. I was 5ft 10½ in height in bare feet and weighed, soaking wet, no more than 12½ stone, and since I played in the pack, usually at open side wing-forward and since I played against genuinely big men, it therefore followed that I had to be galvanically quick to move from inertia. When faced with bigger and faster forwards, I was doomed. R. T. Evans, of Newport, Wales and the Universe, for instance – a racy 14½ stone and 6ft 1½ in height was a nightmare to play against and shaming to play with, both of which agonies I suffered a lot, mostly, thank God, the latter lesser *cauchemar*. Genuine class, of course, doesn't need size though sometimes I forgot this.

Once I played rather condescendingly against a Cambridge College and noted that my opposite number seemed to be shorter than I was in rugby togs, and looked like a schoolboy compared with Mike Owen, Bob Evans or W. J. D. Elliot. However, this blond stripling gave me a terrible time. He was faster and harder and wordlessly ruthless, and it was no consolation to find out his name afterwards, it meant nothing at the time. He has forgotten me but I haven't forgotten him. This anonymity was called Steele–Bodger and a more onomatopoeic name for its owner would be hard to find. He was, and I promise you, Steel and he did, I give you my word, Bodger. Say his name through clenched teeth and you'll see what I mean. I am very glad to say I have never seen him since except from the safety of the stands.

In this match, this last match played against troglodytes, burned to the bone by the fury of their work, bow-legged and embittered because they weren't playing for or hadn't played for and would never play for Cardiff or Swansea or Neath or Aberavon, men who smiled seldom and when they did it was like scalpels, trained to the last ounce by slashing and hacking away neurotically at the frightened coal face for 7½ hours a day, stalactitic, tree-rooted,

90

carved out of granite by a rough and ready sledge-hammer clinker, against these hard volumes of which I was the soft-cover paperback edition. I discovered some truths very soon, just after the first scrum, for instance, that it was time I ran for the bus and not for their outside-half. He had red hair, a blue and white face and no chin. Standing up straight his hands were loosely on a level with his calves and when the ball and I arrived exultantly together at his stock-still body, a perfect set-up you would say, and when I realised that I was supine and he was lazily kicking the ball into touch, I realised that I had forgotten that trying to intimidate a feller like that was like trying to cow a mandrill, and that he had all the graceful willowy-give and sapling-bend of stressed concrete.

That was only the outside-half. From then on I was elbowed, gouged, dug, planted, raked, hoed, kicked a great deal, sandwiched and once humiliatingly taken from behind with nobody in front of me when I had nothing to do but run yards to score. Once, coming down from going up for the ball in a line-out, the other wing-forward – a veteran of at least fifty with grey hair – chose to get up as I was coming down if you'll forgive this tautological syntax. Then I was down and he was up and to insult the injury he generously helped me up from being down and pushed me in a shambling run towards my own try-line with a blood-curdling endearment in the Welsh tongue, since during all these preceding ups and downs his unthinkable team had scored and my presence was necessary behind the posts as they were about to attempt the conversion.

I knew almost at once and appallingly that the speed, such as it had been, had ended and only the memory lingered on, and that tackling Olivia de Havilland and Lana Turner and Claire Bloom was not quite the same thing as tackling those Wills and Dais, those Toms and Dicks.

The thing to do, I told myself with desperate cunning, was to keep alive, and the way to do that was to keep out of the way. This is generally possible to do when you know you are outclassed, without everybody knowing, but in this case it wasn't possible to do so because everybody was very knowing indeed. Sometimes in a lament for my lost youth (I was about twenty-eight) I roughed it up as well as I could but it is discouraging to put the violent elbow into the tempting rib when your prescience tells you that what is about to be broken is not the titillating rib, but your pusillanimous pathetic elbow.

After being gardened, mown and rolled a little more, I gave that up, asked the captain of our team if he didn't think it would be a better idea to hide me deeper in the pack. I had often, I reminded him, played right prop, my neck was strong and my right arm had held its own with most. He gave me a long look, a trifle pitying perhaps, but orders were given and I went to the maelstrom, and now the real suffering began. Their prop, with whom I was to share cheek and jowl for the next eternity, didn't believe in razor blades since he grew them on his chin and shaved me thoroughly for the rest of the game, taking most of the skin in the process, delicacy not being his strong point. He used his prodigious left arm to paralyse mine and pull my head within an inch or two of the earth, then rolled my head around his, first taking my ear between his forefinger and thumb, humming 'Rock of Ages' under his breath. By the end of the game my face was as red as the setting sun and the same shape.

Sometimes, to vary the thing a bit, he rolled his head on what little neck he had around, under and around again my helpless head. I stuck it out because there was nothing else to do, which is why on Monday night in the Waterloo Road I played the Dane looking like a Swede, with my head permanently on one side and my right arm in an imaginary sling intermittently crooked and cramped with occasional severe shakes and involuntary shivers as of one with palsy. I suppose to the connoisseurs of *Hamlet* it was a departure from your traditional Prince but it wasn't strictly what the actor playing the part had in mind. A melancholy Dane he was though. Melancholy he most certainly was.

I tried once to get myself removed to the wing but by this time our captain had become as, shall we say, 'dedicated' (he may read this) as the other team and had actually wanted to win. He seemed not to hear me and the wing in this type of game I knew never got the ball and was, apart from throwing the ball in from the touch, a happy spectator, and I wanted to be a happy spectator. I shuffled after the pack.

I joined in the communal bath afterwards in a large steamy hut next to the changing-rooms, feeling very hard done by and hurt though I didn't register the full extent of the agonies that were to crib, cabin and confine me for the next few days. I drank more than my fair share of beer in the home team's pub, joined in the singing and found that the enemies were curiously shy and withdrawn until the beer had hit the proper spot. Nobody mentioned my performance in the field.

There was only one moment of wild expectation on my part when a particularly grim, sullen and taciturn member of the other side said suddenly with what passed shockingly for a smile splitting the slag heap of his face like an earth tremor:

'Come outside with us will 'ew?' There was another beauty with him.

'Where to?' I asked.

'Never 'ew mind,' he said. 'You'll be awright. Jest come with us.'

'O.K.'

We went into the cruel February night and made our way to the outside Gents' – black painted concrete with one black pipe for flushing, wet to the open sky. We stood side by side in silence They began to void. So did I. There had been beer enough for all. I waited for a possible compliment on my game that afternoon – I had after all done one or two good things if only by accident. I waited. But there was nothing but the sound of wind and water. I waited and silently followed them back into the bar. Finally I said: 'What did you want to tell me?'

'Nothing,' the talkative one said.

'Well, what did you ask me out there for then?'

'Well,' the orator said, 'well us two is brothers and we wanted to tell our mam that we'd 'ad a . . .'

He hesitated, after all I spoke posh except when I spoke Welsh, which oddly enough the other team didn't speak to me though I spoke it to them. 'Well, we jest wanted to tell our mam that we had passed water with Richard Burton,' he said with triumphant care.

'Oh 'ell,' I said.

I went back to London next day in a Mark VIII Jaguar, driving very fast, folding up and tucking away into the back drawer of my subconscious all my wounds, staunched blood, bandaged pride, feeling older than I've ever felt since. The packing wasn't very well done as from time to time all the parcels of all the games I'd ever played wrapped up loosely in that last one will undo themselves, spill out of the drawer into my dreams and wake me shaking to the reassuring reaching-out for the slim cool comfort of a cigarette in the dead vast and doomed middle and with a puff and a sight mitty myself into Van Wyk, Don White and Alan Macarley and winning several matches by myself by 65 points to nil, repack the bags.

* * * * *

As Richard pointed out in that celebratory piece, it was acting that now directed his energies, not the rugby that others denied him. Certainly his acting was, for the spectator at least, worth the sacrifice. If I had been impressed by Richard's Stratford season in 1951, in 1955/56 I was completely enthralled by his sheer nerve and guts in playing Othello one night and Iago the next. He and John Neville would alternate the parts, each having his own group of devotees. Once, before watching him play Othello, I said to him jokingly, 'The Welsh contingent are here in strength this evening, Richard. I want you to shake the very foundations of this building so that the roof vibrates and the walls cave in.'

He merely smiled. I never seriously thought of him as nervous. But he confided to me later that he was at times paralysed by nerves. He used to stride out with the London police officer on the beat, telling him about me in the police force and a hundred different other stories before a first night – sleep was out of the question. Then he would have one stiff drink – just one – to steady him before going on stage.

But the night I saw his Othello with many of my countrymen, I was not let down. I was spellbound. 'Good God,' I thought, 'is that really Rich? Is this truly the little boy from Pontrhydyfen who has taken London by storm and won the hearts and minds of all these men and women?'

I simply could not hold back the tears and was thankful that the theatre was dark and that no one could see me. It felt as though he were playing for Wales against England at Cardiff Arms Park, taking the ball at great speed and running the whole length of the field, beating man after man and scoring a try under the posts when Wales were six points to three behind, as sixty thousand Welshmen beat the drums of his success!

I had intended to be a dispassionate critic of what I saw on stage but I could not help responding with all of myself – proud older brother, patriotic Welshman, the lot. This extraordinary mellifluous voice, I thought, this subtle change in the atmosphere, this demeanour, language and emotion . . . I could hardly believe I was witnessing it, over and over again.

Afterwards, I would ask him in wonder, 'How on earth do you come down to earth, Rich?'

'Well,' he would say, 'You have to live the part – transform yourself into that individual – for three hours. The best way to come down is to have a pint of beer and relax.'

Then sometimes we would have a meal and talk late into the night.

Sybil was always there in the background, always supportive, as though her main aim was to help Richard stay in peak condition, both physically and mentally. She checked his scripts tirelessly and was such a devotee of the theatre as well as of Richard that it was not unusual for her to attend two performances a day. She had accepted the sacrifice of her own career and now threw herself with her customary fire and energy into supporting her husband. At least that was how we perceived it in terms of his British stage and screen work. How Sybil coped with Hollywood (and all that that meant) I really have no idea. I can only imagine that she was as stoical and accepting as all the reports and other writers have made out. This I do know – she was a very private person and very few people ever got close to her.

The 1953/54 season at the Old Vic was a demanding one. Apart from *Hamlet*, Richard played in *King John* as Philip the Bastard (rather a small part in which Richard's unquenchable presence managed – inadvertently? – to distract the audience from the machinations of the main roles); in *Twelfth Night* as Sir Toby Belch (unsuccessful, in that the disguising costume and ill-advised wig seemed, unexpectedly, to smother Richard's personality); in *The Tempest* as Caliban (well received); and in *Coriolanus* as the title role. Some said that he gave the definitive portrait of this difficult character for his generation, ironically because, at first, Richard had refused the part. Philip Burton, in New York at the time, said: 'I know why. Richard's sympathies were all with the working class'. Michael Benthall asked Philip to use his influence on Richard to get him to change his mind.

95

'So,' remembers Philip, 'on his way back from Hollywood, Richard stopped off in New York, stayed with me for a couple of days, I think, and I started to talk about Coriolanus and we talked a whole night through, literally.'

Philip's argument was that an actor had to play death scenes without dying, murderers without murdering people, and that use of the imagination was crucial. Richard was persuaded. Robert Hardy, in the same production, said later:

> He was stunning in it. And all those curious elements of his physical and mental nature which presented danger and extra power and extra strength that filled the room, however big, were of course usable. One moment an iceberg, and the next moment a flaming meteor, he was tremendous, and always dangerous. I've never seen *Coriolanus* better done. I can't imagine it being better done. And you could see why people loved him in the play and why people . . . hated him in the play. The whole thing was so clear. Richard had a great arrogance of his own which matched an irony all his own. A kind of . . . 'why is it that humankind is so perverse, so weak, so heir to the ills of the world', which, of course, in some senses he was himself, and proved it true. But the irony, the toss of the head, the glance off into a plane which he could inhabit by himself; all were very characteristic of him – and were of course shattering in *Coriolanus*.

He was not the only actor to praise Richard in *Coriolanus*. Laurence Olivier told him, after seeing a performance, that he would never now try to play it. Certainly the final scene – the assassination – was a towering achievement.

'They had built a series of steps,' Philip Burton remembers, 'right down to the orchestra pit, and Richard was alone at the top of the steps, against double doors. And this angry crowd, out for blood, came out of the orchestra pit – a tremendous number of extras. They swept up the stairs until they hid Richard from view, and we saw stabbing going on, though we couldn't see Richard – and all the noise suddenly stopped, and then they came backwards down those steps in absolute silence, leaving Richard covered with blood against those doors.

'And when they finally disappeared, he did an extraordinary fall. He just fell down like that – backwards. It was incredible. He didn't crumble, but remained absolutely stiff, and fell.'

Later, Richard changed his own views about 'the mob' and

identified much more with the part about which he had had such strong initial reservations. He continued to revere, in a sense, the working class in terms of the individuals within it, and the aristocracy too, while having little time for the middle classes. And, of course, he always had time and respect for a good mind, a reader, a thinker.

Philip had an explanation for Richard's scathing view of the mob: 'You can tell he is thinking more of the American audience than those who packed the Old Vic in his famous seasons. By now, he doesn't know what the English theatre is like; you can tell this from the way he describes the kind of thing he would like to do now – playing in small theatres to audiences of genuine enthusiasts rather than in vast auditoriums full of stuffed shirts. Yet there is no use in telling him that this is precisely the kind of theatre that has been developed over the past decades. No – if he comes back to London's stage, it will be to the Old Vic. That is the only theatre he considers seriously – indeed he considered buying it when the Trust put it up for sale.'

Philip Burton had continued to keep a fatherly eye on Richard during his early stage and film career – and did so, intermittently, throughout his life. He it was who took him to Savile Row in the early London days to be measured for his first suit – a far cry from the days of the drapery counter in Taibach Co-op.

Richard, in return, continued to respect Philip for what he had done. He described him in 1956 as one who had been 'the greatest person in my life'. No disrespect to Cis or any other family member was intended here. The relationship was just different. Richard had more to say on the subject: 'He instilled in me the inspiration of the classics; he showed me the way. Even today, when I have to learn lines, I take a short walk round the square. Somehow, though, it's not the same atmosphere in Hampstead.'

Richard also quoted Philip on technique. 'Technique, he says, is in essence the ability to get the biggest possible effect with the least possible effort.'

However the effects were achieved, Richard loved the fruits of his acting. Susie Preece recalls the episode of Richard's first car, a Leigh Francis, from around this time – 1954 I believe. He was eager to show it off to his beloved Cis in Taibach. At the end of his stay, as he was about to leave for London, the local coal merchant,

Will Mainwaring, happened to be passing. His eyes fixed reverently on the vehicle, he crooned, 'Oh, what a lovely car, Rich. How is she running?' 'Oh, wonderful,' returned Richard with pride. He got in and started the engine. Nothing happened. Discomfited, he had another try. Not a murmur. Finally he allowed himself to see the funny side. They all had a good laugh over it.

'Don't worry,' said Will. 'Wait a minute and I'll tow you.'

The prospect of being towed by the coal merchant's lorry must have proved too much for the car, which soon jerked into life.

The early 1950s, then, were the years when Richard let rip in a variety of Shakespearian guises. But Hollywood was never forgotten; nor was Richard allowed to forget it. Unfortunately the next venture, *The Prince Of Players*, was a flop. Why? On paper, it was a splendid opportunity for Richard to shine, a Cinemascope biography of the American actor Edwin Booth, legendary nineteenth-century exponent of Shakespeare, and – useful for dramatic tension – brother of the Booth who assassinated President Abraham Lincoln. In retrospect, the problem lay with the script and the lacklustre direction of the picture. Some have admired Richard's recreations of Booth's various performances, but these isolated turns were not enough to redeem the dullness of the whole picture. Like so much in Richard's life, it was a wasted opportunity; this time however, he can hardly be expected to take the blame. At the very worst, it was an error of judgement, but Richard had not been alone in sensing a hit before the cameras rolled.

At least it did not harm Richard's appeal in the eyes of the studios. United Artists borrowed him from Fox to play another historical character, *Alexander The Great*. I wondered if the *Adventure Story* debacle with Paul Scofield still rankled at all. If so, this was a sweet irony. There were very good intentions behind *Alexander*. Both director (Robert Rossen, an Oscar winner) and star planned to make an intelligent epic, exploring the character of the seductive megalomaniac who endeavoured almost successfully to conquer the then known world. Obviously it would have great battle scenes – no one was opposed to excitement – but the thrills would not be empty-headed. Richard, determined to 'know' Alexander, devoured books on the subject before filming started in Madrid in early 1955. Ivor and Gwen were there much of the time. So were mates Michael Hordern, William Squire and Stanley Baker, for whom Richard had found roles in the sprawling venture; and so too was Claire Bloom.

By this time, Ivor had established his position as Richard's henchman and travelled with him almost everywhere. Ivor and Gwen now had a home next door to Richard and Sybil's at Squire's Mount in Hampstead, and eventually spent much of their time in Richard's Swiss home, Le Pays de Galles at Céligny near Geneva – but more of that later.

This partnership was well accepted by the rest of the family – to us, it seemed natural that Ivor should adopt this supportive role, just as he had taken the lead in our childhood days, organizing the household after the death of our mother. Richard looked to him for fathering in the same way that he looked to Cis for mothering. He could laugh at him too – Ivor the well-known Scrooge of the family, Ivor who even now looked on shopping expeditions with great suspicion.

On one occasion Richard was sitting astride a horse waiting for his cue to start; Ivor was standing by him. The horse suddenly reared fiercely and started galloping towards a couple of hundred extras. Ivor boldly ran towards the horse, held on to the reins with all his might, managed to stop the animal from bolting further and, while Richard hung on with tenacity, brought the horse to a stop. Richard held the view that if Ivor had not taken this decisive action the horse would have dashed into the hordes of waiting extras, causing terrible injuries, if not death.

The family party in Spain was joined by Cis and her daughters Marian and Rhianon, both in their twenties. At one point, Richard wrote to Hilda, one of the very few letters to the family from this period:

Dear Hilda

No doubt you'll be surprised to see these few words from me, the worst correspondent in the world, but since you're in hospital, I thought I'd better find out how you are from you yourself. Cis has arrived here in Madrid and is enjoying herself enormously, the weather is coldish but very sunny, the film is going slowly on its way, Ivor speaks four words of

Spanish, and Gwen reads all day long in a relaxed position. They all, Marian included, shop a great deal and Ivor's face gets longer and longer at the sight of Gwen's parcels! You can imagine him.

We hope to be home at the end of June and we're also hoping that my next film will be made in London and *not* Hollywood. We hate leaving London, though the Spanish are very pleasant people, as are the Yanks. No place like home.

Give my love to Dic bach when you see him and to all the family. If there's anything you need don't forget to let me know. ANYTHING! Everybody sends you love. Get well quick.

Mor o Gariad

Rich

Richard was always very concerned when any of us was ill – Hilda had appendicitis, a serious business when maintaining a home for her four children and our father too. In this letter, Richard was careful to present himself as the solid, dependable, home-loving Rich – a far cry from the worldly prince-actor who was beginning to test the new enticing waters so tellingly symbolised by Elizabeth's 'playroom' in *Meeting Mrs Jenkins*. Richard seemed to need his home base very badly at times – that meant Sybil, Wales, the UK. Only when that base felt solid could he think about jumping off, taking risks.

Whatever the complexities of life off the set of *Alexander The Great*, there were major problems with the film itself. A lot of hard work went into making it; any number of seemingly eloquent and stirring speeches were uttered, any number of battle scenes involving much of the Spanish army were lensed, but the sum of these parts turned out to be an unconvincing mess. Critics found much to dislike in the three-hour venture, and though it had its epic moments, audiences tended to agree with them. But before it even opened, Richard was hard at work on a truly awful film, *The Rains of Ranchipur*. Hindsight is a gift to use sparingly, but it is hard to see why anyone thought that this particular effort needed Richard in it. The point of the picture was to batter audiences with Cinemascope floods, tidal waves and dramatic natural disaster – it was, after all, a remake of the aptly-titled *The Rains Came* – and really, there was no reason on earth why my brother was uniquely

100

suited to the romantic lead role of an Indian doctor. The result was boring and risible.

All stars make bad films even now, when the absence of the rigid studio system should mean that they, or their advisers, are in a better position to decline inappropriate parts. Richard was not alone in appearing in unsuccessful films, nor was he alone in going on to survive the flack. Nonetheless it is piquant to note the contrast between his first three Hollywood endeavours, which were all in their way successful, and the next three which were not. It is important to remember that Richard was a property of a major studio, not a free agent; and neither *The Prince Of Players* nor *Alexander The Great* was cynically conceived as a mindless commercial production – they were, I suppose, well-intentioned failures. Still, the effect of a trio of turkeys was a dent in the career and in self esteem.

But whatever Hollywood did to him, Richard still had Shakespeare: no one at the Old Vic or Stratford wanted to immerse him in ill-advised spectacle. There the magic of Burton could erupt in parts that depended on his individual power and presence.

In the 1955/56 season with the Old Vic, Richard played the title role in *Henry V* and the alternating roles of Iago and Othello mentioned earlier. As King Henry, Richard, now thirty, pulled out all the stops, giving to the part the clenched, taut energy waiting to happen that was youth, combined with the intelligence, discretion and considered self-assurance that was maturity. It worked. Said Kenneth Tynan, he was 'now the natural successor to Olivier'. And as such, he won The Evening Standard Drama Award for this performance. The Othello/Iago swap was not quite so well received by the press, but brought an unprecedented wave of fan hysteria to the normally dignified Old Vic. Both Rich and John Neville had vocal devotees in the cheap seats, and they found themselves purveying the Bard to the almost swooning precursors of teenyboppers. This might have proved distracting on occasions, but the adulation must surely have been welcome. I know my brother's self esteem was boosted by it.

At this point, Richard and Sybil had no children, and there was a plan in the mid 1950s to adopt a Welsh child. We wondered what the problem was – low fertility? was alcohol to blame? My daughter remembers the subject being discussed at Cis's home, in very hushed tones. Two children were considered for fostering, but nothing came of it.

Then, as so often happens, nature intervened and Kate was born in September 1957. Richard took naturally to the role of proud father, and was always devoted to Kate. Now, we thought, he had a proper home base of his own, one that appeared to be rock-solid. Kate was followed two years later by Jessica. Richard happened to be away from home for her birth and was less involved with her from the outset. At first she seemed a perfectly normal healthy child, though my sister Cassie, the only professional nurse in the family, maintains that all was not well right from the beginning. I know that Richard found illness and disability of any kind difficult to come to terms with, and he may instinctively have avoided getting too close to his second daughter.

He had also, he confided to me later, wanted a son. But I am sure that he must have been ashamed of any negative feelings that he had and went to some lengths to conceal them, beginning a process of withdrawal from reality that was to characterise much of the rest of his life.

Early 1957 brought another family crisis which must have affected Richard very deeply. Our father Dadi Ni spent the last years of his life as a gentle old man sitting by Hilda's hearth. Some writers have pondered long and hard about his occasional confusion over his many children. I recall that the confusion was over his grandchildren, which I feel was entirely understandable since there were such a lot of them all about the same age. My daughter remembers being taken to see him and being regarded quizzically: 'Which one is this then?' he would ask. Certainly his muddles were not directed with any ulterior motive at Richard alone. We all encountered them.

In March 1957 he became very ill and was taken to Neath General Hospital. We organised a rota of his sons to keep a nightly vigil there – Tom, William, Verdun and myself. It fell to my turn on the night of 25 March, when he died at 4.30 in the morning. So it was that I was the one present at the death of both my parents. My father's death was nowhere near as traumatic as my mother's had been for her young children, but it was nonetheless a great wrench.

102

Richard and Ivor were, I recall, too busy to attend the funeral. Or was there some other reason – some gnawing resentment of Dadi Ni's early neglect that neither brother had come to terms with? The chapel on the other hand was well represented, despite the fact that our father had always been conspicuous by his absence – as I have said, no fewer than seven ministers of religion attended the funeral. Dadi Ni would have chuckled had he known!

Apart from having two personal crises, Richard, over thirty and no longer the untainted white-hot young hopeful, was finding things to fret about in his career. I think there were two main issues. He had achieved great things on the stage, and now in a sense had no further to climb. Of course there would always be other challenging roles – the older Shakespearean parts; new ones written by up-and-coming dramatists – but having so successfully made his own some of the toughest characters written and having been acknowledged for this, the drive to overcome colossal odds was no longer needed – those particular peaks, once so distant from the valleys, now had the Burton standard firmly planted on their summits.

If this was too much success, the opposite was true where Hollywood was concerned. In 1957 he made *Sea Wife*, the first film for a year, and it was another mistake. The basic outline had great dramatic possibilities. After a ship is torpedoed, four survivors in a small boat make it to a deserted island. The main characters were an RAF officer (Richard) and a nun (Joan Collins). Initially it was to have been directed by Roberto Rossellini, a gifted and imaginative Italian *auteur*, and it offered location work in congenial Jamaica. Sadly, Rossellini left the project at an early stage. Tales of isolation on lonely islands work if they show great fortitude and heroic resilience (*Robinson Crusoe*) or a subtle, likeable comic awkwardness (*Father Goose*). This had neither.

Would *Bitter Victory*, helmed by talented director Nicholas Ray, break the run of bad luck? No. A turgid, uninvolving war story, this was a far cry from the crisp, straightforward pleasures of *The Desert Rats*, indeed all it shared with that earlier, happier story was a desert locale. The plot concerned the acquisition of secret German documents, but a sense of skilful stealth was absent from the finished print.

I think these two failures, on top of three other under-achievers,

wounded Richard's bankability in the eyes of Hollywood producers. This was not unfair – these lamentable efforts had, I'm
afraid, shown that the name Richard Burton could not save a bad
film. The better parts went elsewhere.

So Richard turned with some relief to the theatre again. As 1957
– not one of his better years – began to wane, Richard was offered
a meaty part in New York. Jean Anouilh had written a kind of
romantic comedy, called *Time Remembered* in its English translation. Richard, cast as one Prince Albert, played opposite Helen
Hayes (as a duchess) and the teenage Susan Strasberg, hot from
The Diary Of Anne Frank, as a young milliner. Richard had a very
public affair with Susan, who fell seriously in love with him. The
play itself was pleasantly received, rather to Richard's surprise. It
was not profitable, but at least it was no disaster, which was good
news after the recent films.

Meredith Evans, a Welsh university lecturer, recalls seeing this
production:

> In 1958 we were living as a family, my wife Phyllis, our daughter
> Eiluned and myself, in a flat just off Harvard Square, Cambridge,
> Massachusetts. Sometime in mid-February we received invitations from
> Richard and Hugh Griffith to come to a private St David's Day party in
> New York. Along with the letters were tickets to attend performances at
> two leading Broadway theatres. Richard was appearing with Helen
> Hayes and Susan Strasberg in Anouilh's *Time Remembered*. Hugh,
> meanwhile, portrayed the part of old Gant in a dramatisation of Thomas
> Wolfe's *Look Homeward Angel*, playing alongside Jo Van Fleet. In the
> afternoon we watched Richard's polished and stylised performance as the
> mannered young Prince and in the evening witnessed Hugh's vibrant
> portrayal of the rather pathetic father. It was a fine theatrical experience.
>
> If I remember correctly, Richard had the stage to himself at the
> beginning of the second act. He appeared immaculately dressed in court
> attire, complete with sash across his chest; the coat was, I believe, a
> brilliant purple colour. He came to the front of the stage. We were ideally
> seated within a few rows of the stage; near enough, suddenly, to realise
> that he was wearing a stylish little decoration on his left lapel. It had been
> placed there specifically for us and for any other Welsh people who might
> have been present at that matinee performance: a pleasantly conceived
> in-joke, to which we immediately responded, to the surprise of the
> surrounding audience. The decoration was a tiny model of a leek with its
> green stem and bulbous white root! Backstage afterwards, Richard partly
> prepared us for Hugh's stage entrance in the evening's performance,

describing it as the most dramatic Welsh stage-entrance on Broadway. He was right. Old Gant came roaring from the wings, drunk as a lord, grasping in his left hand a full-blooded, genuine leek, roots and all.

The St David's Day party that followed was held in Lena Horne's flat and attended by theatrical friends, the only exceptions being Phyllis and myself. The rest of the Welsh contingent consisted of Sybil, Richard, Hugh and Philip Burton, while among the actors present the ones that I remember with great pleasure were Mary Ure (a fellow Celt), Ricardo Montalban, Robert Preston (appearing, at the time, in *The Music Man*) and Robert Webber. Phyllis and I sang our Welsh folksongs, endlessly so it seemed at the time; Hugh read some of Goronwy Owen's poems (*Hiraeth am Fôn* – 'Longing for Anglesey', in particular); Richard read some Dylan Thomas poems, with great effect, along with singing one of his favourite folksongs, *Ar lan y môr* ('By the sea's strand') and, of course, we sang some well-known Welsh hymns. Dawn was breaking when we left. Two seasoned New York policemen were climbing the stairs to meet us, in good-humoured mood, 'just to pull the lid down a bit', as we made our way to our hotel.

As the 1950s drew to a close there was, at last, a film worth having – *Look Back In Anger*. It was based on John Osborne's epoch-making play, and Richard had met its author at a bizarre reception with a Cockney theme, hosted in New York by Laurence Olivier. Over robustly proletarian fare consumed on a boat sailing at considerable expense up the Hudson River, Osborne and Richard struck up a rapport and discussed Rich's appearing in the film. Unlike many party-inspired enthusiasms, this one came to pass.

Filming took place in England under the direction of Tony Richardson, and the finished article had undeniable power, assaulting the senses with violence of language and extremes of feeling. Rage, cynicism, unkindness and rank brutal selfishness were transferred without diminution from the play. Impressive it certainly was; escapist it was not. There are audiences for unflinching film dramas from time to time, but they are fickle. It is a gamble which Richard later won on *Who's Afraid Of Virginia Woolf* – but this time he lost. Nonetheless, I am very proud of his work in this film, and I think Richard was too. So many moments and scenes sear the memory after viewing it; surely a tribute to both the writer and his chosen star. It was a vigorous, even uncompromising note on which to end a decade.

105

*

When Richard was actually with Sybil and Kate, they enjoyed life in the Swiss villa which Richard had bought to enable him to live as a tax exile. He called it Le Pays de Galles – Wales in French. Wales was literally his home again. Over the years we all visited Céligny and enjoyed Richard's considerable hospitality.

In August 1960 my sister Cassie and her family spent a holiday in Paris. After a week they decided impulsively – typical of Cassie – to travel by train to Geneva and from there to Céligny to see Richard and Sybil. They had no idea where the actual villa was, or even if Richard and Sybil would be there. They bought return tickets and planned to have a look round, 'Just to say we've been.'

They had never even visited Switzerland before and were struck by the beauty, cleanliness and the clarity of the light. They understood then why Richard had bought a house there, though there were the financial reasons too.

They were walking past a restaurant in Céligny – the now famous Café de la Gare – when Cassie suddenly heard a scream of delight. 'Cassie! Cassie!' It was Sybil who had spotted them. She, Richard, their lawyer and his wife were all having a meal together. Returning to Paris was now out of the question. After the meal was over they all went back to the villa. More surprises – Kate and Jessica were there of course, but so too were Ivor, Gwen, Gwen's brother and his family.

Ivor was particularly thrilled and immediately booked the family into a nearby hotel overlooking the lake. Five days of luxurious living ensued, Cassie recalls – wonderful!

They spent most of their time together, infected by Richard's enthusiasms: they swam in Lake Geneva each morning before breakfast; they played cricket, badminton, squash, boules; they watched little Kate and Jessica, and Ivor taking up his customary parental role with them as he taught Kate to swim. Richard was thrilled by this, but was reluctant to show it. He alternated between displays of fatherly pride and classic bursts of frustration and impatience at the baby's crying and at the general tedium of life with small children that even rich and famous fathers cannot always escape.

There was a complication. Cassie recalls that it was at this juncture that the first question mark arose over Jessica: was her crying normal? was she happy? was she healthy? what was the cause of her tantrums? The term autism was not then mentioned, but something was clearly not right. Richard meanwhile was more troubled, and expressed his true feelings less, than anyone else.

Richard was well on the way to amassing his eventual collection of 11,000 books. 'Those books will need some dusting,' remarked Cassie. Hearing this, Richard was reminded of Cis's first visit to Céligny. There had been a conspiracy among Richard, Sybil, Ivor and Gwen to conceal every conceivable duster from our relentlessly houseproud elder sister.

On day one, they thought they had got away with the ruse – Cis said nothing. But she was not so easily deterred. Early next morning she was up before anyone else to greet the daily help, who innocently agreed to supply Cis with dusters. By the time the others got up, Cis was dusting away methodically, much to the amusement of all. Clearly, changing Cis's approach to life would require something more radical than hiding dusters.

Even later, when Richard had bought her a house in Hadley Wood, at the other end of the garden from her daughters, she would not give up. She continued to mother the entire family whenever possible. And to be fair, all of us, Richard included, found her hard to resist.

On Cis's second visit to Céligny, Richard and Ivor, meeting her at the airport in a Rolls Royce, presented her with a parcel – a magnificent collection of multicoloured dusters. Luckily her sense of humour was as indestructible as her maternalism. Richard confided to her that a similar parcel would be placed in her coffin –she would be so distressed, would she not, if a speck were to be found in her last resting place.

As the years went by Richard was less inclined to refer to Cis's mortality, let alone joke about it. He came to dread the prospect of losing her, of not having her there to turn to, however infrequently. None of us ever dreamed, of course, that she would outlive him.

Chapter Eight

Richard and Elizabeth: from scandal to marriage

The 1960s began very well for Richard, with two very different performances that both depended on the shrewdly-used majesty of his voice.

First of all, Richard made one of the finest television programmes of the decade, though he never actually appeared on screen; a twenty-six part series called *The Valiant Years*, based on Sir Winston Churchill's wartime memoirs, and Richard's contribution was the voice-over as Churchill himself.

As I have said earlier, Churchill had been highly impressed by Richard's vocal power, and had asked for Richard to take his part. This was a challenge to any actor – to portray a living person, whose voice was distinctive and individual, without lapsing into parody or caricature. Richard concentrated on the text, the fluency of the words themselves, and, as he noted in a celebrated interview, based the Churchillian accent on a Peter Sellers impersonation of an upper-class twit. Unorthodox and indeed risky it sounded, but the result was a stunning achievement, making Churchill come alive without surrendering to an obvious impersonation.

There was an unexpected coda to Richard's Churchill. One summer's afternoon in August 1981, my wife and I visited Blenheim Palace in Oxfordshire. We approached the golden Baroque mansion as the slowly setting sun brought out an amber richness in its turrets and porticoes, and in my mind the place looked more like a fantasy from ancient Olympian mythology than something you would find in the English countryside. Suddenly, inexplicably, a magnificent voice boomed from the vast Classical pile: 'We shall go on to the end,' it said, 'we shall fight in France, we shall fight on the seas and oceans. . . .' The words were familiar to me, but something else tugged at my memory –

then the realisation hit home. It was Richard's voice, speaking the great Churchillian speeches from *The Valiant Years*. The voice, the words, the setting all conspired to make this a very moving moment for me.

Playing Churchill allowed Richard to let rip with his greatest attribute – that marvellous voice – and the disembodied eloquence of his reading thrilled millions, here and in America.

It was a good time to impress America, because he now embarked on a venture that demanded unquestionable star power to pull it off. Alan Jay Lerner and Fritz Loewe, writers of *My Fair Lady* and *Gigi*, had come up with a musical based on the Arthurian legends, and Richard was offered the part of Arthur. Could he sing? Yes, his pleasant, musical voice had been heard at several Hollywood parties, so there were no doubts on that score. Was the musical ready? No, it most certainly was not. Others have chronicled in detail *Camelot*'s labyrinthine saga of try-outs, re-writes, versions that did not finish till the wee small hours of the morning, and songs disappearing from the score, or, worse, making their debut twenty-four hours before an opening. Then there were the misfortunes afflicting those involved – illness, serious heart conditions, self-doubt. One surprise is that it ever reached Broadway at all; another, perhaps, is that the undisputed rock on whom all around depended, in this cavalcade of chaos, was Richard. Tireless, unflappable, energetic, supportive, tolerant, he kept everyone else alert to the possibility of success in an atmosphere that could so easily have engendered failure.

The Broadway opening in December 1960 had huge advance sales, but it was noticed with concern that many patrons were restive, some even leaving at the interval. Mutterings abounded to the effect that once the advance tickets had been used, *Camelot* would be in trouble. Luckily an appearance on the *Ed Sullivan Show*, billed as a tribute to the composers, which became a preview of *Camelot* for most of America, with all the great songs from the show, turned the tide. *Camelot* swept all before it, earning huge sums each week. For Richard and his co-star Julie Andrews, this was a magical time of triumph. In 1961, Richard was rewarded with the New York Drama Critics' Award for the best performance in a musical. I wish I had seen this marvellous show, the talk of all Broadway, but really there was no chance for a policeman to dash across the Atlantic, however much he wanted to. Needless to say, though, we all took great pride in yet another theatrical conquest by my brother.

Meanwhile, as Richard was scoring such a hit in one legend, another was being readied in Europe.

Because of the repercussions it had for the Burtons and the Jenkinses, for the film industry and, for that matter, the entire newspaper-reading world, I think it worthwhile to pause and look at the whole disordered history of *Cleopatra*.

In 1958, producer Walter Wanger bought the film rights to an Italian novel, *The Life and Times of Cleopatra*. It was a time when comparatively inexpensive features with an ancient world setting – variously referred to in Hollywood as tits and toga epics or, more chastely, sand and sandal pictures – were seen as profitable and a spate of them had flooded, like the Tiber itself, from most of the studios. Wanger went to Twentieth Century Fox, where sufficient enthusiasm was mustered to set up the project with an English actress as the siren. The plan was to film in England with a budget of around one million dollars, but the film dragged a little in its initial stages, and scheduling problems meant that the original star was no longer available. Undeterred, Wanger, after considering one or two others, hit on the idea of approaching Elizabeth Taylor at the height of her fame. Her price took the film into a different league when she signed on late in 1959, since she was to receive approximately as much as the entire budget of the first incarnation of the project. The movie was now evidently going to be a major one and the budget rose to six million. Filming would start in England in autumn 1960, with serious talent on board – Peter Finch would be Julius Caesar; intense, saturnine Stephen Boyd would be Marc Antony.

Almost immediately, there were problems. Exceptionally bad weather made a mockery of attempts to give Pinewood a sultry look, and worse followed when the chilly autumn contributed serious illness in the star. Such was the tenacity of her ailment that it proved impossible to film around Miss Taylor as the producer had initially hoped, and the whole production was shut down, even though overheads were reported to be $45,000 a day. This, and additional difficulties with the script, led to the resignation of the director, Rouben Mamoulian, at the start of 1961. While the costly sets stood unused, the producer searched for a replacement and persuaded Joseph Mankiewicz (universally admired for such films as *Suddenly Last Summer*) to take on the task. Unfortunately before he could even pick up the reins Elizabeth was ill for a second time, and now it was 'flu turning into an almost fatal form of pneumonia. At one point many feared for her life; it was reported that she stopped breathing on five separate occasions. Her understandable period of convalescence meant that she would not be fit enough to work on the cold set for some months.

The result was that the film came to a complete halt once more, but the delays meant that both Peter Finch and Stephen Boyd had to be released to honour commitments now pressing upon them. Faced with such fundamental upheavals, in mid-1961 Fox decided to abandon filming in England altogether, so the sets were taken down and a future start was settled for the third attempt, at the warmer and more appropriate Cinecitta Studios in Rome. To replace the two leading men, Wanger and the head of Fox, Spyros Skouras, approached Laurence Olivier for Caesar. He said no. They approached Rex Harrison. He said yes. And for Marc Antony? Skouras had been involved with *The Robe*, so he knew Richard could bring power and dignity to ancient world subjects, however extravagant the decor around him. Skouras wanted Richard now.

Cleopatra would certainly be a more prestigious operation than his two most recent films. Both had been disasters: the first, *The Bramble Bush*, had a New England setting for its drab tale of murder and adultery; the second, *Ice Palace*, covered the story of Alaskan history, as reflected in the life of one mercurial man – Richard's character. As I have said of earlier efforts, the mystery lay in why Richard was chosen for them. They did nothing with his screen presence. So after yet more downers, *Cleopatra* by contrast offered Richard the sort of lyrical grandeur that suited his skills. However at this point, early autumn 1961, he was contractually tied to *Camelot*. Skouras worked out a deal whereby Richard was released from the musical – there was a payment of $50,000 to the musical's backers – and so my brother was told to be available on the Rome set for the end of September 1961. It transpired that the rest of 1961 was almost exclusively taken up with scenes involving

111

Caesar (Harrison) whom Marc Antony would supplant in Cleopatra's affections, and Richard did virtually no film work at all. He and Sybil, and the cronies he managed to have around him, enjoyed an unexpected, heel-kicking holiday at Twentieth Century Fox's expense.

Finally, in January 1962, Richard and Elizabeth played their very first scene together. Reports elsewhere have indicated that Richard was rude about Elizabeth before they actually worked with each other. These I cannot prove or disprove: he may have resented her vast salary and the way the whole elephantine production revolved, creaking, around her, while he and his prestigious co-stars were very much eclipsed. It is entirely possible that the hugeness of the undertaking, and the doldrums that had becalmed his career, conspired to make him ill at ease and nervous. Whatever he had felt before he came into daily contact with Elizabeth, once they were in close proximity, playing scheming lovers, a quickening of the pulse was sensed. Almost immediately, rumours of an attraction began to circulate, quietly at first, then with a deafening racket. The world's press flung itself into chronicling every move, nuance and event of the Richard/Elizabeth romance with more than its customary fiendish delight, and with correspondingly scant regard for the feelings of anyone concerned. For Richard it was hell, albeit one of his own making. Years later, he confided his experiences of journalistic outrages to me, echoing some things he had written earlier in *Meeting Mrs Jenkins*: 'You should have seen the paparazzi, Dai. They would crawl through the undergrowth, or shift between the cars, like soldiers on manoeuvres, in the frantic hope of catching us – Elizabeth especially – in an unguarded moment.'

Around that time, the peak of invasive publicity, I received through the post a cheap magazine describing Richard's early days in the most sensational and scathing terms. This was not an isolated incident. Over the years we had all been subjected to unpalatable doses of humiliation and embarrassment. We had had to develop a mechanism for coping with this, but when this particular magazine appeared on my doormat, I phoned Richard feeling very bruised.

'You should take action against them, Rich.'

He sighed grimly.

'Do you know, Dai,' he said with resignation, 'if I were to take action against these people I would probably spend more time in the courts of law than I would on the stage.'

I could see his point. But he was not always around to share the hurt. Often these articles would appear when he was out of the country and he would know nothing about it; or so we imagined.

While the public seemed to be clamouring for more and more stories about Richard and Elizabeth, we began to long for privacy, for anonymity. We kept wishing that all this was happening to someone else – someone not related to us. It was very hard to accept, but by the nature of things, somehow we had to deal with it all.

The family's reaction to these rumours, when reports first reached us, was one of heart-felt disbelief. Having had a world- renowned star in the family for fifteen years, we were already well acquainted with the dubious habits of journalists and their capacity for unfounded exaggeration. Besides, this was not the first time Richard's name had been romantically linked with a co-star. Nothing serious had ever come of his transitory entanglements: Sybil and the children came first, always. Whatever was happening now was no threat to the stability of Richard's marriage and family. Or so we convinced ourselves at first. The self- delusion, however, was impossible to keep up for long. Unlike Ivor and Gwen, the rest of us had never spent much time with Sybil, but we felt very close to her now. She was Welsh, she was one of us, she was part of our family, and, we felt, she must be suffering terribly.

For despite Richard's early denials, the basic story, we came to see, was clearly true. There was a great deal of turmoil and agitation within the family at this time. On one occasion, Ivor threatened to punch Richard – I never found out whether he actually did or not.

If I leave to one side for a moment the sensationalism that shrouded the filming of *Cleopatra* I have to acknowledge, with hindsight, the striking parallels between the relationship between Richard and Elizabeth and that of the characters they portrayed. This is particularly apparent in the words of the Shakespearean scholar, R. H. Case:

Admittedly it is far from the noblest kind of world, as the two main figures are far from human nature at its noblest. But, being what they are, they

113

are by their mutual passion lifted to the highest pitch to which they are capable of soaring. It is the merest fatuity of moralising to deny the name of 'love' to their passion, and write it off as 'mere lust'. No doubt it is not the highest kind of love; it is completely an *égoisme à deux*, and has no power to inspire to anything outside itself; but it has in it something that should be an element in the highest kind of love; and at least it is the passion of human beings and not animals, of the spirit as well as the body.

When the filming of *Cleopatra* finished in July 1962, Richard, desperate, I think, for some privacy and for the support of the family, came quietly to Wales for a short visit. He was accompanied not by Sybil but by Dai John Phillips, an old family friend and brother-in-law – Ivor had married Dai's sister, Gwen. I was stationed in the village of Gowerton, near Swansea, about twelve miles west of Pontrhydyfen, and was living there with my wife and daughter, when Richard and Dai John turned up at our little whitewashed police house one Saturday afternoon.

'I'm going to take this daughter of yours out to dinner tonight,' announced Richard. My daughter Susan, then thirteen, was suddenly struck by an incapacitating attack of shyness (much regretted later) which ruled out the dinner. But Richard still had Dai John as his chaperone, and in front of him we talked about everything but the one subject in the forefront of our minds. I had the definite feeling that Dai's presence was being used by Richard to forestall any awkward questions I might ask about what was happening in Rome. The atmosphere was certainly strained, and I did not enjoy my growing sense of unease.

I took them both out of my home to see the nearby police station and divisional office where I had recently taken up a new job. Dai, for some reason, marched briskly ahead. I looked at Richard, and then seized my chance. 'Is it true, Rich,' I ventured, 'about this romance with Elizabeth Taylor?' He looked impassive, as if he had been expecting the question. He stared resolutely at the cracks in the pavement. 'No,' he said.

It was clear that he did not want to talk about it. It was also clear – uncomfortably clear – that he had not told the truth. I felt there was little use raising the subject again. We moved uneventfully through the rest of the day. I drove Richard and Dai to the North Gower Country Club, introduced them to the delighted landlord and some of the staff, and we talked. Although it was all convivial enough, Richard was subdued and there was a conspicuous absence of his usual eager questioning and reminiscing about the family that gave an artificial awkwardness to the proceedings.

When Richard and Dai were gone, I speculated on what might happen. Until then I had never seriously thought Richard might leave Sybil for Elizabeth or for anyone else, but his evasiveness, his unwillingness to meet my eye and his transparent lying suddenly made me afraid for Sybil and the children. For the first time, the real seriousness of the situation was brought home to me. Divorce was a concept alien to our family – marriage was for life. Furthermore, the children, Kate and Jessica, were so tiny. It would be mad to leave all he had for Elizabeth Taylor, known to be a notorious divorcee and a wrecker of marriages who discarded husbands like unwanted suitcases. Could Rich not see through her?

We all felt very protective towards Sybil, although we had no contact with her and very little with Richard. Day by day, we read the newspaper articles like everyone else – Richard's and Elizabeth's movements were constantly being reported. Their denials of a romance and repeated requests for privacy went unheeded. Day and night, the pair of them were relentlessly hounded and the stories that emerged were a source of deep embarrassment within the family. We were stunned and shocked beyond belief: this kind of thing happened in Hollywood, yes – but to one of us? Richard's fame we could cope with, but not this shame.

If we in Wales were suffering at a remove, Ivor and Gwen were almost in the spotlight with Richard and Elizabeth. For years, they had been with Richard and Sybil almost constantly. Next door in Hampstead, at Le Pays de Galles in Céligny, Ivor and Gwen had come close to sharing Richard's life. Now they were Sybil's main source of support, and like her, they were devastated. The three of them waited and waited in the house in Celigny for Richard's promised return, perpetually delayed. Reports reached them that he was with Elizabeth at her villa in Gstaad, also in Switzerland. We learnt later that he had been anxious to get back to Geneva to sort things out with Sybil. He also knew that Ivor would be waiting for him, and that Ivor, unlike me, would not accept a shifty, monosyllabic denial.

115

But if Sybil was tormented by jealousy, so at this stage was Elizabeth. She knew that Richard was agonising over the choice he had to make, and she feared that once back in Celigny he would be swayed by loyalty, fatherhood and – not least – Ivor. So she acted on the sort of impulse that was entirely in keeping with her reputation. She burned all Richard's clothes in an incinerator, ensuring that his return to Celigny would be delayed still further. I never did discover how Richard had reacted to that gesture; neither do I know at what stage he eventually made the trip back to Celigny. What I do remember is how we, the family, finally learnt the truth after months of uncertainty. In common with thousands, millions of others to whom it was just a fabulous entertainment, we watched grim-faced as Richard made a statement on television.

'I love Elizabeth,' he declared stoutly to the world, as he had done privately some time earlier to Emlyn Williams, 'and I am going to marry her.'

From the perspective of the 1990s it seems hardly credible that adultery and impending divorce in the world of film stars could have caused such a sensation. But the combination of the prevailing moral climate, and the aura of fascination in which Richard and Elizabeth were held, ensured that the story not only hit the headlines but stayed there for months.

When the decision was made and arrangements were underway for Sybil and the children, Ivor knew that there was no longer any place for his masterly powers of persuasion, his appeals for stability, for loyalty, for the family. Distraught, he reacted with a silence that was as violent, as wounding, as his roughest speech. He refused to speak to Richard at all. This was no mere token of disapproval; the silence between the brothers lasted a year. Indeed, Richard confided to me much later that Ivor's reaction had shattered him. It was in some respects, he said, the worst year of his life.

Of course, it was not only over Ivor that Richard suffered. He must certainly have tortured himself when trying to decide whether to leave Sybil. Although their relationship had had its stormy moments, she had been the most loving and supportive of wives, part of his existence from almost the birth of his career.

116

They had been through so much together, experienced so many of the unrepeatable excitements of a star in its ascendent. They had made so many good friends together. Unlike many married couples they had always known how to laugh, how to enjoy life and live it to the full. In many real senses, their marriage was a partnership. And on top of all that she was one of his most loyal friends – not always the case in a marriage.

Not only would he be bereft without his wife. There were the children. Richard had been besotted by Kate from the very moment of her birth in September 1957. He had always missed her very deeply when absent filming. Now of course he would see even less of her – it was naturally assumed from the start that the children would stay with Sybil.

And Jessica? On the subject of Jessica, Richard steadfastly refused to be drawn. He would clam up and look darkly at us if we talked of her – eventually we all learnt to avoid mentioning her at all. She was finally diagnosed as autistic at the very time that Richard and Sybil's marriage was ending. Short of questioning Sybil in a way that I am sure would be painful for her even now, I can only recall, here, the murmurings within the family, the uncomfortable possibility that Jessica's illness had been triggered by the emotional storm building up around her. So little was – is known about autism. We do know that Jessica had just begun to talk when Richard left; then, abruptly, all communication ceased. She became locked in her own mysterious world, where she has remained ever since.

Regardless of the origins of Jessica's illness, the trauma experienced by both Richard and Sybil was now compounded. Ivor and Gwen suffered terribly, too. Childless themselves, they adored Kate and Jessica; and 'I-I and Gen', as they were affectionately known, were treasured by the little girls in return. They were among the few who had made some headway in communicating with Jessica, and they passionately believed that Richard's departure was at least partly responsible for her condition. Ivor's long hostility towards Richard sprang as much from this conviction as from his more general abhorrence of adultery and divorce.

Both Ivor and Gwen were desperate to help Jessica, and even wanted to adopt her. Sybil gently rejected this offer, but it was to them that she turned for emotional support, not only then but for years to come.

And in all this personal upheaval and unhappiness, what was happening to careers? After the havoc surrounding *Cleopatra*, only a part of which was to do with the proper business of film-making, Richard and Elizabeth had to decide what projects do do next. Several were considered, but the one that came up trumps was a mild, pleasant bit of jetset fluff called *The VIPs*. It came about like this. Anatole de Grunwald, who had given Richard his break in *The Last Days Of Dolwyn* – how long ago that now seemed! – had a script by Terence Rattigan which dealt with the upmarket concerns of a group of VIPs stranded in the lounge of Heathrow Airport, playing out their dovetailed dramas as they wait for the fog to lift. Grunwald shrewdly calculated that this effort could be made speedily on a few cheap sets and therefore could be brought to market at the optimum moment for cashing in on the press's feeding frenzy for anything Burton/Taylor. Richard was to play an international businessman; Elizabeth his wife who was on the verge of leaving him for another man – a situation not without marketing angles. Quickly he set up his deals; the film was suddenly a go project.

Richard and Elizabeth came to the Dorchester – Elizabeth's London home – and booked separate but adjoining suites. At this time, of course, his marriage to Sybil still existed. It was a tough time emotionally for everyone, but at least the filming went well. Co-starring Louis Jourdan, Elsa Martinelli, Margaret Rutherford, Maggie Smith and Orson Welles, *The VIPs* was entertaining, and as befits a Rattigan script, had passages of dry wit and subtle pathos. Really it was no more than a wordy but well-crafted West End piece somewhat inflated beyond its station, but its cast – two of them in particular – meant money at the box office when the film opened just after *Cleopatra* in September 1963. By then, Richard was hard at work on *Night Of The Iguana* in Mexico. Elizabeth was with him. He was filming with John Huston; she was showing the world how much he meant to her, and discovering a delight in the exotic Mexican locations.

In the meantime, Richard had not been not idle for long once *The VIPs* had come to an end. Almost immediately he was involved in *Becket*, based on Jean Anouilh's play about the murdered twelfth-century archbishop of Canterbury and his exasperated king, Henry II. Thomas à Becket had been a fellow rollicker with his royal companion until appointed to the archbishopric; then he stood firm and opposed the king's attempts to reduce the power of the Church. Offering a dramatic personal *volte face* and a struggle between two institutions as personified by Becket and Henry, Anouilh's drama contained great parts both for Richard as Becket, and Peter O'Toole, fresh from *Lawrence Of Arabia*, as Henry II.

The perhaps long-suffering director was Peter Glenville, who had worked with Richard over fifteen years before in the London theatre. Here he elicited creditable performances from his two stars (Richard was nominated for an Oscar) and from the distinguished supporting cast which included Sir John Gielgud as the king of France.

Cassie visited the set and was amazed by the way Canterbury Cathedral was recreated, convincingly, in what looked like papier mâché. On one occasion, she and her husband Morgan had a light lunch with Richard and a few journalists. Cassie was talking of things in general when Richard pointed out to her, in Welsh, that every word was being written down. It was a reminder of the ever-present interest of the media, and it gave Cassie a brief insight into the world that Richard now inhabited, where popularity had to be paid for with wariness and with being always (when sober, at any rate) on one's guard.

Richard told me that during filming in Northumberland, he and Peter O'Toole made a pact to avoid the hard stuff for two months for the sake of the picture. I cannot vouch for the longevity of that vow, but what I saw on screen was certainly the work of two fine actors at their peak, so perhaps they stuck to their pledge – or perhaps they so mastered the effects of drink that it did not impair their acting.

By late 1963, Richard was ready to talk more freely to friends (and even to the occasional journalist) about Elizabeth and about himself. He would often romanticise his childhood, describing it as idyllic: 'I remember train journeys and bus rides and friendly faces and packets of potato crisps and the warm womb of the village. That is my background. Solid and charming. I still get a tremendous kick out of going home. I took Elizabeth there just before we left England. I told her it was a squat and ugly place, full of rain. But she adored it – said it was the most beautiful place in the world.'

A lot of water had passed under the bridge since Richard's morose, monosyllabic walk around Gowerton with me and Dai John Phillips, only a year or so before.

'Falling in love', he used to say, 'isn't anything instant. It's an accumulation of detail, a slow storing up of knowledge. That's how it was with Elizabeth, anyway. I knew it would cause havoc in my private life. With my wife, and children, and brothers and sisters. But that is finally, painfully, unavoidable.'

He was clearly proud of Elizabeth and enjoyed showing her off. 'Receptively intelligent,' he called her, 'remarkably practical . . . for a so-called raving beauty.'

Finally, the inevitable happened: Richard and Sybil were divorced. Sybil, financially secure, had already settled in New York, there beginning the process of establishing herself as an independent individual. For her the worst was over. She had suffered most when Richard was indecisive, shifting uneasily between Sybil and the children in Hampstead, and Elizabeth and her entourage at the Dorchester. Now Sybil could begin to rebuild her life, and with her admirable, innate strength of character, she did so. Supported by a strong band of loyal friends and colleagues, she made her life her own and became manager of a highly successful nightclub, Arthur's. She eventually remarried and had a third daughter, Amy.

Meanwhile, the Burton-Taylor parade moved on. Richard and Elizabeth were married in Canada, with Bob Wilson, Richard's American aide whom I was to meet later in Rome, as best man. None of the family was present. For us, as for the rest of the public, it was an event happening outside all our points of reference. We just saw what other people saw: the glowing photographs, the media accounts which quoted Elizabeth: 'This marriage will last for ever.' None of us had even met her.

We did eventually meet, later that year, when Richard brought his new wife to Wales. They were en route for Ireland, where *The*

120

Spy Who Came In From The Cold was to be made.

The timing was sound from everyone's point of view. The sensationalism that had initially swamped any understanding of their relationship had receded somewhat, leaving something calmer, something acceptable, something not altogether inconsistent with sitting in armchairs in Cecil Road, Gowerton, sipping cups of tea and chatting with careful casualness. It was still quite an event, of course, having Elizabeth Taylor to tea. You could not help giving quick glances at her eyes just to check whether they really were all they were claimed to be. She looked stunning, I thought, sitting there in knee-length lavender suede boots which, she exclaimed delightedly, matched our sitting room carpet.

The neighbours, not least the wife of my superintendant, were installed behind their lace curtains for the duration of the visit and emerged quite by chance as the pair were leaving. To my great amusement there was a shameless scramble to sit in the chair she sat in.

Needless to say, Elizabeth's beauty mesmerised my male colleagues. When news of the visit percolated (at top speed) down to Gowerton Police Station, the Chief Inspector there rang at once and asked me to bring the celebrated pair to my workplace. Everyone there was agog with excitement and work rather fell by the wayside. Chief Inspector Austin opened a bottle of whisky and the atmosphere was not that of a clinical, busy police station at all! Richard, seeing the booze, said, 'Now the party's starting,' and he rather than Elizabeth was the talkative one. But it was she who drew all glances to her. My immediate superior, the late Superintendant Joe Hewlett said to me, 'My God, Dai, Elizabeth looks simply wonderful. I feel like putting my arms around her!' It was a sentiment shared by many of my seemingly unflappable brawny mates. But perhaps the best comment came from one of our neighbours. 'Oh, such beautiful features, Dai. All I can say is, she is the reincarnation of the Madonna herself.' Mrs Austin in particular paid special attention to Elizabeth's appearance, and lo and behold, in the next edition of the Glamorgan County Police Magazine, every detail of Elizabeth's outfit was meticulously recorded.

And what of our reaction to Elizabeth, after all the months of speculation? When it came to it, we found her quite charming and not at all ostentatious; a little nervous even, anxious to be accepted by us all. Elizabeth must certainly have been aware of our attachment and supportive feelings towards Sybil. In fact, by then we had had to do so much adapting that our longing for a vanished past was somewhat diminished. We still felt for Sybil but she had accepted the situation by now, and everybody, with the exception of Ivor, was prepared to move on.

Richard's method of acclimatising us to Elizabeth was to introduce her to small sections of the family at a time, with little advance warning. A little while before the meetings in Wales, Hilda and Edie happened to be staying with Cassie in London, when a telephone call came from Richard. Would they like to go to the Dorchester for tea? Elizabeth's parents would be there as well.

My sisters duly set off to the Dorchester for their first meeting with Richard's prospective new wife and parents-in-law. They found them extremely charming and got along very well together. Richard was on great form, and skilfully dissipated any lingering awkwardness.

I was always fascinated to observe the interplay between Richard and Elizabeth. If he was gifted, eloquent, openly persuasive, she was subtle, quietly convincing. In a sense they always competed with each other – but at best the interaction was healthy, open and humorous.

Richard used to say with pride that Elizabeth could get what she wanted merely by look or gesture. I witnessed it – it was true. And her charisma worked with me as well.

Our meeting Elizabeth was the beginning of what was to become a long and close relationship, one which would outlive their marriage, and Richard himself, by many years, though at the time we would never have dreamed of such developments.

In the midst of the drama of his marriage, and the helter-skelter rush into films, some good, some bad, all demanding, Richard found time for his neglected first love, Shakespeare. The play was *Hamlet*, and Richard, asked to give his views on the play at the time of the 1964 New York stage production to commemorate the 400th anniversary of Shakespeare's birth, came up with the following response:

122

If one man believes that *Hamlet* is the tragedy of a man who cannot make up his mind, and plays it that way, then that is, for three and a half hours, what *Hamlet* is. If another believes him to be a frustrated soldier, envious of 'the delicate and tender Prince . . . with divine ambition puffed', then that is what he is. If another chooses to mince delicately on high heels, scornful and scorning, to his deadly appointment with Laertes's rapier, then that is what *Hamlet* is. These actors have but to have enough power of personality to command your attention and their Hamlets are for a couple of hours what these actors choose to be, or cannot help being.

Someone once told me that the first *Hamlet* you see is the one that dominates the rest of your life. I've asked this of other people and apparently it is not true; in my case however it is. The first *Hamlet* I ever saw was in 1944 at Oxford. The actor was Gielgud. I was lucky. I saw – and see in my memory – the golden renaissance Prince, witty, scholarly, loving, high-poetic, infinitely, smilingly and heartbreakingly melancholy. His was indeed so near perfect a performance that he nearly killed my ambition. Who could match him, I thought. Who could match him? It was Sir John himself who later on when I became friends with him persuaded me, by inference more than by direct statement, that every man is his own Hamlet, that *Hamlet* (assuming that there is the initial talent) is so massive that there is room for all.

Who in two or three hundred words, or for that matter, two or three thousand books can throw light on *Hamlet?* Thousands of volumes, philosophical, psychological, idolatrous, religious, political and hate-filled have been written about this most inconsistent and disjointed creation of Shakespeare. He is so illusive that he can be (and has been) played as a homosexual, as a man of action (someone once told me that Olivier's performance of *Hamlet* was the best performance of Hotspur he had ever seen), as demoniacal, as one suffering from satyriasis, as a poet, as an intellectual, as a brilliant but tragic comedian and so on, through endless permutations of these and many other labels. He has even, as we all know, been played by women. My own theory, if you can call it one, is that no actor has ever been right or perfect as Hamlet, and that everybody has been right and perfect. Let me quickly qualify this by adding that any weaknesses or strengths of the

123

individual actor will be exaggerated under the blinding light of this most searching of parts. You'll see the man reveal himself for what he is when the great Prince gets at him – exciting, vulgar, envious, perversely witty, obscene, poetic, exotic, brave, cowardly, cynical, romantic, empty, mystical, posturing, lovable, charming, self-pitying – a combination of some or all of these things and more, or that most dreaded revelation of all – prosaic, inadequate and dull.

I have played Hamlet many times and in many ways. I played him first with no thought of his inconsistencies but with sheer delight in the verbal magic of each individual scene. I later played him with some attempt to connect up all the apparent incongruities. (I found this exhausting and fell back easily into self pity.) I played him again, as Hugh Griffith put it, as a Welsh preacher, bewildered but determinedly sonorous in the labyrinthine ways of Elsinore. I tried him once as a crafty (but poetically gifted) politician, anxious that never again would anyone pop in between the election and my hopes. I am, at the time of writing, playing Hamlet again and there is no knowing in this production (and no Hamlet has been given greater freedom or more help from a director) how this *Hamlet* will turn out. But whatever the verdict, I hope that whatever happens, I will *not* qualify for the last three words of the previous paragraph.

* * * * *

And so Richard, at thirty-eight, took on *Hamlet* in Gielgud's production, which opened at the Lunt-Fontanne Theatre, New York, on 9 April 1964. Richard Watts of the *New York Post* summed up the critical reaction:

> The fact to be stated at once is that Richard Burton is a very fine Hamlet indeed. His Prince of Denmark is forceful, direct, unpretentiously eloquent, more thoughtfully introspective than darkly melancholy, with the glint of ironic humour, and decidedly a man of action and feeling. And John Gielgud's production of Shakespeare's towering masterpiece is stirring and skilful, with Hume Cronyn presenting a memorable characterization of the blundering old Polonius.

There were other excited statements. The *New York Times* noted that 'Richard Burton dominates the drama, as Hamlet should: this is a performance of electrical power and sweeping virility.' Power and virility indeed – I have always believed that these were two of Richard's greatest attributes as a stage actor, ones he could bring with mesmeric effect to some of his most unsettling, insidious, unforgettable creations.

John Gielgud also talked about the production:

> I told him not to strain himself in certain scenes, where a relaxed lower tempo would help to make the higher possible effect and he said that was a help. I could never get him alone. He never seemed to want to rehearse very much. I used to write long notes – seven or eight pages and put them on his dressing table and he would go on the stage and try two or three of them that evening without any rehearsals and discard the rest – quite rightly probably. The amazing confidence with which he just tried two or three new things during the performance amazed me!

Richard in turn always spoke highly of Sir John Gielgud. He said that he was the best director he had ever worked with on the stage:

> Certainly he was marvellously instructive about *Hamlet*, but didn't dominate in the sense that you must do this or you must do that, or you must go here or you must go there because there were certain rules that I had for myself, "don't come near me, leave me alone," which he understood. . . . I think he thinks that I'm very undisciplined and for that very reason I have to have a lot of space on the stage, a lot of space so that I can move without being bothered by too many people. John said that I was very undisciplined and he is probably right. Then I wouldn't want to be disciplined. I wouldn't want to be that kind of actor who goes on the stage perfectly every night giving the same cadence, the same speech every night for days and days and days on end. I would prefer to be free so that I'm invited to be bad some nights.

This production of *Hamlet* turned out to be such a huge success, 'bad nights' notwithstanding, that it broke the previous world record for the number of consecutive performances of the play.

My sister Cis was invited to see it, so three weeks before the end of the run she and Elfed arrived in New York to stay with Richard and Elizabeth. Cis still remembers the event with tears of pride. 'I shall never forget Richard's wonderful performance,' she says. 'On the last night as we left the theatre there were thousands of people, all ages, all backgrounds, all waiting to shake his hand and give him a tremendous send-off. The car was being pushed one way and then another. It was quite incredible. The tears of emotion were running down my face and I turned to Richard and said, "Oh, Rich, if only mam could see you now".'

It was a very precious moment. The 'scandal' stories were rapidly receding into the past. Elizabeth was accepted, and was content for now to give Richard, literally and symbolically, the centre stage. Richard was at his peak theatrically and physically.

I shared all this, like the rest of the family, only indirectly. But my response was almost as emotional as Cis's. To get as close as possible to the production itself I managed to obtain a record of some of the key scenes. I have played it over and over again and it has never failed to thrill and move me. In my imagination I am right there in the theatre with Richard up on stage, his voice rising to a crescendo, every look fixed upon him, every syllable absorbed by an audience whose breathing is all but suspended. When he pauses we know that if a flake of snow were to fall it would be clearly heard.

The reviews included their customary dose of anecdotes. Someone had overheard Richard mentioning that he particularly enjoyed the traditional Welsh breakfast of bacon and laverbread. Next day the *New York Times* carried a strange headline: 'Actor Burton Brought Up On Seaweed'.

This time I was more amused than angry. They might have added, I thought, that the Welsh laverbread is equivalent to caviar.

The incident was one more example of the fact that everything Richard ever did, ate, drank, shouted or muttered was subject to the closest scrutiny, tossed around, perhaps distorted, treated in all manner of ways to maximise its news or gossip value. And of course we were invariably affected. Such is the price of fame in a family.

During this period, 1963 to 1965, Richard and Elizabeth certainly made a magnificent living out of a combination of their talent and their notoriety. After *The VIPs*, they went their own separate ways, at least professionally, for a couple of years. Then they made *The Sandpiper* together. It was certainly one for those who like life, or rather the cinema, to be full of enjoyably vexing emotional tangles. Richard played a married priest who falls for a free-spirited female artist, yet who still has feelings for his wife. It was directed by Vincente Minnelli, who knew a thing or two about drama on screen and off it, but the film which could have been moving and human ended up overblown and facile. Critics hated it, and, though it did well enough – Burton and Taylor in an eternal triangle was still a hot ticket –, it was a disappointment for those of us hoping for a high-quality study of love and its repercussions.

Early in 1965, Richard began making one of his finest films – *The Spy Who Came In From The Cold*. John le Carré's novel concerned an ageing, disillusioned agent, using some people, used by others, loving nothing in particular and life least of all. In contrast to earlier parts, this called not for bravado and the grand gesture, but for a deep-rooted emptiness. Richard played a grey lonely man lost in a fatal way of life; a man no longer young, blooded and exhausted by experience. It was a superbly conceived character and all praise to the film's makers, especially director Martin Ritt, for preserving – indeed enhancing – the book's study of introspection and despair as well as the more obvious set pieces of pursuit and bluff.

It was made in Dublin, which then had any number of suitably decayed streets. Elizabeth came too, and relations on the set were, I believe, not always relaxed. Claire Bloom, playing the female lead, had once been dear to Richard. Now, according to all accounts, he was cool to the point of rudeness and unkindness. I am saddened to think that reports of his ungallant, discourteous behaviour are probably true, but I suppose he was in a difficult position.

Nonetheless what was seen on the screen, whatever the circumstances of its making, was wonderfully atmospheric, and Richard's muted, world-weary spy was a revelation to those who expected the usual Burton intensity. Richard's performance was rivetting, and critics were delighted by it. He deserves an Oscar for this, was the general concensus.

Soon afterwards, Richard and Elizabeth collaborated on what many think is their greatest film together – *Who's Afraid Of Virginia Woolf?* from Edward Albee's play. It describes the tortuous bickering of an American university lecturer and his childless wife, and the corrosive effect this tirade has on a younger, impressionable couple unfortunate enough to be their dinner guests. Not for the emotionally squeamish, the film, like the play before it, was a *tour de force* of savagery, cruelty, misanthropic manipulation, selfishness and hopelessness, made more piquant with a dash of truly venomous wit. In other words, great drama. Not easy to play, it exhausted all who took part (Sandy Dennis and George Segal were the other couple) but the results were worth it.

As I recall, both Richard and Elizabeth were particularly proud of this film. At the end of the summer of 1966, Richard, echoed by Elizabeth, recommended it to me warmly. 'Go and see it, Dai. We don't look pretty in it. But it's worthwhile – it has something to say about relationships.' When I did see it, I was struck and moved by the courageous humility which enabled Richard to play George so brilliantly opposite Elizabeth's Martha.

The reviews were full of admiration; the film made Hollywood history for its open, casual use of profanity – the first time this had been permitted in a mainstream studio picture; audiences allowed themselves to be battered by on-screen torment in rewardingly large numbers; and both stars were nominated for Oscars. Elizabeth got one, Richard did not – a slightly sour note in what was otherwise a brave foray into dangerous waters that paid off brilliantly for both of them. They looked round for another test of their mettle, and Richard found it; *The Taming Of The Shrew*, to film in Rome in 1966.

Chapter Nine

Life with Elizabeth

For August 1966 I had planned a holiday in Geneva with my wife, daughter and a family friend, but towards the end of July my wife became ill with bronchitis, and we began to worry that the stress of the journey and even the hotel itself might prove too much for her. We wavered, and seriously considered cancelling.

Around this time, there was a family tragedy: my sister Edie died. Then living in London, Edith had suffered from rheumatic fever when she was fourteen and was very ill with it for a long time. Later, in adult life, she complained of being continuously tired. Doctors discovered that the valves of her heart had corroded and needed replacing. This involved major surgery and, sadly, she did not recover from the operation.

Richard and Elizabeth, filming *The Taming Of The Shrew* in Rome, flew to London for the funeral. Although we had long been prepared for her death, it was nonetheless a deeply moving episode. Edie was the first of the eleven of us to die, and the fact that she was one of the youngest made the event especially poignant. All the family attended the cremation service, held at Golders Green. As always on these occasions, we 'talked light', avoiding the sadness that had reunited us all. I spoke to Richard of our forthcoming holiday, and my doubts about it. To my astonishment he reacted immediately.

'Why not come to Rome and have a fortnight with us instead?' he said. 'It would be much more relaxing than a hotel – and we'd take care of the travel arrangements. The whole thing could be stress-free.' He went on to describe their rented villa – spacious, in huge grounds, with its own pool, comfortably away from the bustle and heat of Rome, just a short run from the studio where we could go along to watch the last scenes of *The Taming Of The Shrew* being shot. There would just be the six of us, he said, plus

Elizabeth's three children and their jointly adopted daughter, Maria. And the servants.

I was beginning to wonder just how relaxing it would be – not that I believed anything would come of it. Richard was notorious for making rash promises and then forgetting all about them afterwards. We returned home and put Richard's unconfirmed offer to one side – until the plane tickets arrived one morning. It was fixed: we were going to Rome.

Our excitement mounted as the departure date drew nearer. Not only was it our first flight, but our first-ever holiday with Richard, and of course, Elizabeth.

We arrived in Rome to the anticipated blaze of sunlight and publicity. Richard and Elizabeth, looking mildly anxious, were on the runway. Naturally their appearance caused a sensation among our fellow passengers, and there was a surge of autograph-hunters, whom they obliged in a good-natured way. Then the anxious look was accounted for. 'The most dangerous times are taking off and landing,' said Richard authoritatively. 'Those are the times I worry about.'

How extraordinary, I thought, that one of the most travelled people in the world should be so worried by the prospect of a statistically improbable plane accident. . . . But, of course, his great concern had always been for 'the family' and here he was demonstrating his sense of responsibility for keeping it intact.

Having struggled through the throng we made for the airport buildings – Elizabeth and I walking ahead, Richard and the others following. I was wearing a light two-piece suit which had been made for Richard to wear in *Sea Wife* in the Caribbean, nine years before; Richard clearly remembered it.

'Hey Dai!' he called after me, loud and jocular, 'you're wearing my suit!'

I decided to ignore him and retain some dignity. Elizabeth backed me up. 'Don't take the slightest notice of him,' she urged me warmly.

We seemed to bypass the customs. At any rate it was all done with great speed, and we climbed into the two awaiting cars – a magnificent Tornado and a long sleek Lincoln Continental, the choice of presidents. A pattern was hereby established for the entire holiday; whenever the six of us went out together, my wife and I travelled in the Lincoln with Elizabeth, and Richard accompanied the two girls in the Tornado.

We sped through the outskirts of the city and dry, dusty streets gave way to greener, more affluent suburbs made up of pristine white houses. Finally we turned off towards what looked like the lodge house of a grand estate, and elaborate gates opened instantly to admit us.

'That's where they keep the guard dogs,' said Elizabeth as we passed one rather grim building, 'and there are the snakes,' she murmured, indicating another. 'Good God,' I thought, 'what kind of security service is this?' Though we never did have a close view of the dogs, much less the snakes, we were thus made aware, very early on, of the extent of the security precautions that Richard and Elizabeth's lifestyle compelled them to take.

The cars swept up the winding drive to the villa, typically Roman in all its flat-roofed Italian splendour. Surrounded by thickets of dark Cypress trees and, closer to the house, a formal landscaped garden as far as the eye could see, all elegant Renaissance terraces and verandas, plus a huge, dazzlingly blue swimming pool and high hedges, this display of ostentation and luxury was to be our home for two weeks.

As we drew up the Burton/Taylor children and some of the staff appeared in the front porch. Bronzed and lean in their Bermuda shorts, Michael and Christopher Wilding, aged thirteen and eleven, peered anxiously at us through long fringes. Then Liza Todd, nine, came out: long dark hair and a triangle of a face, as Richard frequently and fondly described her, with enormous eyes. Finally there was Maria, five, fair and elf-like, every movement a dance-step.

Maria's early life had been a tragedy. She had been born with her legs growing almost at right-angles to her body; abandoned and resourceless, this was how she seemed fated to remain. Elizabeth had discovered her in a West German orphanage, and captivated by the tiny mis-shapen child, almost instantly resolved to adopt her and give her the best medical care. The transformation, many operations later, was dramatic; once we had heard the story, we marvelled every time Maria danced into view.

The house-staff greeted us like welcoming hosts. We soon understood that Enzo, who cooked and served our food, swam with us, played with the children and joked with us, and Karen, who had special charge of the children, were almost totally integrated into the family. Or were they? Enzo served our meals but did not share our table; Karen ate separately from us with Elizabeth's children. This routine was apparent from the first. It seems strange now that it did not occur to us, even to my daughter Susan and her friend, to question the fact that not only did the staff eat apart from us, but more bizarre, the children never once shared their mother's table.

The first meal, as always when Richard and 'family' came together, was full of cheerful reminiscing of Welsh days over mounds of buttery green vermicelli steaming enticingly on huge pottery platters. Elizabeth's eye caught mine a couple of times conspiratorially. 'My God Dai,' she remarked when he was briefly out of earshot, 'he can't half talk!' Richard's flow of jokes, reliving the family legends, imitating voices from the past, so very Welsh in so alien a setting, continued unabated.

They seemed very united, very contented together, just like a fond married couple of many decades standing, their manner serving to underline this impression. Elizabeth would say something like, 'We hope you don't find it too quiet here . . . we just lead a very simple life.' Richard might then add, 'When we come back from the studio we just like to relax – no high living. You won't be bored, will you?' It was all remarkably low-key for a couple whose 'high-living' had shocked and thrilled the popular press just a year or two before.

So began our simple holiday – if anything can be called simple which is set in a private, high-security villa populated by two world-famous film stars, an assortment of children, a visiting family and a retinue of servants – not to mention the rather menacing presence of those dogs and snakes! The staff themselves brought their own idiosyncracies, some quite startling, to me at least, in the mid-1960s. One of the secretaries, for instance, appeared at the poolside one day with her own child – a robust toddler. Nothing unusual in that. But Richard was keen to explain the background: she had reached her forties childless and, aware that time was limited, resolved to conceive. She therefore approached an acquaintance of hers – Richard warmed to his tale and there was clear admiration in his voice – to co-operate in the conception. The infant crawling around us was the result – reared, as I understood it, entirely by his mother alone.

There was something almost wistful in Richard's account. Not only did he approve of the pluckiness of his secretary, but he envied her the opportunity he himself was denied; after all, he could not bear a child at will. Moreover, this child was a boy, and although he loved his own daughters dearly he badly wanted a son. Even more perhaps, would he have wanted a child of his union with Elizabeth. True, Maria had been adopted by them both, but she was really Elizabeth's find. And, at that time anyway, Richard seemed to me to have more proprietary feelings towards Liza and the boys than towards Maria; perhaps about Liza most of all, as Elizabeth's true love-child. He was fond of saying, apparently without jealousy, that if Mike Todd had lived there would have been no space in Elizabeth's life for him. But to have a child with Elizabeth – that was a dream he could not even voice. Elizabeth, for her part, did talk of it – at least when he was not around. 'We so much want a child together,' she would say with longing, 'but it just can't happen.' She never went into details. I assumed that Liza's difficult birth, combined with Elizabeth's back problems since, made it impossible for her to bear any more children. I never felt it was appropriate to mention the subject to Richard, close though we were.

His fondness for Kate, his own first-born, was paramount. Jessica he could not or would not talk about, any more than his thwarted desire for a love-child with Elizabeth. Kate on the other hand he was full of, Kate who had recently visited the villa, 'my friend Kate,' as Liza reported. Richard showed us her most recent photograph with paternal pride; 'You can tell who she takes after, can't you Dai?' I reflected privately how much she resembled her mother, and wisely forbore to comment until Richard had answered his own question. 'A real Jinks. Look at her eyes! Look at that mouth!'

Anyone daring to suggest otherwise would have done so at his peril. No doubt there was his need to dissociate himself from Sybil, from the painful break with his past; but also there was an element that had always been characteristic of him: his need for continuity, to put the Jenkins stamp on the next generation, to create a kind of immortality of his own.

On a day-to-day level Richard strove to establish a good family atmosphere, with himself clearly at the head. Certain rituals had to be observed: kissing, for example, at the start and end of the day. The children complied willingly enough, but were inclined to forget, especially in the mornings. So Richard's paternal reminders became themselves a ritual. 'Where are the kisses flying around here this morning?' he would say sternly to everyone and no one. The children would shuffle around and respond. In fact this question, or a variation of it, could be taken as the daily indication that Richard's day had begun.

Then there was the business of Liza's donkey. She had her tenth birthday while we were there, and the donkey was her main present. The arrival of the unsuspecting animal was quite an event. We assembled in the front porch while the horse-box wound its way up the drive. Liza was undisputed queen of the occasion – even Elizabeth (perhaps *especially* Elizabeth) slipped into the background and enjoyed her daughter's pleasure. Richard on the other hand took to the role of father with great assertiveness. 'Now,' he organised, 'you have a ride on the donkey first, Liza, then let each of the others have a ride in turn.'

Liza obediently trotted round the garden, got off and waited while the other children did the same. Richard had presented a polaroid instant camera to my daughter immediately beforehand, so that the jubilation of the young equestrian and her family and friends could be captured for posterity.

For the next few days the donkey was the most important inhabitant of the universe as far as Liza was concerned. She fed, watered and tended it with true maternal affection. Then the novelty began to wear off; grooming sessions, even meals, were missed. Richard put on his paternal hat again.

'What about the donkey, Liza?' he would say sternly at intervals, but with little apparent effect. Finally he gave her a good dressing-down in which all the little carelessnesses and arrogances of rich children were addressed. He threw himself wholeheartedly into the part; fiery words flew across the stately sitting-room. Elizabeth stood by discreetly, not participating but clearly the supportive co-parent. 'She has to learn to take responsibility,' she remarked softly to us on the side lines. 'She has to go through this.'

134

Liza eventually stopped looking defiant and sobbed repentant tears. End of Act.

Richard found it easy to be a father to Liza since her real father was dead, whereas the boys' father, Michael Wilding, was very much alive. About a week after the donkey episode, the boys began packing for their trip to the States, getting ready for their summer visit to their dad. They were greatly excited about the prospect and were ready days in advance.

Then on the eve of the flight, there was a telegram from their father. The boys' grandfather was unwell; the trip was off. Both boys were disconsolate, especially thirteen-year-old Michael. They shuffled around, hurt, and in a state of limbo. Richard hovered anxiously over them, feeling their disappointment, and perhaps even more so, his own relative insignificance to them, his powerlessness to lift their spirits. He approached them hesitantly, gruffly: 'I'm sorry about your trip boys – I'm sorry about your grandfather.' They acknowledged his sympathy in monosyllables and went on nursing their wounded feelings for some days, consoling each other, slouching around the grounds of the villa.

But if the boys were, understandably, sometimes off-hand with Richard, they were at all times fiercely protective towards their mother. Thirteen and eleven now, they must have been bruised, if not scarred, by the relentless media onslaughts during the *Cleopatra* episode, when, after all, they were very young and vulnerable. In particular the much-promoted image of their mother as a breaker of marriages must have been terribly distressing to them. It was clearly important to them to view her (and to project this view to others) not only as the good mother, but also as the beautiful woman – especially if anyone dared to voice any criticism of her on that score. On one of the rare times when we received visitors at the villa, such an occasion arose.

Richard and Elizabeth's work schedule was unusual that day: they were free until early evening. In the morning, then, a couple drove up with their striking, raven-haired teenage daughter. She must have been about fourteen. As they were ringing the doorbell Elizabeth suddenly panicked. 'Oh God, I can't remember his wife's name.' Richard, predictably, was no help. Somehow the introductions were managed, and the daughter, with a somewhat superior air, began a tour of inspection of house and gardens.

135

Richard, observing her with quizzical eye, found a cue for his first anecdote and thus a way to feel at ease with the guests, who did not seem to be much more than acquaintances despite the enthusiastic exchanges of 'darling' and other theatrical endearments.

Richard recounted the occasion when the daughter had apparently been first · told of a remarkable resemblance to Elizabeth. When, shortly afterwards, she met the lady in question for the first time, she reacted with horror.

'My God! Am I supposed to look like that?'

Richard, of course, played his part with relish, keeping a humorous eye on Elizabeth all the while. The latter reacted with characteristic cheerfulness, as we would have expected.

The boys were not there at the time, but my daughter was – and later in the garden she mischievously recounted the anecdote to them. Michael had anyway been eyeing the visitor with some suspicion as she prowled around silently. Now on hearing this, he exploded. 'Am I supposed to look like that?' he echoed, his face reddening dangerously. All chances of anything approaching friendly contact were henceforth lost. At intervals during the remainder of the day, Michael was to be heard muttering unkind observations about flat-chested teenage girls, and the unrivalled beauty of his mother.

Later, when Richard and Elizabeth had gone off to the studio, we sat down to supper with these guests of theirs. It was an odd situation; not only did we barely know them, their connection with Elizabeth and Richard also seemed rather tenuous. While we all searched for promising conversation topics, the new-comers chimed in with tales of the friendship with Richard and Sybil. So that was it. Clearly they had felt deeply for Sybil throughout the whole trauma.

'And how do you compete,' said the man, wryly thoughtful, 'with the most beautiful woman in the world?'

There was little room for conversational development here. I think we confined our talk to the food after that.

But to return to the boys . . . Richard was, of course, aware of the role Elizabeth's sons had played in protecting and defending her, and he was very conscious of their somewhat ambivalent feelings towards him. Out of his own need, then, to be more fully accepted by them, he was very cautious in his manner with

Elizabeth when they were around, even to the extent (it seemed to me) of avoiding direct verbal exchanges with her in their presence. This was made easier by the fact that, as I have said before, meals were taken quite separately, and also by Richard and Elizabeth's schedule of work which mostly took them out before the rest of us were up. The 'together' times, as I recall them, were patchy affairs – adults and children meeting almost in passing in the sitting-room or garden. Richard, always alert to his responsibilities as co-parent, then confined his communication to direct exchanges with the children.

When the children were not around it was a different story. At meal times press speculation about their relationship were frequently discussed by Richard and Elizabeth.

'They say it won't last, that it's a self-limiting affair. We're just going to have to prove them wrong – in twenty years time, when we're still together, they'll be forced to admit they were wrong!' They would chuckle with anticipatory pleasure at the thought.

Another safe topic which they expanded on delightedly was their friendly fighting – often over the most inconsequential things, such as who should switch off the alarm, who should take a shower first, and so on. In affectionate banter she would call him 'pock face'; he retorted with 'Fatso'.

Elizabeth, as Richard well knew, had a tremendous appetite. When she was ill – which was often – it took on more eccentric forms, and it was not unusual for her to down several Bloody Marys for breakfast.

We later heard that Elizabeth, at times, relied on medication and had long periods of dependency on sleeping pills. Sometimes Richard would be at his wits' end trying to cope with her. Cassie remembers her arching her back pitifully so that Richard had to straighten her up. It was an odd kind of emotional and psycho-logical seesaw. Often when Elizabeth most needed care, Richard was sober and endowed with a kind of almost maternal energy. At these times he was so much more fastidious than Elizabeth, being almost fussy in the way he ate, drank and so on. Yet when his own drinking led to a loss of control, the picture was reversed and it was Elizabeth who was the strong parental one.

But back to Rome. During the 'Roman Holiday' period of

August, when many city residents flocked to the summer resorts and there was less danger of being besieged by autograph hunters, Richard took us out to one of his favourite restaurants. We were ushered to a private room as soon as the manager spotted us – then no sooner had we sat down than three violinists began a serenade. Richard, in the best of humours, sang his beloved 'Sosban Fach' to them; in no time they had picked up the tune, and there we all were, in the heart of the Eternal City, singing the nonsensical 'Sosban Fach' to violin accompaniment.

One beautiful balmy evening, Elizabeth, on the point of retiring to her bedroom, paused at the foot of the magnificent white marble stairway. We all knew that she had fallen off the donkey while filming *The Taming Of The Shrew*. (This was the same donkey that was presented to Liza on her birthday!) Elizabeth had injured her foot which was now heavily bandaged and she was obviously in pain.

Richard, my wife, daughter and the rest of the family were present in the lounge when Elizabeth said to me, 'Dai, will you please help me to go upstairs?' Richard immediately interjected, and said with a smile, 'You watch her Dai, she's only trying to attract your attention. There is nothing wrong with her foot. She is merely feigning injury.'

I gave what assistance I could and the matter was resolved. However the next day Elizabeth was taken to the hospital for an X-ray which revealed that she had fractured a small bone in her left foot and her foot was placed in plaster for a few weeks.

Sometimes we joined Richard and Elizabeth at the film studios. One afternoon while we were there an unexpected celebrity appeared – Princess Fatimah Al Sabah, a great fan of Richard's. She was the daughter of King Farouk, no less. King Farouk! She could not know that the name would conjure up the image of 'Ivor Stern' for us. What an irony!

The Princess asked Richard for a photograph, so he promptly arranged for the studio photographer to take one of us all. I was given the task of posting it to her in London after our return.

Elizabeth must have been filming while this episode took place, for the first she knew of the visitor was when she found her dressing-room occupied, much to her astonishment; Princess

138

Fatimah had unwittingly taken it over for the afternoon. Elizabeth flew at Richard. 'What is going on?' she said accusingly.

'Well after all, she is a Princess,' said Richard with a naughty twinkle.

'You are so gullible,' mocked Elizabeth. 'She's no Princess.'

'Oh yes she is!'

And so on. It all seemed to be part of their need to demonstrate to us that all was well, that the level of disagreement was utterly superficial and good humoured. But was it? Something they never alluded to, but which I witnessed, was the hostile rivalry savagely played out by in Richard late in the evening, when in the grip of tiredness and – inevitably – drink.

One episode in particular sticks in my mind. By the time of our arrival, filming of *The Taming Of The Shrew* was almost finished and the winding-down process was underway. Richard in particular was beginning to relax and, ominously, to drink more freely each day. Increasingly, an evening excursion would be planned. Richard would say to Mario, 'Is there a club where we can take the family tonight?'

'The family', of course, fitted in readily enough. Sometimes a whole range of social activities was crammed into one evening. Once we drove to the coast, stopping at some exclusive boutique on the way to buy the girls new swimsuits. Elizabeth was immediately swamped with attention by the manager and showered with an assortment of garments, including bikinis as gifts for the girls. Richard stood near the door, tapping his feet and looking mildly sceptical. It was hard to tell whether he was silently objecting to Elizabeth's collusion with the attention, simply feeling a little left out, or both. The pair of them climbed into the cars in silence.

We drove on to the coast where the new bikinis were christened under the strict supervision of two bodyguards. Richard and Elizabeth stood with us on the balcony of a bar indulgently watching the closely guarded swimmers. We had a few drinks and eventually moved on to a nightclub where a singer known to Richard was to perform. We met him at the ground floor entrance. With unusual insensitivity, Richard pushed my apprehensive daughter into trying out her school French: 'Ask him what he's going to sing tonight.'

'Qu'est-ce que c'est . . .' she faltered, 'que vous chantez, ce soir?' The singer looked blankly at her, then at Richard. 'Qu'est-ce que tu chantes, ce soir?' Richard barked scornfully, showing no interest in any reply. He called for drinks. I began to feel just a little concerned; irrational displays of impatience usually led to some sort of eruption later.

We eventually moved down to the club in the basement where Richard danced sporadically with the girls, drank and looked morose. There were signs of hostility to Elizabeth but its source was unclear. It was almost as if he was seeking a fight as a diversion. The end of filming was a classic time for this sort of thing to happen where Richard was concerned.

Richard perpetually looked forward to having more time and space for himself, but paradoxically he also viewed this with disquiet, and invariably reacted with some discord; as now when he was building up something out of nothing with Elizabeth.

As the evening wore on, Richard's moroseness deepened and was matched by his almost defiant attention to the girls, sixteen and wide-eyed at their first-ever experience of a nightclub. Elizabeth gave her attention to us, the adults, but it was clear she was waiting in the wings, not without some nervousness.

The climax erupted shortly before the journey home. As always, we were using two cars in the habitual split – Elizabeth with us in the Lincoln Continental and Richard with the girls in the Tornado. When Elizabeth made moves to indicate it was time to leave, Richard looked antagonistic – 'I'll race you home,' he announced to her in a tone that was anything other than playful, and she knew it.

'Richard,' she began firmly, but was immediately silenced. We took ourselves off to the cars with feelings of trepidation. The girls were with Elizabeth this time while I was with Richard, and I could see that he was in a mood to stir things up. Full of devilment, he leant forward to the chauffeur: 'I want you to go like hell and beat them to the villa.' The driver naturally stepped on the accelerator. He obviously knew Rome like the back of his hand, and Richard was mildly placated when his car was clearly ahead of Elizabeth's, but even so, he did not let up – the tense posture and verbal pressure on the long-suffering driver were maintained.

Richard and Elizabeth swept upstairs in a heavily-charged

140

silence. Any further explosions were strictly private.

We were left musing sadly over the mysterious ways in which this most serious-minded brother of mine could be driven – or drive himself – to such pathetic outbursts; alcohol, of course, playing its part in the distortion.

Although Richard had discovered on the set of *Cleopatra* that life with Elizabeth was lived in the spotlight, the 1967 premiere in London of *The Taming Of The Shrew* was the family's first real exposure to its dazzling glare. Elizabeth had grown up a star and had always treated the Dorchester Hotel as her London home; and it was there that the festivities surrounding the gala took place. There were more than two hundred guests from all over the world, most of them, unlike us, able to take the Dorchester lifestyle, its revolving doors, sumptuous bars and attentive waiters hovering reverently with cocktails at one's elbow, in their stride. If they were blasé about such glamour and comfort, I found it hard not to let my jaw drop at the unaccustomed luxury of it all.

It was without doubt an important occasion – the film had been chosen for The Royal Command Performance and Princess Margaret was in attendance. The screening was held at the Odeon Leicester Square – vast Art Deco flagship of the cinema chain, and worlds away from the tattiness of the fleapits of our youth. Before the film was shown, Richard stood in front of the audience, introducing his beautiful co-star and making an eloquent polished speech of welcome to us all. Once again, it was impossible for us not to be proud of our extraordinary brother. Who would have thought, twenty-five years before, that the little boy from Pontrhydyfen would be instrumental in holding up the traffic in London's West End, and that we would all be ferried in gleaming Rolls Royces to the opening of one of his efforts?

Richard's speech to the celebrity audience that night was a good one, his wit to the fore. He said that the press had suggested facetiously that the Jenkins family had taken over the entire Dorchester. Well, he said, his name was Jenkins, and up there in the circle was a young lady called Maggie Jones, so it was only an understandable attempt to keep up with the Joneses! He was referring, of course, to Princess Margaret, whose married name was Armstrong-Jones.

The film was a joy to watch. Director Franco Zeffirelli had perfectly caught the sense of fun in the play and the pleasure for us was the marvellous rapport between Richard and Elizabeth. We had always known that Richard could do Shakespeare – it was his patch – but here was Elizabeth matching him in power, making Kate a voluptuous, feisty, spirited woman that any man would want to woo, despite the price to be paid! In addition, the look of the picture – warm browns, rich oranges, sunlit courtyards, caressing flesh tones – made it a visual feast far removed from the austere majesty and grimy battle-scenes of most films of Shakespeare. This was a Bard to revel in as well as admire.

The rest of the world thought so, too. The picture was seen by millions of delighted filmgoers, and not only that; it rightly pleased those critics who had the sense to look beyond hidebound tenets of what Shakespeare should be.

During our 1966 stay in Rome, Ivor and Gwen had been frequently mentioned, indeed they had seemed very much present, though they had actually been in London at the time – we had visited them in Hampstead before flying out. By this time, Ivor had come round, slowly and very reluctantly, to accepting Elizabeth. Richard was hugely relieved and glad to have Ivor back as his guide and mentor. He would say to us frequently, 'I don't know what I would do if anything happened to Ivor.'

And we knew it was true. If Cis was mother to Richard, Ivor was very much the father; not that anyone ever thought anything *could* happen to Ivor. He was so strong, so robust, so apparently indestructible. He had a vigorous presence that belied his sixty or so years. Ivor and Gwen's base was in Hampstead, next door to the house in Squire's Mount which had been Richard's and Sybil's, but they were often with Richard in Geneva and other parts of the world.

In 1968, just two years after Rome and the making of *The Shrew*, Richard was in London when there was a phonecall from Céligny. The gardener who had worked for them for many years, now an old family friend, had died. There were no relatives so Richard, Ivor, Gwen, and Kate flew out to make the necessary arrangements.

After the funeral, the men repaired to the Café de la Gare for food and drinks, especially drinks. Then they decided to go back to Richard's villa although the women were installed in a hotel.

There are conflicting versions of what followed. As far as I can establish, Ivor went ahead to open up the house, which involved switching on the mains electricity from somewhere in the grounds. There was some sort of metal grille you had to step on in order to do this. Ivor, uncharacteristically, tripped. He fell awkwardly and broke his neck. He was never to walk again.

What led to the fall? Was it drink? horse-play with Richard? Or the more acceptable explanation – the awkward layout of the place and the darkness? Richard was never able to talk to any of us about it. He was utterly devastated by the accident, and by Ivor's helpless misery during the remaining four years of his life. Of course he did everything possible for Ivor, who was transferred as soon as possible to the specialist Stoke Mandeville Hospital in England. But despite the tremendous efforts by the staff and by Ivor himself, he remained paralysed, and it was appalling to see him, a shadow of the Ivor we remembered. Out of all of us, it was Ivor who had valued his physique most highly, Ivor for whom it was a top priority to keep himself fit and strong. Ironically, it was probably because of his unusually strong constitution that he managed to survive in a wheelchair for as long as he did.

We would all visit him and put on brave faces, and he did the same for us, but nothing could hide the fact that it was appalling to see him in such a state. I know Richard found it almost unbearable and his own visits grew less frequent. Ivor's accident and its tragic consequences took their place in the shadowed, taboo area of his life along with Jessica and her autism. Moreover, if Ivor never recovered, neither did Richard. A light had gone out in his life and he was the poorer for it.

Of course, there was still Elizabeth – very much so – and there was a brighter side to these years. Richard himself captured it on paper.

The Trials Of Travel With Liz

Travelling with Elizabeth Taylor is a kind of exquisite pain. Let me explain why this is: I am ferociously over-punctual, whereas

Elizabeth is indolently the opposite. I love Elizabeth to the point of idolatry, but – let's repeat that 'but' – she will unquestionably be late for the Last bloody Judgment. And, infuriatingly, she is always breathtakingly on time. She actually misses no train, or plane or boat, but of course misses the fact that her husband has had several minor heart attacks waiting for her while he shifts a shivering Scotch from his trembling hand to his quivering mouth to his abandoned liver, waiting, waiting, waiting for her to come out of the lavatory.

And the hooters howl or somebody says, 'All aboard' or 'last call for flight 109 to Los Angeles,' and not standing there is my stupendously serene lady, firmly believing that time waits for no man but will for her. In a sense I am one of the original boys who watched the train go by and lusted for London and, indeed, I finally caught that train and never went back and never will.

Elizabeth is not the only one of her sex who thinks that a hair's-breadth is half a mile wide. I have a sister-in-law who for years has been catching the 10.55 from Paddington to Port Talbot, resolutely believing that it's the 9.55. She has never understood why the train is always an hour late. But travel has become to us, as to most itinerant professionals, a part of our lives. We have been forced by habit to become doomed nomads, incapable any more of being sweet stay-at-homes, sweet lie-a-beds, forced to work around the world. We find nowadays that staying in any one place for more than – shall we say – three months is intolerable. And there is no place we've been to that we don't love.

We love New York (but not in June) and Los Angeles and London and Paris and Rome and San Francisco and Puerta Valarta and Gstaad and that rough country of my heart, Wales, and even Ireland, though the land is so unharsh that it gives a cragged moored felled fenned man like me a touch of the creeps.

We sit around in the middle of the night wherever we are and dream of places we have been to – my wife is a bad sleeper and worries about spiders and mosquitoes – and the middle of the night is sometimes an open forum as to where you would like to be now. And she says, or I say, perhaps in Paris, 'Wouldn't you sell your soul for an ordinary drugstore where you can have hamburgers or coleslaw or corned beef hash with an egg on top?'

And then again we're in New York and again we awake at the

dying time of night and dream of a bistro in Switzerland or some of the remoter regions of France unspoiled by Michelin or a trattoria in Italy nestling at the foot of a hill at the top of which is a magnificent church and there is a turbulent red wine and salami and a cheese that crumbles in the hand, falling down its own face like a landslide. We separate countries into foods.

Then there is, of course, the press. I mean photographers. If they are not there to meet us off the plane or train or boat, I lament the end of our careers. If they are, I blame Elizabeth for being too notorious. What can you do? What can she do? You're damned if they're there and you're damned if they're not.

However, travelling with Elizabeth has its compensations. She loves it. Porters and stewards and even stewardesses reward her with enormous over-attention and therefore I get a little on the side. Customs men from Port Said to Porto Santo Stefano grace her with a kiss on the hand. Grim men at Chicago and Dover wish her well. I remember once going into a restaurant, a famous one, in the South of France, and there were so many cars outside that we couldn't pull up to the entrance. We had two of our dogs with us. They ran ahead and up the steps into the restaurant. We had forgotten that dogs are forbidden in this place. The head waiter came out in a passion of outrage looking like an impersonation of Peter Ustinov impersonating a head waiter and with a shuddering admonitory finger was about to order them out when suddenly he saw Elizabeth and the cosmic gesture of dismissal turned, in a flash, into the most sycophantic leering smile of welcome that it has been my privilege to see. I laughed for the rest of the day. So much so that I allowed them to overcharge me. After all, $100 for two bowls of soup and two *quenelles de brochet* and two *mille-feuilles* is going a bit far, I think. They fed the dogs too. By hand. Very sweet. We've never been back.

But back to the drawbacks. How would you like to have a shoe of your wife's stolen off her foot by some fanatical fool at an airport – one of several thousand fools on this particular occasion – and feel the urgency of the crowd toppling you inexorably, it seemed at the time, into a trampled and affectionate death? How would you like to pass your small daughter over the heads of the madding crowd to a friend, all of us shouting in a language we didn't know? How would you like your wife to be hit in the

145

stomach by a paparazzo because he wanted an unusual photograph? It happened, you know. No jokes. Honest to God, he hit my wife in the stomach. I wasn't there or I would have long ago walked Death Row. Or how would you like to travel from Paris to Geneva with two nannies, four children, five dogs, two secretaries, a budgerigar, and a turtle who has to be kept permanently in water, and a wildcat, and 140 bags and Rex Harrison edging his way through the narrow bag-besieged foyer screaming in a low mutter – this was in the Lancaster Hotel in the Rue de Berri – 'Why do the Burtons have to be so filthily ostentatious?'

Well, I'll tell you, it's a tough old ride, but I wouldn't swap the privilege of travelling with Elizabeth for anything on earth.

* * * * *

Richard also enjoyed writing and talking about his notorious presents to Elizabeth. He was certainly generous – not only to her but to everyone close to him, as well as to innumerable causes and charities. Elizabeth, of course, was something special when it came to presents. She would tease him about them. I remember him telling me of her reaction to the famous Krupp diamond, which he presented to her wrapped in tissue-paper.

'It's lovely, darling,' she said, 'but not quite me. Do you mind if I take it back and change it for something else?'

Richard rarely, he said, gave her presents at Christmas or anniversaries or birthdays. He always said that surprise was the most important element. Once he bought a sapphire costing £27,000.

'You could wear it on the chest or the finger,' he said. 'I was working at Shepperton, so I asked her to lunch. She came in most days. Then I asked Liza to give it to her when she thought I was out of the room, but I was watching. Liza played the part beautifully. She said casually, "Oh, Dad forgot to give you this".'

'And then,' went on Richard, smiling at the thought, 'to watch her face when she opened it and saw it for the first time. . . . Elizabeth is so easy to buy presents for. Especially jewels. I have, in fact, a wife who is devoted to the idea of LARGE diamonds, LARGE rubies, LARGE emeralds and LARGE sapphires. She is . . . one of the world's greatest experts on large gems.'

The Krupp diamond was Richard's greatest secret. He explained how he had arranged with eight people to bid for it at an auction in New York. The press said that someone anonymous had bought it. And still he did not tell her. Then it was flown in from the States with one of the bidders, who arrived, flanked by two police guards, one Saturday morning. 'Even I,' said Richard, 'who have no eye for colour, could see the absolute power of the thing.'

He used to justify his presents for Elizabeth as a way of investing. He would say: 'I believe in putting money into bricks and mortar, or a piece of grass, or a jewel. But it must be a big jewel, not one of those fancy made-up pieces.'

He disliked buying her dresses because it was such a waste, he used to say, that she could only wear them once. 'And to spend £300 on a dress for one occasion seems a lamentable waste of money.'

And for himself? Paintings, if they were the right ones, and books. 'The only thing you can give me and be certain that I will enjoy it is a book.'

Richard was asked once what would happen if Elizabeth lost one of the jewels. He described one occasion when he took her out to lunch at the Guinea Restaurant in London: 'We were sitting at the table munching our lamb chops and she looked down and the sapphire I had bought three days before was missing. It wasn't insured. Well, we searched the Guinea, we searched the waiters, the waiters searched us. We went back to the hotel and searched the foyer, the lift, the flat, and finally in despair we went back to finish our lamb chops. On the way home we found it in the car. It had fallen off her chest and slipped down between two cushions.'

Richard sighed. 'But for an hour or two,' he said, 'I was in a foul sweat. I've never got used to money on that scale.'

A far cry indeed from that first ever present, the little print of the *Mona Lisa* he gave to Cis because, he said, she looked like her.

Meanwhile, there were films to make, ambitions to achieve. Richard never forgot his interest in Oxford University, nor his debt to Nevill Coghill. It had long been a dream of Richard's to help set up something really worthwhile to promote drama at the University, and now that he was one of the wealthiest and most powerful actors in filmland, he began seriously to pursue this personal Grail again.

One tangible effect of this enthusiasm was a performance of Marlowe's *Doctor Faustus* with students from the University, actually in Oxford itself; and with one Elizabeth Taylor in a minor role! The affair was somewhat rushed and chaotic from time to time, as all student productions are. Nonetheless a spirit of optimism, excitement and generosity was clear for all to see, and the carping of critics over this endeavour has always annoyed me.

The next phase was perhaps too optimistic. Richard and Elizabeth organised a party of undergraduates to come to Rome to film the play. Amateur drama is one thing; amateur Hollywood is another, and the film was patchy. Yet again though, this was Richard the great star trying to do something practical for a cause he believed in, and his input was more than a cheque, airily waved to the recipient. The episode cost him a lot in lost potential earnings. Whatever you think of the finished product, Richard's involvement was no mere empty gesture.

What Richard talked about most, and what I gather the undergraduates remember most vividly, is the series of seminars he gave on literature. These extended to long sessions, hugely popular, in the pub with both Richard and Elizabeth. Then all the old stories from Wales would come out – the rugby, and the miners, those aristocrats of the working class for whom Richard had as much reverence as he did for the academics who were now temporarily his colleagues.

For serious filming, of course, Richard and Elizabeth still had Hollywood (and its accountants) at their feet. They were seen as a licence to print money, able to make a commercial success of almost anything. After all, not many stars could get the public in to see Shakespeare the way these two had. So, not surprisingly, the offers came in from all over. Richard was wary of rubbish, and wanted something that, like *Who's Afraid Of Virginia Woolf?*, would combine artistic integrity with financial rewards. Rich they might be, but their lifestyle – owning yachts, staying at that cliché, 'only the best hotels', buying jewels, presents – needed a constant input of cash.

They chose a Graham Greene novel, *The Comedians*, set in Haiti and dealing with a steamy cocktail of politics, voodoo and individual tests of character. Richard would play a former Catholic, immured in a dive and in the throes of a relationship with a diplomat's wife – Elizabeth. Echoes of *The Sandpiper*, but on a loftier plane? One would not have thought so at first, as this was intended to be a high-class project with the two stars ably supported by the finest talent – Peter Ustinov, Alec Guinness, Lilian Gish: the nobility of the profession, steeped in experience and the subtleties of their calling. Somehow, though, the mix, such promising ingredients, turned out to be to no one's taste. Many critics have said that Elizabeth was not right for her part, but it usually takes more than one actor to undermine an otherwise sterling effort. It was not all her fault. The characters do not seem sufficiently moulded, nor do they interplay with conviction. It was a muddle of splendid parts, but finally, muddle it was.

Never mind; it was an honourable failure and now Elizabeth had a project of her own with a part for Richard, written by her favourite Tennessee Williams who had provided her with such a brilliant creature to play in *Cat On A Hot Tin Roof*. His play in question had an even longer title: *The Milk Train Doesn't Stop Here Any More*, but this would change during production, eventually becoming simply *Boom!* Elizabeth's was the central character – at one point the film was to be called *Goforth* after her part, Flora Goforth – as the plot revolved around a rich widow living in luxurious isolation on a Mediterranean island. Into her life comes a dangerous gigolo, pertinently named the Angel of Death, despite the warnings of a langorous elderly neighbour (from a neighbouring island, that is) charmingly called the Witch of Capri. Richard was the Angel, Noel Coward the Witch, so the calibre of the cast led to expectations of witty, waspish fireworks with an undercurrent of menace thrown in.

Sadly there were many problems with the picture. I have read that the filmmakers' initial choice for the Angel was James Fox, who a few years earlier had brought such a refined air of dissolution to *The Servant*. Certainly he was younger than Richard, and I mean no disrespect to my brother when I say that gigolos are by their very nature supposed to be youthful. Another problem was the way the characters were drawn. Many Tennessee Williams roles are exaggerated and artificial, but at his best the author could make us care deeply about their predicaments, no

149

matter how pathetic, deceitful or foolish they were. Here the characters had no redeeming qualities; they seemed just rich, self-indulgent bores.

Hollywood had paid a lot of money for the Burtons in this film, and to be fair, no one thought it would be a dud during production. When it opened, the first few days saw hefty ticket sales, but the truth got out with damning speed – hostile word of mouth slashed at the attendances, and reviews were punitive. The influential trade paper *The Hollywood Reporter* succinctly described it as 'an ordeal in tedium'. Within two weeks of the opening, the cinemas were almost empty.

This was exceptionally bad news. Richard had had a decent failure, with *The Comedians*, not finally something to tarnish a reputation. By contrast, *Boom!* was corrosive. It was a laughing stock, and one which irked the moneymen in Hollywood. Commercial success would be the only acceptable apology. Luckily Richard now made an astute choice, and early in 1968, went into the phenomenally popular *Where Eagles Dare*. It had all the right credentials for a late 1960s action hit: it was based on an Alistair Maclean novel; it had no end of plot twists, double crosses and explosive confrontations with evil Nazis; and it co-starred the king of westerns, Clint Eastwood. Richard was still young enough to convince as a man of action, and anyway nearly all the tricky stuff was done on the set at Pinewood. Certainly the producers thought Richard was essential to the film, as they paid him one million dollars plus a percentage of the gross, and gave him approval over most aspects of the package, including his famous co-star.

When it came out, the film proved everybody right, becoming MGM's most successful film of the year. Richard showed once again that he could rise above a tide of dross and bounce back, as great a star as ever. I think all the family enjoyed *Where Eagles Dare* (though it was a bit violent for some!) and it left Richard with a very healthy bank balance. From this unassailable position of strength, he could have had almost anything as his next film.

He chose *Staircase*, a tale of the strained relationship between two homosexuals, in which his lover was played by Rex Harrison. Both were hairdressers, notionally in London's East End, but for complex reasons, the film was made on a set in Paris. The main

150

element in this odd choice of location was the fact that Richard and Elizabeth, filming separate pictures simultaneously, wanted to be together. Her film, *The Only Game In Town*, was set in Las Vegas, but that too had to be recreated in Paris. *Staircase* was serious, and bold for its time (only two years after homosexuality had ceased to be illegal in England). The film was played for pathos and a feel for the disintegration of a once loving relationship in more than usually trying circumstances. Sadly it rarely got beyond the superficial, and while audiences may have appreciated that the two leads were obviously playing against type, they did not really care about the result. It flopped. Perhaps it would have done better with two comparatively unknown leads, who did not bring the baggage of their previous reputations to the parts; perhaps a better script would have helped; whatever. The point was that Richard had gone from an ironclad smash to yet another worthy damp squib.

Now Richard decided to play safe. When offered the role of Henry VIII in *Anne Of The Thousand Days*, to be made in England in the summer of 1969, he took it. Henry was undisputably larger than life, and here he was in his early middle age, a bit of a monster but not yet inhabited by total, syphilitic madness; in other words a multi-facetted monarch, one for Richard to explore with brio.

Anne of the short duration was played by a comparative newcomer, the Canadian actress Genevieve Bujold (who would go on to a very successful career, in *Earthquake*, *Dead Ringers* and most memorable of all, *Coma*). The storyline had winning elements: the king without an heir ditches his devout Spanish wife in ungallant circumstances, bewitched by a youthful adventuress with many enemies at court, who ironically also fails to deliver the male goods (she was, to be fair, responsible for Queen Elizabeth I) and so is despatched to the scaffold by means as nefarious as the ousting of her predecessor. As well as the charismatic royals, the plot required all manner of devious courtiers, dishonest statesmen, nobly suffering women and worldly clerics, and the film was well furnished with character-acting talent, including Anthony Quayle, so instrumental in Richard's career almost twenty years earlier, as Cardinal Wolsey.

It was inevitable that Richard would one day play Henry VIII.

'It is rather like being a reputable French actress who must eventually play St Joan,' Richard explained. 'In the same way, if you are an English actor or in my case, a Welsh actor grown up within the body of English literature, there are certain parts that, if you are lucky enough, you should play, like Hamlet, Lear, Macbeth and some of the other major figures not really touched by Shakespeare. Every actor given half a chance wants to play Henry VIII, and I was very excited about the opportunity.'

There must be aspects of every part that an actor identifies with. In this one it was undoubtedly the desire for a son – devoted father of Kate and Jessica though Richard was. Henry's lifelong obsession was to have a son and heir. Richard, who had grown up as the 'son' of one sister and the darling of the others, and who had fathered two daughters, would have loved a son of his own. And a child with Elizabeth would be the natural celebration of their marriage – but it was not to be. After the birth of Liza we later had our suspicions confirmed, Elizabeth had been advised that it was too risky to have more children. So – no son; no fruit of his marriage with Elizabeth. It was not difficult for Richard to enter fully and empathically into certain aspects at least of Henry's character.

Ironically Kate, now twelve years old, made her film debut in *Anne Of The Thousand Days* by curtseying to her father in the role of a Tudor serving-maid. Liza too had a walk-on part, as a beggar-maid.

Authenticity was almost an obsession with the filmmakers. It was made at Hever Castle, once home of Anne Boleyn's family. Many of the scenes recreate history on the very spot where it happened, a factor which added to the performance given by the actors. Some settings, of course, had to be replicated because nothing like them now exists. The most elaborate is a set of Greenwich Palace's main hall, scene of two balls. The set took 150 men three months to build, with minute attention to detail.

The film made its desired impact. Just over two months after filming was completed, it was selected for the Royal Film Performance of 1970.

Once again Richard was at the peak of his form with everything in his life going well. There were some amusing moments – as when the stand-in John Bailey, hair dyed brown to match Richard's, found that the summer sun had bleached him back to blond.

'Not to worry,' he was told. 'Richard wears his hat through most of the film.' But in the studio, in a love scene with Anne, Richard impulsively threw his hat in the air. Bailey metaphorically turned grey!

Then there was the time when Richard looked just a little too real for Penshurst Place's current owner Viscount de L'Isle, who declared: 'The last time Henry was here, in 1521, he beheaded the owner, and took the castle as death duty.'

Anne Of The Thousand Days was not the huge hit everyone had hoped for, nor was it accorded the critical reception of *A Man For All Seasons*. On the other hand it did respectable business and Richard was nominated yet again for a best actor Oscar – and yet again, he lost out. On balance then, this was a sensible film to have chosen, and Richard was still a world star after it.

But the 1970s were more difficult than the 1960s. The film world was more confused, more doubtful than ever. Costly industry projects like *Darling Lili* or *Paint Your Wagon* had lost millions; cheap, druggy youth pictures heralded by *Easy Rider* coined it. No one could predict what would work and what would fail. At the same time, Richard and Elizabeth, though unquestionably a news item of the greatest interest, were no longer guarantors of bottoms on seats. In this rather fluid, uncertain atmosphere, Richard made some unfortunate choices.

The immediate follow-up to *Anne Of The Thousand Days* was *Raid on Rommel*. The odd thing about this is that it used up chunks of battle scenes left over from *Tobruk*, made a few years earlier. *Raid On Rommel* was not a bad film, just a fairly minor one, in a genre suddenly running out of steam. It was a strange choice for a serious actor whose most recent film had been a big budget historical piece and whose last true hit had been a thrilling adventure yarn.

Then there was *Villain*. This at least gave Richard the opportunity to display almost Jacobean extremes of wickedness, as he threw himself into the part of an East-End ganglord with the morals of a shark. The screenplay was by the highly-talented team of Dick Clement and Ian la Frenais, and the occasional if repulsive power of their endeavours is undeniable. I do not believe that it was very successful with audiences, however.

After this, Richard set up a project closer to his heart. A long-time admirer of Dylan Thomas's work (and, perhaps his self destructive way of life?), Richard had always cherished *Under Milk Wood* and now realised an ambition to film it. A brave ambition, this; *Under Milk Wood* was primarily a radio drama, one intended to work in the listener's imagination. It was not a real place, nor were these real characters. Instead Thomas had created images and emblems of a Wales that was, for all his cynical observation, almost a mythical place. How could such a cerebral creation survive the translation to the precise, literal vision of the cinema?

Rather well is the answer to that. Despite many problems with the finished film, it is enjoyable, and I for one delighted in seeing Richard in something worthwhile. His supporters in this endeavour were Elizabeth – of course – and Peter O'Toole. I think they enjoyed themselves.

Less enjoyable was the next project, *The Assassination Of Trotsky*. Richard played the Russian revolutionary of the title and Alain Delon, the great French leading man, was his co-star. Some of the film was made authentically in Mexico, which at least provided variety, but the subject matter was of academic rather than popular interest. Richard had a fine director here – Joseph Losey. The completed film should, I think, have been better than it was, given the talent involved, but instead of making a puzzling and complex character fascinating for the audience, the film only confuses and, unforgivably, bores the viewer. I wonder why Richard took on this work? How can he have thought it would be a hit? Did he really think the film-going public, such as it then was, would warm to the nature of the story?

And so to early 1971 and *Hammersmith Is Out*. This was very promising on paper. Richard was a psychotic who escaped from a mental institution and embarked on an unhinged riot across America with an alluring but impressionable waitress from a cheap diner (Elizabeth) and a gullible young male nurse (Beau Bridges), all under the direction of that maverick talent, Peter Ustinov. I know that Richard had high hopes for this one and who could gainsay him when it dealt with danger, lunacy, menace and unpredictable excitement at a very adult level? At this time the public was taking to adult-themed stories and road movies; this

154

could have been one of the best in both genres. For whatever reason, however, it was not. Again, something which could have been meaningful and disturbing was instead uninvolving and faintly repellant.

This failure was, I think, an important one. Richard and Elizabeth had somehow failed to please in an intense, complicated drama of the kind that should have been their forte. Still, Richard was far too great a star to lose box office appeal overnight, and soon embarked on a sexy serial-killer thriller, *Bluebeard*, in Budapest, which brings us to the great event of 1972 – Elizabeth's fortieth birthday party.

Well almost. Before that, let us return to Richard the letter writer. Some of Richard's letters have survived from the later years with Elizabeth, the early 1970s. They were written, as always, in the calmer, jocular spells. This, to Hilda, is typical.

Dear Hilda,

Don't pass out but this is from me. Chiefly it's to tell you that Elizabeth has found a lot of clothes that she doesn't wear any more and wondered if you have a jumble sale or something or give them away to old colliers or do what you like with them. Some of them are out of style but she says that a needle and cotton can work wonders. A large parcel will be arriving shortly and all customs duties and carriage should have been paid. If not let me know and I'll create a fuss.

We've just spent six months in Mexico where we have been doing a film [*Hammersmith is Out*] with Peter Ustinov and are having a little holiday here in Gstaad before going on the yacht at Monte Carlo and probably sailing to Israel, if the Egyptians promise not to bomb us. Then work again.

We shall be back in England for a couple of days in August to see (hopefully) Elizabeth's first grandchild which is due then. [This was Michael's child.] After that we shan't be back for at least a year I should think. I am working in France until December and then we work in Hollywood until the Spring sometime after which I go, I think, to Jugoslavia to do a film.

All very healthy as we hope you are. Love to you and Dai. How he puts up with you, I don't know, though people say the same thing about Elizabeth. 'How the devil can she put up with him?' *Dyna'r Saes i ti*. (That's the English for you.)

All love,

Rich

P.S. I enclose a present for the holidays.

So many years after those early letters from Canada, Richard still aimed at telling the recipients the things they would want to hear, with a touch of the old humour always present.

Chapter Ten

Parties and parting

For us, Elizabeth's fortieth birthday was the event of the year, if not the decade. On 16 February 1972 Richard and Elizabeth sent the following telegram, via Graham, to the whole family:

> Dear Graham, will you do favour and read out following message listed – Dear Tom and Hyral – Cis and Elfed – Will Scotland and Betty – David and his Betty – Verdun and his Betty – Hilda and Dai – Cassie and Morgan. Can you possibly get time off to come to Budapest, on the 25th February, for Elizabeth's birthday party on the 27th returning London 28th or 29th casual dress for Saturday night – Sunday best for Sunday night – Stop – All expenses paid including caviar and bloaters – Stop – Try and persuade your various bosses of the importance and uniqueness of occasion – most important know immediately how many – which ones are coming for visas, plane reservations, hotel etc return address Hotel Duna Intercontinental, Budapest, Hungary – Stop – Suggest you all meet in London and come on same plane – Stop – Please contact Marjorie Lee – Dorchester Hotel, London for any questions. Much love from us both.

> Elizabeth and Richard

This was not all. We next received a telephone message from Marjorie Lee, public relations officer at the Dorchester, informing us that we could all stay at the hotel on the Thursday night before travelling to Budapest on the following day. It took place in Budapest because Richard was there, filming the title part in *Bluebeard*. We accepted with relish, and celebrated the start of the event in the Dorchester with champagne and Welsh songs – reverent and otherwise.

Richard had made two requests: could we bring out a video of the British Lions rugby team, and a fresh supply of laverbread from Penclawdd. He hadn't changed!

On the Friday morning, Dorchester hangovers notwithstanding, we took up our places in the Rolls Royces provided for our trip to Heathrow. There were some familiar faces on the plane:

Professor Nevill Coghill from Oxford; Susannah York; Michael Caine; Frankie Howerd, and a host of others. Gradually the connection dawned on us: the entire aircraft was occupied by Richard and Elizabeth's guests. Not surprisingly, there was a festive atmosphere right from the moment of take-off.

Richard met us at Budapest Airport, his customary anxiety evaporating into relief as we appeared on the runway. I remember that one of the first remarks I made to him was of how much I was looking forward to meeting Princess Grace of Monaco. No sooner had we arrived at the hotel than I was whisked down to her suite to be introduced. I was not disappointed! She was charming and excellent company, as well as being almost startlingly beautiful.

Our own suites were as luxurious as that of the Princess. Elizabeth had personally decorated each one with flowers. Richard in his turn had organized the drinks: there was a loaded tray in each bedroom bearing champagne, whisky, wine and vodka – Russian, of course. We were so enveloped in comfort that the poverty around us seemed almost unimaginable. We caught only glimpses of the other face of Budapest during our occasional expeditions around the city.

Elizabeth's presents were, to us, even more unreal. Richard's was well documented by the media: a huge diamond designed by the Prince who had commissioned the Taj Mahal. Richard more than once remarked that it had 'more carats than you would find in a greengrocer's shop'. For his part, he said, he was more than content with his laverbread.

We had chosen something original to remind Elizabeth of Richard's town of origin: a stainless-steel rose. As two of my brothers had worked at the steelworks, it seemed fitting. Who knows – by a different quirk of fate, Richard might have ended up there himself. Elizabeth seemed just as thrilled with her humble presents as with her more elaborate ones.

On the Saturday night a huge party was held in the ornately cobwebbed Tokaj wine cellar. Richard pointed out the cobwebs as he led the way down and suddenly grinned: 'Cis will have something to say about this. Better warn her they're not real.'

He was only partly joking. We all knew she was eminently capable of rolling up her sleeves, finding a broom and sweeping away the cobwebs with great relish. She saw the funny side herself.

And instead of a broom, she held a candle, like all the rest of us, as she was led down to the cellar buffet – an impressive banquet of goulash, sauerkraut, sausages; the very best of Hungarian food.

At first the band played Hungarian music. Later we began singing some Welsh hymns and to our surprise the young men quickly picked up the tunes and accompanied us. Soon we were well away – we might have spent weeks rehearsing. Certainly we seemed to make a fine impression: Princess Grace among others asked for several encores. We were duly flattered.

By midnight we were dancing; now Elizabeth's birthday had arrived and we greeted it with the customary rendition of 'Happy Birthday', first in English, then in Welsh. Elizabeth stood up.

'I think it is fantastic!' she announced. 'Forty always sounds important. The big Four 0. It's halfway or more through life, but I find it appealing. I've always wanted to be older.'

She sounded as if she meant it, I thought. Not that she looked anything like middle-aged; she positively sparkled all weekend, and not just because of the diamond. She and Richard seemed fine together. He was drinking, but not to excess, and threw himself wholeheartedly into hosting the event.

The next day was of course the official day of celebration, although we felt as if the party had begun four days earlier in the Dorchester. The party proper was held in the Belle Vue Supper Club on the twelfth floor of our hotel. Here, instead of cobwebs on the ceiling, were festoons of red and gold balloons, and the room was an explosion of flowers – hyacinths, lilac, roses, cyclamen, daffodils. . . . Everyone you could think of from Hollywood was there, it seemed, including Raquel Welch (filming *Bluebeard* with Richard) with her right arm in plaster and coated with innumerable autographs.

Richard had prepared a surprise for Princess Grace: a 'Proclamation' inviting her to become Princess of Wales as well as of Monaco. (There was no Princess Diana, of course, in those days!) The document was duly read and solemnly signed by each member of our family.

Princess Grace received it shortly after midnight, and was moved to tears by Richard's reading of the proclamation and our emotional rendering of 'We'll keep a welcome in the hillside'. Certainly she made a tremendous impact on us all and when I heard, driving one day through the rain in mid-Wales, that she had died tragically, I felt as if I had lost a friend, albeit one I only met once.

We eventually returned to Wales bursting with anecdotes of the high life. It was quite an adjustment returning to the everyday. I wrote an enthusiastic letter of thanks to Richard and, a few weeks later, back came this lengthy reply:

Dear Dai and Betty,

Thank you for your lovely letter and particularly thank you for thanking us for something we should thank you for, that is to say that it is pretty fascinating to have a family which does you honour with every conceivable class of person, and that you behaved with brilliant but never dull courtesy to everyone from Princess Grace to Professor Coghill and with a couple of Frankie Howerds and Spinettis and Ringo Starrs in between. Almost everyone that we've heard from including the above-mentioned, repeat ad almost nauseam, how magnificent they thought Richard's family were. The fact is that nobody is being a bit 'shwd ichi heddi' ['How are you today?'] and sycophantic and polite when they assure Elizabeth and thine that were it not for *the family* the party and parties and the weekend itself might have been a failure. Elizabeth's family too, in a very different way, did us proud. In fact the combination of intellect and intelligence, of scholarship and willingness to learn, of extraordinary humour from all, of passionate, but not too much Welsh singing and of nobody trying to show off or be above him or herself was as much a tribute to Elizabeth's genius for getting the right hodge-podge of opposites and curious adjacencies slotted into a kind of perfection as to the people themselves. Arcanely enough (have fair vocabulary) I try to make everybody, *force* everybody, to look up at least one word in my letters otherwise the buggers won't remember that I've written.

I am reminded more and more how much my success stems from a happy collection of genes labelled roughly Jenkins – Thomas – Wales, for almost everybody said, 'Your family, Richard, though they're all so different, have such extraordinary vitality. We,' they say, 'thought you were unique but now after meeting your family we realise that it was luck all the time. Why aren't some of them as famous as you?' 'Luck,' I reply.

Anyway, thank you for your sweet letter. You don't know how odd it is to live in a place where every word you say in an enclosed space – like our suite for instance – is recorded and entered into some eventually dusty dossier for the perusal of people who will be greyhounding around when we are long dead.

I have now been officially made by order of the Queen no less, an official 'Fellow' of the University of Oxford. It is the kind of honour that gives me a subtle satisfaction. By comparison a knighthood is blatantly ostentatious. Many actors have been made knights but I am the first and possibly the last actor to be made a 'Fellow' of either Cambridge or Oxford. Larry (Lord) Olivier and Sir John Gielgud and Sir Uncle Tom Cobley and a great many other splendid actors have been knighted and Larry has even been a peer of the realm but none of them has been invited to be or has become a 'Fellow' of Oxford. Also, though the newspapers will say that I 'bought' it because Elizabeth and I have given so much money, as a result of *Faustus* etc., the objective reality is that you cannot buy so great an honour. They give such honours for misted and dim reasons of their own. In this case I have a shrewd suspicion that part of the dimness and the mist is called Elizabeth Taylor. At least I'd like to think so.

She is that *rara avis* who compels the imagination of unknown millions and very well known idiots. Like myself.

Anyway, thank you again for your marvellous letter and we are both delighted that you enjoyed it. Give our love to that girl who pretends to be your daughter and tell her that anytime she wants to improve her Spanish she can go and live in Puerta Vallarta, Mexico – fare paid, all mod cons, three servants, a private swimming pool, a vast library and the Pacific Ocean facing and the river sending a rich smell of genlect and expatriate Americans blind drunk from dawn to dawn and Marijuana. (Ask her, by the way, if she is semantically interested, whether she has realised that 'Marijuana' is the Spanish for Mary John or Mary Jane, depending on the gender. Once you realise that it becomes as oddly innocent as the name.) Tell her never to take it – even as a dare.

Hope all goes well with you. Let us know if any emergencies come up that we can help you with. You know of course that any time you wish to be Chief of Police of Monte Carlo all you have to do is to drop a line to Princess Grace! We have a lovely letter from her which adds a P.S. saying that the 'Jinks Proclamation is framed in gold and hangs on the Palace Wall.' I have a funny feeling that Prince Rainier is a bit jealous!

Before we had received this letter, the sad news came of Ivor's death. There was to be another reunion, then, one that was a far cry from the elaborate festivities of Budapest that had brought us so much happiness.

He died on 19 March. We had long expected this, and all of us, Richard especially, had been through so much distress over the four years of his suffering that when the end finally came, it was a relief.

Cassie remembers Richard's visits to Ivor. 'It was agony for him

161

to watch,' she said. Ivor the strong, the invincible, was now totally immobilised and having enormous problems in adjusting to the related loss of pride, loss of power, loss of control over his life.

Cassie, always ready to step in when there was a crisis, gave up her job and went to look after him for the last six months. Her children were grown by then, so she slept at Ivor and Gwen's and devoted herself completely to his care.

'He was such a proud man,' she says, 'and there was no dignity in it. He had always been such a dignified man. I had never seen him drunk.'

Richard used to visit Ivor when there was usually sport on the television. The sport acted as a link and eased Richard's discomfort.

'But if there was no sport on,' adds Cassie, 'he was like a cat on hot bricks. Then he would have to talk to Ivor and he just didn't know what to say. The whole thing was so painful for all of us – four years of absolute hell.'

Richard had, of course, adjusted to the loss of Ivor as big brother, as his protector and guide. But with the finality of Ivor's death, he turned more than ever to Elizabeth for protection, especially when the going was tough.

I remember one occasion around this time when the three of us – Richard, Elizabeth and myself – were being driven over the Black Mountains to Aberystwyth to visit Elizabeth's son Michael.

Elizabeth announced that she was thirsty and suggested we stop at the next pub at Llangadog.

'What about Richard?' I queried, rather anxious. He was on the water-waggon at the time.

'Oh, it's all right,' said Elizabeth soothingly, like a nurse. 'I've just given him his tablet.'

'I don't want to drink if it's going to upset you,' I said to him.

Richard looked meek, patient-like. 'Don't worry about me, Dai,' he repeated over and over again. 'I shall have a glass of Perrier water. I shall be all right.'

Where was the Richard who had written so confidently from Budapest? The one who, just months before, had joked with me in Fishguard about his career when filming *Under Milk Wood*? I had watched him at work on a scene.

'Do you get paid just for walking along there, Rich?' I queried playfully.

'It's money for old rope, Dai,' he grinned. 'Money for old rope.'

The same day a budding actor approached him with the time-honoured question: 'How do you become a star?'

Richard peered down at him with a smile in his eyes.

'How do you become the President of the United States of America? How do you become the leader of any country?'

There was no boastfulness in his answer. It was the natural pride of one who knew he was gifted.

Later on the Welsh trip I learnt for the first time that Richard had been in hospital in Los Angeles to 'dry out'. It was disturbing news but also a relief. At least he was really tackling the problem now. And that tackling had to come from him – none of us could really try to influence him. We knew it would be counter-productive. The only exception was Cis, 'more mother to me than any real mother could have been' (*A Christmas Story*). Cis never withheld what she was thinking and feeling. She is by nature nothing if not forthright.

But now – what was really going on, when the parties were over, the scenes had been shot, the curtain was down? Gradually it became clear that the problems, the under-the-surface tensions we had witnessed in Rome six years earlier were still there, and were threatening Richard and Elizabeth's marriage.

In the late summer of 1973, there were statements about separation, albeit temporary. The rift between the pair was confirmed when my daughter, who had hoped to take Richard up on his offer to stay at Puerta Vallarta for a while en route to Venezuela, had a message from Valerie Douglas: things were 'not so good', and since the Mexican house was more Elizabeth's than Richard's, it might be better to defer all plans for a while.

Plans were duly deferred; in fact the visit never took place. Richard and Elizabeth fluctuated for another three years or so between separation and reconciliation, between marriage, re-marriage (in Botswana, 1975) and finally divorce again in 1976.

Early in 1976, Richard and Elizabeth called to see my family at our home in Sketty (a district of Swansea), before going to New York where Richard was about to take over the lead in the stage play *Equus* – a very demanding role he was later to take to the screen. Apart from the Oxford *Faustus* – a short run – he had not done any work in the theatre since *Hamlet* in 1964 when he had been in such superb form. I looked at him and seriously wondered, perhaps for the first time, whether he was really up to this, whether he could possibly do himself justice. I knew the play and had some idea of the intensity of the performance that would be required – a psychiatrist exploring the root cause of a young man's neurotic blinding of horses.

Richard, sitting at our house, simply did not have that 'presence' which we had grown accustomed to thinking of as his birthright. Normally when he came his personality and charisma would shine through like beacons. Now he seemed to have lost much of his vitality and spiritedness.

Elizabeth, too, was subdued and lacking in verve. They did not confide in us, but we sensed all was not well between them, despite their quite recent remarriage in Botswana. Later, of course, it became clear that this second marriage was also doomed.

I watched him leave us with a heavy heart, and later I approached the *Equus* reviews with misgivings. I knew he was no longer drinking; that he was going on stage, for perhaps the first time ever, *without a drink*. With his morale so low, how would he cope? So I was amazed to read that he had been regarded by the critics as a huge success – 'performance positively brilliant' and so on. How had he done it?

'Rich,' I thought to myself, 'I didn't think it could be done – not this time. You must have revived that ox-like constitution after all.'

What I did not know was that someone else was now involved – supportive, strong, beautiful Susan, offering him the kind of nurturing he most needed in order to cope with life.

Around this time, Maggie, a friend of my daughter's, happened to be working for a Knightsbridge nursing bureau when she was called one night to the Dorchester. Richard Burton was the patient. He had recently remarried Elizabeth, that she knew, but went along not quite knowing what to expect.

Would they not be experiencing, literally, a second honeymoon? Yet if she was being summoned to Richard Burton at night, it could only mean something to do with drink.

Sure enough, her brief was to keep him calm for the night and to stay there.

Maggie duly arrived at the suite. Richard sat on the bed in his pyjamas, looking belligerent. 'What have they sent you for?' he barked. 'You look like a bloody horse!'

Maggie thought very quickly. No point in being over-sensitive here, she decided. She looked at him quizzically.

'Well,' she said, 'For twelve pounds an hour you don't get Raquel Welch, you know.'

At this, his whole demeanour changed, she told us years afterwards. 'He began to regard me in a friendly, even respectful way.' Richard started telling stories to her. The first night it was all Welsh *hiraeth* and the family. Elizabeth did not appear. Eventually he fell asleep.

The next night, Maggie was summoned again. Richard was pacing the floor looking theatrical. 'My Lord Buck is dead,' he announced sorrowfully.

'Oh well, I might as well go home then,' said Maggie, turning to the door.

'No, no, come back!' came the still-powerful voice. So she returned for a long session of theatrical anecdotes.

She remembers the whole thing with an overwhelming feeling of pathos. Occasionally Richard would pause and lean over confidentially. 'Couldn't you give me a finger of Scotch?'

'I don't know what it is,' replied the nurse innocently. Richard looked suspicious for a moment then returned, uncomplaining, to his anecdotes.

On the third night Elizabeth was there, pleasant, warm, supportive. Richard became calmer – the side-effects of withdrawal from drink were fading.

Richard's film career in the later years with Elizabeth, their remarriage and final divorce was erratic even by his standards. One of the strangest choices he ever made was to appear as Marshall Tito in a Yugoslavian celebration of that man's wartime activities, *The Battle Of Sutjeska*. Certainly this was a man of drive, of bravery, of his own ruthless personal vision. But a film produced by his own government could not be expected to be a study in candour, nor present a shrewd character analysis. Richard was, quite frankly, mad to agree to do it. The fact that there was an abrupt hiatus in filming hardly helped. I have never seen the film and know no one who has – I am not even sure that it was properly released in this country or America.

At least 1973's *Massacre In Rome* was made available to a

somewhat indifferent public. Here, Richard played a German colonel in Rome in the Second World War, faced with the order to kill 320 Italians in revenge for the deaths of thirty-two German soldiers at the hands of Italian anti-fascist partisans. Without doubt this was a terrible and tragic story, and with Marcello Mastroianni in the cast, the film had moments of stature and dignity. It was uneven, true; but it marked a partial return to form for Richard and I only wish more people had seen it at the time. When shown on television, it still packs an emotional punch and stays in the mind after the end-credits have rolled.

Unfortunately this quality was not maintained in his next foray. In 1974 *The Klansman*, a dreary and repugnant look at racism in Alabama, received some of the worst notices of Richard's career. According to *Variety*, Richard's role was 'a damp challenge to Burton's surviving abilities, and he fell 'flat on his face'.

A dramatic contrast was needed to wipe away the memory of *that*. So from Deep South mayhem, Richard turned to *fin-de-siècle* elegance in the shape of Vittorio De Sica's swansong, *The Voyage*. Taken from a tale by Pirandello, this had many of the virtues so painfully absent from *The Klansman*, and starred Sophia Loren; a rare creature of beauty and refinement. Perhaps it did not set the world box office alight, but it glowed with its own special qualities, and many people I know admire it.

In 1975 there was the unpleasant episode of *Jackpot*, a film abandoned for complicated reasons half way through its making. For Richard it was, at the very least, an infuriating and unprofitable waste of his time.

This disaster was of course balanced by his triumphant playing in *Equus* on Broadway; proof again that Richard had not lost the knack of bouncing back when it really mattered. But nor had he lost the unfortunate ability of picking losers by default. This time, it was *Exorcist II The Heretic*. The first *Exorcist* had been one of the most successful films of all time, a genuinely frightening subject presented with that subtle kind of seriousness (and emetic special effects) which made the idea of demonic possession horrifyingly credible. The return match between doubting, believably-flawed good and mocking, self-confident evil was expected to repeat the box-office bonanza of the original. Unfortunately it failed spectacularly, committing the unforgivable sin, in many reviewers' eyes, of not being scary. As a consequence, although it opened brilliantly in June 1977, trading on expectations of unlimited terror, its earnings plummetted as the word got out of its mildness (comparatively speaking – it had its fair share of deaths). The reviews were terminal, but at least Richard by and large escaped a personal savaging.

I believe the point of taking on that film was to be in a no-nonsense smash before the demanding intensities of the film of *Equus* unsettled the public. In fact, Richard did not need any easy return to screen fame. When it came to it, his playing in the *Equus* film largely redeemed the dross of recent years, and earned him yet another Oscar nomination, which, I am sorry to say, proved as empty a hope as all the others.

But I am rather jumping ahead of myself: by the time he made *Equus*, his marriages to Elizabeth were, once and for all, a thing of the past, and Susan was very definitely Mrs Burton.

Chapter Eleven

Richard and Susan

When Richard was strong (and that usually meant when he had a strong woman supporting him) then he could give unstintingly of himself, of his support and his warmth. Such a time occurred when Cassie's husband Morgan died suddenly and prematurely in the winter of 1976. Richard had recently married Susan, in August of that year in America, and was at one of his peaks – one of those rare times when high spirits and contentment were in perfect balance. Perhaps because his own happiness was so great he could be all the more sensitive to Cassie's tragic loss.

'He was a rock of support – they both were,' remembers Cassie. 'Nothing was too much trouble for them. They came to see me' – Cassie lived in London at the time – 'they cossetted me in London, then they drove me to Wales calling at Susan's parents on the way.'

By this time Susan had been welcomed and accepted by the family. Although we were sorry that the second marriage to Elizabeth had not worked out, Susan could hardly be blamed. And she was very natural, endearing and straightforward. We liked her almost before we met her, from Richard's description of their meeting at a ski resort. 'There was this gorgeous creature,' he said, 'about nine feet tall . . .'

A close friend of Richard's once summed up, very well I thought, the contrast between Elizabeth and Susan.

> For Richard and Elizabeth it was a second childhood. With Susan, I think it's quieter, less ecstatic, but also less torturous. This is better for him and easier to bear, now that his salad days are over. For Richard's sake, I hope it develops into a true, lasting love.

Certainly we all liked Susan immensely. Physically she commanded attention and respect – she was tall and gracious, without being pretentious. Her English background was totally different from ours, but we communicated easily with her. I am firmly convinced that had it not been for the drink, she would have remained with him until he died.

Richard himself remarked during his time with Susan:

> I went through a period of seven or eight years when everything tasted bad. I think it happens to everyone. I've also had periods of immense depression. But you know what it is like when you're depressed and then suddenly everything comes alive? I've been coming alive the past few years.

Elsewhere he said of Susan, 'She saved my life'. 'I feel as though this is the second prime of my life,' Richard went on. 'I'm in better shape than I've been for years. For the first time I am mentally content with my private life. My wife Susan is largely responsible for that. She's wise far beyond her years.'

Hilda's daughter, my niece Siân, once stayed with Richard and Susan in Los Angeles before their marriage. Siân, like everyone else, got on extremely well with Susan. The atmosphere was calm and Richard seemed very happy. But Siân, knowing her uncle well, was not altogether surprised to witness daily telephone calls between Richard and Elizabeth. One of Susan's many strengths was that she was able to accept this quite naturally. She was unaffected by jealousy or possessiveness. She was capable of that rare phenomenon – understanding love.

I remember one of my own early exchanges with Susan, on one of their trips to Wales. 'You're very tall and very slender,' I remarked, 'but I've never seen you in a skirt.' She grinned. Next day we met again. She motioned downwards with her eyes. Sure enough she had put on a skirt. My turn to smile.

It was clear from the start, however, that Susan was under no illusions about Richard. I am quite sure no woman could live with him, even for a month, without being aware of the shadow as well as the sunshine that encompassed him, and at times the shadow reduced the sunlight to a mere flicker.

On one of Susan's early trips to Wales the darker side was much in evidence. They travelled down to Wales for Tom's funeral – Tom, my much-loved oldest brother, had died after a long illness. The family assembled, as always, this time at Margam Crematorium, close to Port Talbot. Tom had been a stalwart member of

169

the Cwmavon male voice choir, which turned up in strength for his funeral. He had selected two of his favourite hymns well in advance, and the singing was the most powerful and impassioned I have ever heard. Richard and Susan were both extremely moved –Susan in particular, whose background had never before exposed her to anything remotely like this outpouring of emotion.

It was afterwards that the trouble started. Graham led the men up to the Pontrhydyfen Rugby Club.

'Come on Rich!' he said briskly. Richard didn't need much persuading. But Susan looked glum. She knew already what a brief trip to the rugby club might mean later on.

She confided to Verdun that she found Richard's language sometimes very hard to take. And Verdun, the unshockable, who had come out with some choice expressions in his time, was concerned. 'Rich, I'd rather sell *Echoes* every day than hear you in that state,' he said sorrowfully.

At another time when Richard and Susan were staying, he had been off drink and was coping well with Susan's support; but on the second day he had an overwhelming bout of *hiraeth* and started drinking again. The family rallied round and made a huge effort to protect him. Someone gave Richard a glass of whisky which was virtually 95% water. Richard looked at us doubtfully and took a sip. He held up his glass. 'Well,' he said. 'Now I know Dai must be unemployed.' (Hilda's Dai had spells out of work.)

Susan grew accustomed to it. And she needed to – there were several years more to come. It was during their six years together that Richard's operation took place – vertebrae were removed from the top of his spine. It was a very painful episode. Many said that Susan gradually transformed herself from wife into nursemaid, cutting off other sources of help and support for Richard. I believe she simply did what had to be done. There was no guile in her, no malice; she cared deeply about him and tried her utmost to save him from the darker side of himself – which of course invariably involved drink.

Later, much later, when Susan could take no more, she confided to Cassie that when things were really bad, she used to sleep next to the bottles, just in case Richard made a semi-conscious effort to reach them in the middle of the night. Sometimes her efforts would be enough to dissuade him, sometimes not.

As regards the stage, Richard had one undisputed triumph in this period. On 27 July, 1980, the *New York Times* carried the following headline and review: 'Richard Burton triumphs in Camelot.'

> Who says you can't go home again? Richard Burton returned to the kingdom of Camelot, and it was as if he had never abdicated his throne. He remains every inch the King Arthur of our most majestic storybook dreams. He doesn't merely command the stage; he seems to own it by divine right. By the time he sings for a final time of that one brief shining moment that was known as Camelot, the audience is ready to weep for every noble ideal that ever has been smashed on the hard rocks of history. In Camelot he is our once, our present and – who knows? Maybe our future king.

Others agreed: 'Richard Burton still wears the crown in *Camelot*. He is an even more assured and engaging King Arthur than in 1960, and with a large, well drilled cast and scads of scenery and costumes. It is bound to be the thing to see!' Douglas Watt in the *New York Daily News*. 'Richard Burton's voice is one of the great instruments of the English-speaking stage. He will make *Camelot* prosper.' T.E. Kalem, in *Time* magazine.

It was Sir Laurence Olivier who once said to him, during his highly publicized marriage to Elizabeth: 'Make up your mind, dear boy. Do you want to be a household name or a great actor?' 'Both,' was Richard's retort. And in my opinion, at the State Theatre in Lincoln Center in New York he achieved both. As a household name, he returned to *Camelot* to recreate the role of King Arthur he had created twenty years before. His box-office appeal wrapped up the greatest advance sale in the history of the theatre – more than $2½ million.

One of the many qualities we admired in Susan was the energy she poured into supporting Richard's career. Let me make no bones about the demands put upon her. She had married an extra-ordinary talent, but one who was now in his early fifties, one on whom a lifetime of alcoholic indulgence, and subsequent dependency, had begun to take its toll. Film-makers knew all too well the bad as well as the good; if Richard was to win good parts in the face of younger, fitter competition, he had to deliver the goods, sober and on time.

The film he made after *Equus* was an intelligent paranormal mystery called *The Medusa Touch*. Richard's character aptly describes himself as 'the man with a gift for disaster', for he had the ability to cause catastrophes, large and small, by the force of his will. By the end of the film he had demolished a cathedral and crashed an airliner into a skyscraper just by concentrating hard. This sort of plot could have been wholly preposterous in the wrong hands, but director Jack Gold elicited credible performances from Richard, Lino Ventura, Lee Remick and Harry Andrews amongst others, and the film, made in England – Susan rented a homely base near the studios – was popular.

By contrast, conditions on location for *The Wild Geese* were anything but homely. Not since *Where Eagles Dare* had Richard been in an honest, manly romp. Now he was teamed with bankable action stars (Roger Moore and Richard Harris) top-notch support from the likes of Stewart Granger, and an old hand at this kind of picture, director Andrew V. McLaglen. If anything was a surefire hit, it was this. The challenge was the need to avoid alcohol, and indeed to stay fit enough to work, in the ferocious heat which pounded the crew day after day (the film was made in Northern Transvaal). By all accounts Richard was a model of professionalism, at least to his colleagues, but the burden on Susan must have been a heavy one.

Thankfully Richard's rather unreliable instincts for what would be a hit were spot-on this time. The action sequences were vivid and explosive, the occasional banter between the almost self-guying leads pleasantly light, and the come-uppance of the villains appropriately bloody. It was the ideal Saturday-night-out film, at least for the male half of the audience, and the box-office returns were far from insignificant.

Richard, delighted by this honest success, went on to appear in the same director's *Breakthrough*, a sequel to Sam Peckinpah's *Cross Of Iron*. Both were violent World War Two stories, told from a German perspective. Altogether a lesser film than *The Wild Geese*, it was only a moderate success.

Around the same time he made a thought-provoking British film, small in scale, large in ambition, called *Absolution*, written by Anthony Shaffer. Set in the covertly overwrought atmosphere of a religious boarding school for boys, the film gave Richard the

172

chance to play a priest unsettled by the confession of murder by a coolly amoral schoolboy. In parts disturbing and one one occasion – a murder by spade – genuinely shocking, *Absolution* was not unworthy of the talent appearing in it (which included Billy Connolly) and deserved a wider release than it eventually got.

The next small-scale effort had, it grieves me to say, almost nothing to recommend it. This was *Tristan and Isolt*, a tale of legendary love cuckolding the 'mature' (i.e. old) King Mark – Richard's part. A larger scale effort – *Circle Of Two* – followed later in 1980. Richard now played a 'mature' (i.e. old) artist who never made it, whose wasted life is warmed by a schoolgirl's passionate attentions. Those playing such roles can hope for pathos; they can hope to avoid the ludicrous, the embarrassing. In this case, Richard hoped in vain. Kind reviewers felt sorry for him, which must have hurt; the more acidic took the film apart.

On the personal front, things were also at a very low ebb. By the time *Circle Of Two* was finally released in 1982. Richard knew he had lost Susan. Just how bad things were was only revealed when my sisters went to visit Richard in America.

In 1981, Cassie was supposed to go out to Los Angeles (where Richard was playing in the revival, now on tour, of *Camelot*), with Hilda, Verdun and Betty. An 'official' family voyage on the *Queen Elizabeth 2* had been planned, but then a message arrived from secretary Valerie Douglas: Richard had a pinched nerve. They were sorry, but the trip was off.

By the end of March 1981 Richard had played in *Camelot* for months without a break. Friends commented that he was driving himself to the limits of his energy reserves. I remember being very disturbed when Valerie Douglas told me that he had lost thirty pounds in weight, and I began to wish he would stop, or at least take more breaks. There was something, I felt, unhealthy in this tendency of his to push himself to the boundaries of endurance (when he was obviously not up to it physically). Some driving force, perhaps the need to escape, or the fear of what would happen if he stopped, always seemed present in him.

Despite what they had been told, Cassie and others decided to go independently, partly so that they could see Richard for themselves. They arrived a day after the show had been cancelled. It transpired that Richard was in too much pain to go on, and the matter was literally beyond his control – he had lost consciousness on stage. Contrary to press reports, pain and medication were the core of his problem now, not alcohol, though of course, it was true that if he risked even one small drink in this vulnerable state, he would be finished. He could not function at all, let alone act.

By the time my brother and sisters actually reached him, Richard was as calm and as serene as the circumstances permitted – sitting in the lounge of his rented house, barely able to get up and greet them. They had in a sense defied his secretary by going over. They had taken a chance in doing so, but felt instinctively that he would respond well to their concern. And he did. True to his old self, he put aside any embarrassment or awkwardness he might have felt at being so physically helpless before the family. He concentrated instead on making things as enjoyable as possible for them. Hilda had mentioned, in passing, that cups of tea were hard to come by at their hotel. Next day he had them moved to another, where tea-cups were in abundant supply. He arranged a programme of visits for them so they would get maximum benefit from their stay in America.

All the time, though things got increasingly difficult, Susan cared for Richard. She and Valerie Douglas became very close, and were the central women in his life, now that contact with Elizabeth was less frequent. They formed a two-tier network in which Richard was given total support: Valerie, her office set up in his house, dealing with the practical side of his life, and Susan with the emotional side, along with the twenty-four-hour physical care.

Inevitably the strain began to tell on Susan. She confided to Valerie that she did not know how long she could keep it up. She loved Richard with great tenderness and compassion but their relationship had involved so much giving and forgiving on her part that she almost despaired of the possibility of ever achieving a balance – an equilibrium in which her own needs were also met. Reluctantly she faced reality and planned for the future. She would stay with Richard, unless things became intolerable, until he had recovered from his current illness. Then she would quietly make her exit.

As a contingency plan, Valerie asked Cassie if she could 'stand by' – if she was prepared to return as sister-cum-nurse after Richard's operation, and see him through the convalescence.

Cassie, who, like the others, had managed to summon up some appropriate holiday spirit – partly for Richard's sake – was taken by surprise. From her nursing experience she knew convalescence to be the most difficult stage of any illness; from her perspective as Richard's sister – and one who knew him only too well – she could testify that he was not easy to support at the best of times. That period a few years earlier when he had been strong and buoyant in his marriage, giving out support unstintingly himself, now seemed very remote. My sister, in the light of all this, was reluctant to agree to the plan – but in the end, of course, she did.

Cassie knew of Susan's long-term plan to leave; but Richard, who had to be protected at all cost, did not. As if to consolidate the semblance of normality in this situation, Susan's parents arrived to stay while Cassie and the others were still there. Susan was thus able to receive some much-needed parenting herself.

Shortly afterwards, Cassie and the rest of the family returned home. Cassie, always mindful of a promise, was ready to return at a moment's notice to look after Richard, but the anticipated call did not come – or rather came in a different form, a few months later. Richard rang to say that he and Susan wanted to stay with Cis at her home in Hadley Wood on the northern outskirts of London. Cis, aware that all was not well and nervous of looking after them alone, asked Cassie to join her.

So the two sisters waited; and of course Richard and Susan's eventual arrival was punctuated by all the effusiveness and delight that characterised all Richard's meetings with the family. As always, going to Cis was something extra special for him. It gave him that feeling of going home, going to be looked after, with Cis's fragility balanced by Cassie's practical support.

But after the excitement of the greeting and the first meal together, it was clear that this was not to be a jolly occasion. My sisters' misgivings were confirmed when Richard withdrew to his room at the first opportunity, and then the three women shared their anxieties over him, talking long into the night. Susan particularly needed to unburden herself and to talk about her plans. She had finally, she said with sorrow, decided to leave Richard. She simply could not cope any longer with the complex demands of the relationship. Her own health was suffering badly as a result of it. She was, she admitted, at the end of her tether.

Nonetheless, Susan felt deeply for Richard; her preoccupation with his health and care was maternal.

She explained to Cassie and Cis what medication he was taking. 'These are the drugs he's taking . . .' There were ten varieties. 'Drugs to help him stay off alcohol – painkillers – anti-depressants. He must remember – he can't double up. He must stick to the prescribed dose.'

Susan was almost desperate in her anxiety to make sure he was protected after she had left. She took particular care to warn Cassie that Richard could be very persuasive about his need for more medication. 'Sometimes I know I need something stronger,' he would say, that old determination in his voice.

'You have to listen,' Susan warned, 'and pretend that you believe him. Then you just don't do it.'

Susan's departure was now imminent. The night before she left, Richard was at a very low ebb. Cassie, still awake at 4.30 a.m., heard him pacing about and felt utterly helpless. Next morning Susan quietly left for her parents' house near Aldermaston in Berkshire. Cis turned to Richard, heavy hearted. 'I'm very sorry, Rich.'

And once again there was that irresistible smile, that resilience of spirit.

'Oh, it's all right, Cis. It's only six years they stay with me after all. . . .' Elizabeth, then, was also in his thoughts. His brightness, not surprisingly, was short-lived, and had been put on partly to protect Cis.

Richard stayed on with his sisters, allowing himself to be looked after, eating sporadically, withdrawing to his room. Cassie, on reflection, considers that he was quite deeply depressed. Despite this, his natural vitality was always there, if at some level below the surface, and when it did emerge with the lifting of his mood, it was like a powerful burst of sunshine. The old charismatic Rich was back, reminiscing, entertaining, delighting. Then there were brief spells of respite and relief for Cassie and Cis, as well as for Richard himself.

He wanted so badly to hold on to those brighter moods, to be positive and creative. He would get up early and take his notebooks out to the back lawn. When Cis and Cassie got up, he

176

would be writing earnestly, or poised in thought over the paper. Sometimes he would go off for a while and leave his notebook in the garden; one day when Cassie was passing she could not resist having a peep. She regretted it. On that occasion there were just fragments – broken shadows of the creativity that at other times flowed powerfully. But it was natural enough that Richard's writing should reflect the contrasts and opposites that were so much an integral part of his life. Cassie understood.

One morning Richard got up brisk and determined. He looked at Cassie assertively. 'Will you come with me to Hampstead? I want to visit Gwen.'

Richard decided to drive there himself. Cassie knew better than to try to dissuade him. Nervously she got into the car, knowing it was a long time since Richard had sat behind the wheel. Furthermore, she had misgivings about a trip to Gwen just then. Of course he wanted to be supportive of his sister-in-law, with whom so much had been shared, but everyone knew that Richard needed to be strong to be able to give such support. Now he was the needy one. Was he going to ask her for more drugs? It was known that Gwen had a vast supply. Cassie was filled with trepidation.

They arrived at Gwen's without mishap. Then, as Cassie had feared, Richard asked her to wait in the car when they arrived. Half an hour later, he reappeared and drove off in silence. To question him was unthinkable. You just accepted that this was how it was. But whatever had happened in the meeting with Gwen, over the next few days it became clear that Richard's immediate crisis had passed. He was coming to terms with being on his own again, and was ready to move on.

Guy Masterson-Mastroianni (Cis's grandson) wrote his recollections of his experiences with Richard at this point in his life, which reveal a man still capable of enjoying the spontaneous and the unexpected in life, as well as one with hopes for the future.

Travelling in Richard Burton's Mini-Cooper 'S'

Over the first few days of Richard's stay with his sister Cis, he and I struck up a camaraderie based initially on our mutual avid interest in tennis – it was the Wimbledon fortnight. Before long he began to stray from his anecdotes and talk of things deeper and more personal.

He joked a lot. He used to say of his brother Will's wounded eye, 'He had one eye so beautiful the other couldn't help looking at it!' He also spoke of money and films and great projects and lousy ones. He told me that a rough estimate of what he earned in his life was about £75 million and related a staggering story of how he was paid £100,000 to be narrator on the pop album based on H.G. Wells's *War Of The Worlds*: The makers thought it would take two days to complete, so he was paid his standard £50,000 per day. They flew David Essex across the pole to join him, and he did the entire job in less than eight hours. Finished. Perfect. Six months later he received a cheque for nearly a million dollars in respect of royalties due for the sale of the record – and he couldn't even remember doing the job!

What I remember mostly, however, was the way he talked of Elizabeth. He would talk constantly about her, always fondly and often tinged with sadness. And he would talk of the early days of his career with 'Syb'. He would speak of Kate and Jessica, Ivor and Switzerland.

Around the quarter-final stages of Wimbledon, he did an extraordinary thing – he bought a Mini! Proudly he showed off this tiny little car to me and all I could think was why, when he could afford any car he wanted, had he chosen a Mini. The answer was simple. He'd always wanted a red Mini-Cooper 'S' and had waited a long time for one to become available.

He was really excited by his new toy, and he made me drive him all around Hadley Wood, zooming down country lanes at ridiculous speeds.

Unexpectedly, during the McEnroe–Borg final, he asked me, very quietly, if I would drive the car to Switzerland for him as he was too weak to manage it himself. Faced with such a difficult decision I accepted instantly! What an adventure! He also invited Helen, my then girlfriend.

We were waved off by Mam and a resigned but smiling Cis. Before long we were in Dover, and at the back of an enormous queue of cars waiting for the ferry. I remember thinking how odd it must have felt to Uncle Richard, hitherto used to being ushered to and fro in a Rolls, first-class accommodation wherever he stopped, and protection from the invading gaze of the public. Yet there he stood, totally relaxed, leaning against the car, basking in the sunlight and nodding politely to those who caught his eye. I noticed that he acknowledged people in a way that was courteous, yet would discourage any further advance. But soon a ferry official spotted him and hurried off, presumably to notify his Captain, because within minutes we were invited to drive to the front of the queue, hand the keys to another official, and join the Captain on the bridge for the journey across the channel!

At a tiny roadside café we again tasted Uncle Richard's fame as the owner lavished service on us and then waved away the bill as if it would be an insult to accept Richard's money. There was, of course, the mandatory autograph. Uncle Richard took it all in his stride and smiled graciously. He only once commented on this to me. He said, 'They don't want any money, they want my smile . . . So I give it to them. Besides, it's cheaper!' He said of the owner of that café, 'He'll eat for weeks because we stopped there!'

Around one pm, on a straight road about an hour from Paris, Richard decided that he wanted to drive. Having driven briefly in Hadley Wood, he was aware that the car had a slight defect – between fifty and sixty mph it would wobble. As we had been travelling mostly over seventy, he didn't think it would be a problem. So he took the wheel and sure enough, at fifty-five, the car began to rattle . . . and then shake . . . and then it veered calmly across the road, upon which Uncle Richard corrected, and it veered back. Richard corrected again and this time it veered sharply, and so he corrected sharply, and soon we were zig-zagging virtually out of control all over the road and then, he began to sing 'Waltzing Matilda, waltzing Matilda, oh won't you come waltzing Matilda with me. . . !', I had to reach across and grab the wheel to steady the car, as he was fast losing strength. Eventually we ground to a halt on the wrong side of the road, both of us in hysterics, knowing that the car had been perilously close to flipping over. Helen, oblivious, had slept through it all. 'That girl will never know how close to the arms of Mary she was!' said Uncle Richard.

We arrived, sweaty, grimy and exhausted much later than expected, but having not laughed as much in a long while. We stayed at a plush apartment on the Avenue Kleber belonging to

David Rowe-Beddow, a life-long friend of Richard's.

Once, at Richard's favourite restaurant in Paris, a brash New Yorker approached our table and began telling Uncle Richard how proud he was to be sitting in the same restaurant, how he'd seen all his films and *Camelot* and *Equus*, but there was something he really wanted to know . . . Was it true that Richard Burton wore something red on his person at all times because, as far as he could tell, looking at him there, there was no red to be seen. Uncle Richard immediately removed a boot, took out the cash he was storing there, and showed this man the lining, which was, of course, bright red. The American was overwhelmed. He kept telling Uncle Richard how fantastic he was. How brilliant. For my part, I could not believe that a grown man, obviously quite wealthy and respected, could become so obsequious and ridiculous. Uncle Richard remarked quietly, 'He'll dine out on that one for a few years!'

One day, David came home early from work to pick up Richard, Helen and me to take us out to the country somewhere, as far as I could tell, near Versailles. We were to dine at their friends, the Rothschilds. It was a warm day but overcast and quite windy, nevertheless it was decided that we would play tennis on their private court followed by a jacuzzi and dinner. Uncle Richard, unable to play himself, elected to umpire and duly climbed the steps to the high seat.

He announced that he would keep score using cigarette butts, and there he sat frantically try to smoke enough to keep up with our games. Soon, of course, the match descended to the ridiculous as he altered the rules whimsically to support his smoking habit. And he kept calling the wrong score, which he blamed on the wind blowing the cigarette butts around. It was very definitely his match, not ours!

* * * * *

So the ten days of melancholy and tenderness with Cis and Cassie gave way to another phase. Richard was ready to move back into that more flamboyant world which was also home to him. But for just a little while he had allowed himself to be nurtured by his family and had become, at least partly, a little boy again.

Chapter Twelve

Wagner and a new life

After such a low period, Richard wanted – needed – a good part. He also needed the health and strength to play it to the best of his ability. March 1981, as I've already related, had seen him collapse with terrifying pains in his arms. The diagnosis was severe degenerative changes in the cervical spine, for which the remedy was a traumatic operation to rebuild the vertebrae in his back. This was performed successfully, but the year had another nasty surprise for him. A further collapse in October, just as the convalescence was going well, was found to indicate a perforated ulcer. This prevented him from taking painkillers to ease the problems in his back, and Richard's days were filled with nagging pain.

Then, at last, Fortune remembered his existence. As he was recovering from his second setback, he received the script of an ambitious film-cum-television series, *Wagner*. It was to be as grand and as demanding as its subject himself. Director Tony Palmer had a unique reputation for making intense, memorable films about composers, but this endeavour was huge – a return against all odds to the days of the epic, and an epic laced with intelligence at that. This of course had appeal for Richard – even on *Alexander The Great*, now nearly thirty years ago, it had been his (dashed) hope to stimulate the brain as well as the eyes. *Wagner* was a heaven-sent opportunity to do precisely that. Once all the legal niceties were out of the way, filming started in Vienna in January 1982.

Wagner was one of the most important independent productions ever made, and brought together some of the most sought-after talents in contemporary film and television.

Richard told me that the filming took place in more than two hundred separate locations, over seven months and in six countries, throughout Hungary and Central Europe, including 'mad' King Ludwig's castles in Bavaria, and Wagner's own rooms overlooking the Grand Canal in Venice where he wrote *Tristan and Isolde*. Only an actor of the stature of Richard could have taken on the towering character of Wagner. His co-stars were Vanessa Redgrave as Cosima, Wagner's second wife, and Gemma Craven who portrayed Minna, Wagner's first wife.

The supporting cast was staggering, giving real meaning to that much-abused expression, 'an all-star cast': Sir Laurence Olivier, Sir John Gielgud, Sir Ralph Richardson, Arthur Lowe, Ronald Pickup, Marthe Keller, Franco Nero and Cyril Cusack.

The talented Irish actor Gabriel Byrne, who also had a part in *Wagner*, wrote a perceptive article about Richard during the making of the film. This is an extract from it:

The director introduced us. 'Family, really,' Burton smiled. 'Irish and Welsh. How is dear Dublin? I love it. Have to stick together, us Celts.' He winked as the director inquired reverentially if everything was 'Okay Rich?' 'Don't be nervous, love', he said quietly to me.

During lunch he spoke about Ireland and about Niall Toibin and Cyril Cusack, who were friends and whose work he admired greatly. He had worked with Toibin in *Tristan and Isolt* and with Cusack several times, including his own production of the *The Taming Of The Shrew*. Whenever I met him later, one of his first questions was always, 'How is Niall and how is Cyril?'

There was wine on the table that day but he drank only Perrier water and hardly touched the food. And as on subsequent occasions, he talked and talked of Wales, of rugby, of Dylan Thomas, of Gareth Edwards and Elizabeth Taylor, and his days as a young actor: 'When I was a windy boy and a bit', at Stratford, where Kenneth Tynan first said of him as Henry the Fifth, 'A young Welsh boy shines out with greatness.'

He quoted Myles Copaleen, Shakespeare, Joyce, Yeats all the time, and smoked Marlboro incessantly.

Few people realised that during *Wagner* he was in great pain, having had operations to relieve trapped nerves in his back. He told me that every morning he had to get up at five o'clock for sessions of gruelling physiotherapy. Towards the end of the film the pain was so great he had to be taken to hospital. His work schedule was punishing. He was in almost every scene. He had to

Richard in the mid 1960s, when success and melancholy were beginning to compete with each other. (Hulton-Deutsch)

Previous page: Richard and Elizabeth in Cleopatra, 1963. Almost immediately, rumours of an attraction began to circulate. (London Features International Ltd)

On the set of *The Taming of the Shrew* in Rome, 1966. Left to right: the author, an American secretary, Princess Fatimah (King Farouk's daughter), Richard.

Above: A family gathering at the Dorchester to celebrate one of Richard's triumphs – the Royal Premiere
of *The Taming of the Shrew*. (© *Daily Express*)

Above right: Richard with brother Ivor, to whom he
looked for fathering until his tragic accident in 1968.

Right: Richard and Elizabeth in *The Taming of the
Shrew*.

Left: Richard in *The Spy Who Came In From The Cold.* (Rex Features)

Right: The author with Raquel Welch at Elizabeth's fortieth birthday party in Budapest, 1972.

Left: Richard in cheerful mood, walking his secretary Valerie Douglas's dog in Los Angeles, 1983. (© Valerie Douglas)

Above: Richard on holiday in Céligny a few months before he died. Left to Right: Betty Jenkins, David Owen, Hilda Owen, Sally and Richard. (© Verdun Jenkins)

Right: Sally Burton, some months after Richard's death (1985). (© Douglas Morrison/*Daily Express*)

The funeral. (Rex Features)

speak volumes of words and locations changed almost every day. . . .

"Seventy films, I think I've done. We tried to name all the films in one day for a bet, and we couldn't. I've done some awful films. You never know that when you begin them. So much depends on the director, the editor, the location. The main thing is, to keep working. That's all you can do really."

I met him again in Budapest, two months later. Our call was for 5.30 a.m. Even at that time, there were three or four journalists or photographers, shouting that he and Liz would get back together again. They had been waiting all night.

'Amazing people, journalists – like wolves,' he said. It was so cold, one of the photographer's fingers stuck to his camera and they had to cut the flesh off with a penknife.

'Serves him bloody right,' said somebody at the back of the coach. 'Poor bugger, I hope he's all right,' said Burton. He told me that he regretted not being able to move about unrecognised. There were always crowds and he hated crowds. And always the journalists. Yet he was courteous to them. And once I saw him send a round of drinks and an extempore poem to a group of reporters who were waiting outside.

But the abiding image I shall have of him is in the Gritti Palace Hotel in Venice. He had invited four or five of us to his suite for a meal. He was dressed in his customary red (the legacy of a bet he had made years ago with Peter O'Toole) with a black blazer, and he was drinking Pernod. 'My dear old Dad would call me a sissy if he could see me drinking this stuff. Still, I believe it's good for the brain cells.'

Beside him sat a beautiful dark-eyed Italian journalist from one of Italy's leading Communist newspapers. 'Doesn't she look like Elizabeth?' said Arthur Lowe. He was talking to her about money, as he often did, with a kind of childlike amazement. I don't think he ever got over the fact that he was a working class boy from the Welsh Valleys who had made it, and had become rich beyond his wildest dreams in a business that he sometimes disparaged.

Later, I left to stroll around the city before turning in. Venice by night is full of mysterious and overpowering silence. But that night, as I returned through the dark empty streets his unmistakeable voice rang out:

'And I gave my soul,
A blind slashed eye
Gristle and rind
And a roarer's life.
And I shoved it into the cold
black sky
To find a woman's soul for a
wife.'

It was Burton, hand-in-hand with the beautiful dark-eyed Italian – 'the capitalist and the Communist,' he said. 'We're off to Harry's Bar. Come and join us.'

At five o'clock in the morning, we emerged the worse for wear, carrying between us Eckehard Schall, Bertholt Brecht's son-in-law, behind us the journalist, 'doréed and adoring.'

'Jesus, I filled her with a bottle of Pernod and she's still straight as a ramrod,' he whispered. At the hotel, the night porter eyed us warily. 'Give me a stamp,' demanded Burton.

'What price, sir?'

'Any price. Just give it here.'

Finally, Schall – the leading actor of the Berliner Ensemble – his room number written in eyebrow pencil on his forehead underneath a first class Italian stamp depicting Michelangelo's *David* – was hoisted onto Burton's shoulder, carried up the stairs and deposited on the bed of the astonished Mrs Schall. This was the man who said he couldn't do *King Lear* because he wouldn't have the strength to carry Cordelia onto the stage. . . .

* * * * *

Wagner not only gave Richard the chance to reassess his career, it unexpectedly had the most profound effect on his personal life. As I have said, Susan had come to the end of her tether, exhausted by her superhuman efforts to help Richard in all aspects of his life, not the least of which was wrestling with alcoholism. Not long into 1982, with filming leaping ahead at its breakneck pace, Richard and Susan announced that they were going to be divorced. Richard continued to discipline himself and, though now facing life on his own – something I think he dreaded – unleashed a

184

performance of great potency, as the *Wagner* court trailed around photogenic Europe.

A production of *Wagner*'s scope needed coordination, organisation and structure or it would fall apart. One of those hired to ensure this did not happen was Sally Hay, a bright young woman in her early thirties who had worked with Tony Palmer in the past. She had relished the chance to work on so international and demanding a project and had been on location since November 1981. To her delight Richard, whom she found most attractive, was drawn to her and, a few months into the filming, it became clear to both of them that a serious attachment was forming. When the shoot was over later in the year, she went to Los Angeles with Richard when more tests were needed for the continuing pain in his back.

At this point, rather surprisingly, Richard made a stage appearance in, of all things, Noel Coward's *Private Lives* – and his leading lady (indeed in many ways the *only* lady; the piece is pointedly about one couple) was Elizabeth Taylor. Naturally, to act in such a play at this particular hiatus in his marital status, and with this particular lady, was to let slip the dogs of gossip, but it did no harm to the box office. Reviews were sniffy when it opened in New York in May 1983, and perhaps neither player was truly suited to the clipped, precise snipings of Coward's dialogue, but few who saw it cared about that: they wanted, and got, live showbiz legends.

A few months before, on 28 February, he had been divorced from Susan, in Haiti. In July, Richard made a trip to Las Vegas. He was not alone – the point of the journey was to marry Sally. It was a quiet wedding. Brook Williams was Richard's best man. Richard now had someone to care for him, someone who was devoted to him, and who needed him.

By the 1980s Richard was a self-confessed alcoholic, his health ruined. He knew what drink and cigarettes were doing to his health and fought them both with a grim determination. Sometimes he could isolate himself, drink-free, for a week or so with his books. Then, for some inexplicable reason, he would return to the bottle. There were times when he would get up in the middle of the night for a drink and continue drinking for the next four or five days.

This always happened, it semed to me, when he was resting between films and plays, or when he was not rehearsing. He was happier when he was busy, and hated boredom and enforced inactivity.

I can think of several instances when he was hopelessly drunk. When he was in this state, aggressive and belligerent, it was very difficult to control him.

In October 1982, four or five days before he was due to compere a singing festival at the St David's Hall, Cardiff, he got into such a state of blind intoxication at Hilda's house that Sally contemplated flying him to a health farm in Los Angeles. Eventually we got him into the car, and between them, Sally and Gareth got him back to where he was staying.

We were all very concerned whether he would be fit enough to appear in Cardiff as planned. It was a major event – the Princess of Wales was due to attend. Gareth put Richard to bed; later fed him, because he had been drinking on an empty stomach; and stayed with Richard for forty-eight hours until he was fully recovered. Fortunately he stopped drinking only a few days before he was due to make his very public appearance. Nonetheless, it was heartbreaking to see a highly intelligent man completely taken over by drink. Moreover, it was obvious to me that Richard was not at his best at the show, even though when it came to it he did not disgrace himself; we had all wanted him to do so well, since this marked, in a sense, his professional return to Wales after a long absence.

Towards the end of his life, Richard was prone to discuss his problems with sympathetic journalists. David Lewin obtained a particularly honest response; Richard, he heard, drank to deaden his doubts:

> I became famous at any bar I went to because I could drink anyone under the table. But it wasn't until I was forty-eight that I got a hangover. Then I knew something had to be done and I went into hospital for the first time to dry out.
>
> I swore I'd stay on the wagon or maybe just stick to wine, but I fell off more times than I can count.
>
> When you wake up in the morning and the first thing you want is a drink, you are in dead trouble. I confess that I am alcoholic – temporarily healed now and again – but it is a terrifying disease, as bad as cancer or TB.

The horror is that it's so available, so convival, so nice, just sitting in a bar and watching someone pour. I started to drink because I couldn't face going on the stage without one. It steadied the nerves – and later it broke them.

It wasn't a lot at the beginning – just a couple of Scotches or vodkas, or whatever it was I was drinking at the time – and as I went on with it, I enjoyed it rather more, and I thought it intensified the personality. It was only later I found out that what drink does is just to pull you down and make you soggy.

If you call it self-destruction, in my case it's because the growing pains are caused by reaching for the grave.

You see, it's not really my fault: it's the valleys and the pitheads. My background is there and I'm the victim. I am the authentic dark voice of the tortured part of my world. Although I like to be thought of as all-machismo and tough Welsh rugby-playing, and able to do anything with my own two hands – and yes, take on the world too – that isn't the reality at all.

The reality is that there is a fundamental weakness in me, and that whole image is merely superficial. I need a woman to pull me out of that weakness. And a woman always has, whether it was Sybil or Elizabeth until it got rather foolish, or Susan and now Sally.

It has taken these delicate, fragile, beautiful but strong-minded ladies to save me. Women do cling to me a bit – but for the most part I do the clinging.

Richard shrewdly summed himself up when in conversation with Michael Parkinson. 'How much of a drinker were you?' he was asked. Richard paused. 'I was . . . I was the champion.' A brave admission for a man nervous of live interviews.

I had had little contact with Richard during *Wagner* – after all, the rigorous location work had kept him in farflung places across Europe for much of the last year or so. Now, unexpectedly, events conspired to bring me into close contact with him again, and it is ironic that I should get to know Richard so well in the very last part of his life.

The adult Richard was not renowned in the family for the frequency of his letters. Even when emotion ran deep, he did not usually write, and, we had to presume, also found the telephone an inadequate medium. In August 1983 my wife died of a rapidly-growing cancer. Although I knew Richard of old, and sensed intuitively that he would be feeling for me, the consoling presence

187

of the rest of my family, even the poignant roses, with the note '*Mor o gariad, Rich a Sally*' could not fill the gap. He had not spoken to me. My perceptive eldest sister, Cis, sensitive as always at seventy-eight, sitting dignified at the window in the August heat, noted that gap and felt for me as a mother would. She said nothing.

Months later, in early November, ending her customary birthday greeting to Richard, she added to her card in Welsh, 'You should have been ashamed of yourself. There I was, watching for the postman coming and praying he would be bringing your letter. . . .' ('Well, it was a white lie,' she later confessed to my daughter, 'How was I to know when the postman was due?')

For Richard, the clear note of censure from his adored sister/ mother was enough: he was contrite. Within minutes of opening his card he was telephoning me, oblivious of the early hour, startling me out of a sleep which was, anyway, fitful, – 'Dai, come out. Come and join me.' 'Out' meant Los Angeles. He had just finished the stage run of *Private Lives* with Elizabeth. 'Come out!' I remembered that time so many years before when he had made a similar request from Celigny, for his sake, then, rather than mine – a time when he was alone and deeply depressed. Heavily committed as I was then to a job and family, I felt I could not respond, and had regretted it ever since.

Now, nearly twenty years later, he was beckoning to me, his older brother – grieving, job and family responsibilities over, and facing alone the first chills of the Welsh winter, which I hated.

Three weeks in Los Angeles! Even as we talked I was planning: a hunt for my passport, keys to the trusted Williams family, the gas bill.

On Monday 14 November 1983, four short days after Richard's fifty-eighth birthday and the surprise 'phone call, I climbed, still somewhat incredulous, into a TWA plane bound for California, with a suitcase hurriedly packed for a few weeks (I little dreamt that my stay would be much longer). Richard had recommended a dinner suit for a forthcoming dinner to honour Frank Sinatra – otherwise I put in two of everything and hoped for the best.

I had collected my first class ticket at Heathrow and assumed the dignity of a regular Atlantic traveller as I nonchalantly downed the

188

first of the abundant (and free) glasses of champagne on my first-ever trip to the States.

At last, I arrived in Los Angeles. The contrast with my everyday life was even more apparent. I stepped from the plane, happily aware that the late autumn temperature was around 70 degrees Fahrenheit, and was soon speeding in my chauffeur-driven car to Richard and Sally's Beverly Hills home.

There were Richard and Sally on the doorstep – Richard, as always, agitated because of the flight. And again, as always, the tension left his face when he saw me and I noted with relief that he looked well – fit and bronzed. One never knew quite what one would find after a long time of not seeing Richard. I, in turn, felt able to relax.

Awaiting me indoors was a huge bouquet of flowers from Richard's secretary, Valerie Douglas. Richard growled. 'Bloody flowers! Dai's a man – give him a bottle of bloody champagne!'

I settled down to contented anticipation of our first meal together, during which, I knew, Richard would regale us with the anecdotes of Wales and his past which the arrival of a member of the family never failed to inspire. I was not disappointed. Sally, her mother Mary Hay (who was on a short visit) and I abandoned all attempts to savour or digest our meal, and collapsed in fits of laughter for the entire evening. Richard's *hiraeth* – that Welsh term to which the English 'nostalgia' and 'homesickness' do scant justice – had clearly been acute before my arrival, and was, partially at least, eased by my presence. He was now exploiting this *hiraeth* to the full by plunging headlong into his past, even lapsing into his native Welsh, drawing on the rich tapestry of his family and national heritage, treating us to a privilege no stage or screen audience ever witnessed – that of hearing the natural story-teller at the height of his powers.

So began my stay. When I finally wound my way to bed, reminded as I passed the massive groaning bookcases of Richard's passion for reading, I was more invigorated than tired. Once again I was aware of that strong family bond and greatly relieved, as an elder brother, that Richard was in good form and that all seemed well.

One of my earliest experiences on this trip was that of dining out for breakfast – a far cry indeed from our Pontrhydyfen childhood! Early one morning Richard knocked at my door and asked me to join him for breakfast at the oddly named 'Pink and Turtle' restaurant about a mile away. He drove me there in his Cadillac, obviously pleased at the chance to take me out on his own. Sally respected this need to have a brother to himself and to be able to reminisce in complete freedom, so she did not join us on these expeditions.

On the first breakfast date, I revelled in the luxury of an outsize portion of grilled bacon and eggs, hashed brown potatoes, wholemeal toast with marmalade, coffee. . . . We had, of course, been given the red carpet treatment from the moment my brother was recognised.

Towards the end of the meal I muttered something about my shaver needing an adapter. Richard whisked me effortlessly to the nearest store – what pride he would take in meeting his family's every need when he 'hosted' us. In the Beverly Hills store he selected a new shaver with adapters to suit every conceivable voltage in the world. My shaving troubles were over.

Then came the inevitable fan attention. While Richard was scrutinising the new shaver, I became aware that an attractive brunette in her twenties was staring at him in disbelief as if he had dropped in from outer space. Finally, she gasped, 'Is it really you? I simply cannot believe it. It cannot be true. Are you the real Richard Burton?'

He peered at her over the shaver slightly amused, and said quietly, 'Yes, sure.'

At this reply she suddenly grabbed his arm and asked him if her father, who was standing right behind her, could take a photograph of them together. He agreed.

'Sure.'

Her face lit up and she promptly asked her father to take a snap of them. At this stage the shop assistant intervened and told him that he would not be able to take a snap because there was no light flash in the camera. They had probably just bought it. His daughter looked anxious and said to her father quickly, 'Please get one fixed at once,' in case he might walk away and the opportunity would be lost for ever. She kissed him on both cheeks and was obviously highly elated at her sudden and unexpected good fortune. A few snaps were taken and she pleaded with her father to take a few more.

I noticed that she spoke with a foreign accent and I wondered where she came from. We discovered that she was an Iranian on holiday with her parents in Los Angeles. She held on to Richard like a leech, and pleaded with him to give her his name and address or telephone number. She then added, 'May I come with you now or this afternoon?'

Richard looked at me slightly amused and said to me in the Welsh tongue, 'Dai, I had better go or I will be in serious trouble.'

Finally, he said to her, 'But I am happily married to a lovely lady.'

I quickly decided that this was the time to whisk him away. I felt sure that if this Iranian girl had possessed a straight-jacket she would have shipped him back to Iran there and then.

As we left the store, I reminded Richard of the old quotation:

I expect to pass along this way but once.
Any good thing therefore that I can do or any
kindness that I can show my fellow creatures,
let me do it now. Let me not defer or neglect
it for I shall not pass this way again.

That was the end of *that* episode.

Later, just after we had crossed the road at a busy junction, a huge car swung around the corner with the screeching of brakes. The driver and his three companions shouted, 'Hi, Mr Burton. How are you? You look in great shape. You are the greatest!'

It is as if he were some heavyweight prize fighter getting fit for his next contest, I thought. Richard enlightened me as to their identity: four members of the Mafia. Richard returned the compliment and waved back at them, saying jokingly, 'I have to keep in with them.'

They kept on waving until they were out of sight.

We avoided further encounters by returning home. As this was Sally's mother's last day in Los Angeles, Richard and Sally decided to take us to the sea-front at Malibu, some twenty-five miles away. Sally drove the Cadillac through the warm November sunshine, and we reached Malibu just in time for lunch; the customary red-carpet treatment was meted out as soon as Richard was spotted. I was beginning to get used to this, but God knows, I thought, how Richard puts up with it as a way of life.

Next to the restaurant was a large off-licence. A member of the staff happened to pass with an empty trolley. He acknowledged Richard, and a few minutes later returned with the same trolley full of beer. He had made a huge card and pinned it to the front, 'For Mr Richard Burton.'

I never did discover whether the irony was intended. Richard in fact had not touched a drop of alcohol since my arrival. I noted with admiration the apparent ease with which he was able to sip his mineral water while we downed glasses of wine or champagne with our meals. Perhaps because I sensed the gathering clouds within him, I did not feel I could question him about it.

Another excursion, during this early light-hearted phase of my stay, was on bicycles! I mentioned to Richard one morning that I would like to explore Beverly Hills by bike, particularly as the actual hills were some safe distance away. With his typical eagerness to satisfy my every need, he telephoned Valerie Douglas at whose home two bicycles had been stored many years ago. He and Ivor had cycled along these roads before many of the houses had been built; both bikes were still in excellent condition.

I had been out several times on my own, when one day to my surprise, Richard decided to join me. There we were, Richard all in red for Wales and on the ladies' bike, me representing England in white, cycling cheerfully along territory normally reserved for the Rolls Royces of the multi-millionaires. We had not gone far when three women in an open tourer spotted Richard. They stopped their car in the middle of the highway, and a number of others followed suit until there was heavy congestion of traffic. Everyone stared in amazement at the grinning man in red on his bike, who was otherwise occasionally to be glimpsed in the back of his white Rolls. They looked and smiled, and Richard said, 'Yes, it really is me.'

Another group went round the block and came back to take a snap of him. More cameras appeared. At this stage, as a former police officer, I had visions of a pile-up, so I steered Richard into a side road from which we were able to make our escape. As we took the corner Richard jokingly reminded me to keep on the right hand side as we were not in Pontrhydyfen. As if I needed reminding!

One sunny afternoon, while Richard and I were walking along the main boulevard towards down town Los Angeles, a large limousine turned the corner and a tall, slim, and pleasant-looking man stood in front of Richard with open arms. They greeted each other like long lost brothers, then I was introduced to Brian Hutton, who had directed *Where Eagles Dare*. 'Where have you been? We have been trying to contact you for months to direct another film. What has happened to you? We have tried and tried to locate you.' Brian Hutton said that he had left the business for a more lucrative job in the building industry.

Richard held him at arms length and took a good look at him and said, 'You have the same scruffy sweater and trousers, and the same dirty shoes and socks that you were wearing when I last saw you.'

One thing I had worried about, before setting out from Wales, was Richard's drinking. You never knew until you were with him what the situation was – how far he might lose control. I remember making a mental note that if things got out of hand I would not attempt, as I might have done years before, to straighten him out. I would head right back home.

Opting out? Perhaps, but with Richard you were bound to acknowledge, sooner or later, that you were up against the immovable. You would make a terrific effort, only to be forced in the end to admit defeat. At nearly seventy, I was also interested in self-preservation.

But in Los Angeles I found, to my great relief, no evidence of a crisis. Richard was on the water-wagon. Moreover, he was making a valiant effort to cut down smoking. Every morning when he smoked his first cigarette he would mark the packet with the date and the total number remaining – on a good run, he was nothing if not meticulous. At the end of the day he would study the numbers on the packet with satisfaction.

'Dai,' he would declare triumphantly. 'I'm down to only eight cigarettes today.' I began to share his elation.

However, an alcoholic cannot modify his drinking as a smoker limits his cigarettes. And Richard always found it hard to cope with holidays. His last spell of working – *Private Lives* with Elizabeth – began to recede into the background, and the novelty of not having to get up, of not having to stick to a schedule, was wearing off.

Gradually I came to accept the pattern of his days. Nobody would disturb him in the mornings (unless, of course he initiated one of those breakfast excursions); he would lie in bed with several volumes from his vast library. Brook Williams, who was not living with us at the time but had a place nearby, was there as a kind of personal assistant, and he would busy himself in the mornings, while Sally did the shopping and dealt with some of the private correspondence. Richard just wallowed in solitude – his thoughts and his books. There was no approaching him in the mornings.

I was more than happy to enjoy my brother's books, the sunshine, swimming pool, and generally soak up the luxurious living on my own. When Richard did surface, towards midday or later, he was always extremely solicitous and concerned as to my well-being – as though the latter was his main preoccupation in life (well, it probably was for the time being). Richard, Sally and I would sunbathe at the side of the incredible heated pool – sunbathing in November was something for me to savour – and do some reading.

Neither Richard nor Sally ate lunch; I got used to raiding the fridge by myself. As the day wore on he would gradually come to life, working up to fine anecdotal form over dinner and later into the night.

I adapted my routine to his and came to expect a five a.m. call from his library: 'Dai, are you awake? Come and have a chat.' Then all the family in turn – our brothers and sisters, our parents, Elfed, the whole lot – would be selected for scrutiny, for analysis, for unrepeatable and hilarious mimicry. The self-imposed exile had taken its toll, and rootless Richard craved the secure continuity which was his birthright. But he knew better than anyone how impossible it would be for him to return to Welsh parochial life now. So he got as near as he could to it when one of us was around.

Drinking undoubtedly provided an escape route which was always available, one that did not have to be flown in from Wales. That autumn in Los Angeles, Richard lasted about three weeks without touching a drop. He stuck to mineral water or soft drinks with no apparent difficulty. Then, one morning, there was a clear sign that things had changed: empty bottles were lying around. For some reason apparent to no one else, and perhaps not even to Richard himself, he would get up in the night and go through a couple of bottles of wine with a good helping of Drambuie thrown in. He was invariably ill afterwards. During these bouts of drinking it was distressing to be with him – there was a total personality change. He would talk incessantly, becoming less and less coherent. At times he could be extremely funny and make the most outrageous statements – declarations that made me thank God there was no journalist to hear them.

But if any of us tried to calm or caution him, woe betide us – the aggressor took over. Sally had learnt in her year with Richard to be wary of him at such times. I had made that discovery long ago. In fact, while we were still in Los Angeles his drinking bouts were usually relatively mild. Nonetheless we all felt helpless because we knew there was absolutely nothing to be done. Banning alcohol from the house was impossible because he was so determined that *we* should be able to drink. Before he opened the first bottle there might have been a chance of dissuading him, but he nearly always chose the dead of night when, not unexpectedly, we were sound asleep. The night appeals for reminiscing were at his initiative only; I was not afraid of him, but somehow I would not have dared to suggest it at whim. Richard was unspoken master of his house; there was no mistake about that.

So, for a spell of a few days, Richard was completely lost to us. Then he would stop the drinking just as abruptly as he had started. Next morning he would get up somewhat earlier than usual, and behave as if nothing had happened. He would pick up a book, look around convivially and say, 'That's it Dai, I won't drink for another month.'

An audible sigh of relief passed around the three of us – Sally, Brook and me. Following Richard's lead, we would try to dismiss the episode from our minds. An inquest was out of the question; it would only aggravate matters. I must say, I found it difficult to take this line, but I had learnt over the years that I had no choice if I was to continue as his friend and confidant.

Richard was well aware of his plight and was particularly sympathetic to that of fellow alcoholics. Once a woman – a distant relative of ours – confided in him about her own battles with the disease. He went to great lengths to help her, even giving her his private 'phone number in the States. This was something he rarely did. She could ring him, he said, at any time of the day or night.

One of our evening excursions took us to ¬ of all places – a Welsh chapel in the heart of Beverly Hills.

Another – on a late November Sunday, was to an all-star gala in recognition of Frank Sinatra's generosity to a Los Angeles hospital. Richard was one of the guest speakers. As always when dressed up, he looked impeccable and supremely confident. Sally, head to foot in white silk, might have been a star's wife for decades. I felt mildly self-conscious in my dinner-jacket, but was looking forward to the party. Frank Sinatra had not been told of the precise arrangements or the names of the guest speakers; the whole affair was to be surprise for him.

We walked into the studio which was so powerfully lit that it seemed you could see all two hundred guests at a glance. Cary Grant and Zsa-Zsa Gabor were there; Michael Caine and his charming wife Shakira; the entire cast of *Dallas*; Frank Sinatra of course, with his wife and daughter Nancy. Richard marched up to the top table, where Sinatra greeted him like the old friend he was. I tried to behave as though I attended this sort of gathering all the time. It was not difficult; the faces were so familiar. And the presence of the television cameras – the party was to be televised just before Christmas – seemed the most natural thing in the world.

Eventually, Richard got up to pay his tribute to Frank. Completely sober, he was impressively relaxed, and held the floor and his audience completely. I sat back in unashamed admiration. So, later on, did Richard Nixon, watching the programme on his television set at home. He took up his pen to write to Richard, congratulating him on his brilliant speech. The letter arrived around Christmas time. Richard was pleased, of course, but very casual – just another fan letter. So it is not just the family who are unstinting in their praise, I thought.

After the speeches there was more entertainment: a succession of musicians took to the floor, including Julio Iglesias, who gave an impressive rendering of 'Begin the Beguine'. Richard, always aware of nervousness in a performer, muttered to me that the strain of performing before Frank Sinatra was certainly showing.

Later a cocktail reception was held in the studio. The champagne flowed; I no longer had to make an effort to relax. Richard was steadfastly drinking Perrier water. I admired him. Somehow he seemed to find it easier to keep off the drink in gatherings like this than when he was alone with his thoughts. If he could stay sober in company, he retained his dignity; perhaps as he grew older the need to present a dignified face to the world was more powerful. The fact that others were drinking in his presence posed no problem.

Alone with the family, he could revert to that childlike self; always a part of him. 'I've been a naughty boy, Dai,' he would say, sheepishly, when the 'one little drink' that acted as a trigger had taken its toll. He seemed to need to draw from me the concern, the attention of a big brother. It was hardly difficult. This little brother, who had scarcely known his own mother and father, could bring out the parent in all of us, despite the paradox of his superior status in life.

The battles to ward off the temptations of alcohol and tobacco were matched by an almost obsessive faith in the powers of vitamin pills. Once, on the way to the Beverly Hills house, Richard stopped the car outside a huge drugstore, and we all marched in. He knew we would shortly be leaving for Haiti and it was vital that he did not run out of pills while we were there. Out he came with bottle after bottle of the whole range of vitamins – there must have been two dozen altogether. I could not help thinking he had fallen prey to the North American myth that no matter how much you abuse your body, a collection of chemically prepared capsules with health-giving names will magically restore health and balance – or at least protect you from steady decline.

It might not have been a bad idea if Richard had given his meals the same careful consideration. As it was, his eating habits were haphazard. He rarely had any breakfast, our excursions apart, and I could not help feeling that the latter were purely for my benefit. Lunch was another non-starter except, presumably, when he was filming or rehearsing. It was nothing for him to go all day without food, and then sit down to a hefty meal quite late in the evening. Best of all he liked rare steak, fish and stew – my brother Verdun's wife Betty had a standing request to make some *cawl* (a special Welsh stew) whenever she went to Céligny.

But as a result, he got hungry at odd times of the day, and had a weakness for fruit-and-nut chocolate, which he stored in a corner of the refrigerator like a secretive child. He used to sneak down and help himself at all times of the day and night.

For nutritional 'balance' however, Richard relied on the bottled vitamins. At least vitamin pills were infinitely preferable to the other kind of drugs, I thought. As far as I knew he had never even experimented with marijuana, though he must have had innumerable opportunities. Perhaps, like some avid teetotallers, he was afraid to touch soft drugs in case he got hooked and moved on to the hard stuff.

One morning we were sitting companionably reading in the lounge when the telephone rang; I could not help overhearing Richard's side of the conversation, such as it was. I had never heard him, sober, sounding so meek and submissive, so uncharacteristically subdued. I gradually realised that it was one of his doctors on the line, clearly giving him a firm and fatherly warning about his health. Richard replied in words of few syllables, 'Yes. No, I see – no, I understand. No I won't go into hospital. I've had enough of hospitals. . . .' He confirmed afterwards that it had indeed been his doctor on the line.

I discovered later that shortly after *Private Lives* had ended, Richard had complained of severe stomach pains. His Beverly Hills doctor had suggested he went to hospital for a series of tests, but he refused. Now, under pressure again, he was still refusing. The conversation, albeit one sided, went on at great length. I could all but hear the warning: 'If you don't take care . . . your liver . . . you absolutely have to stop drinking. . . .' and so on.

'I'll try,' said Richard, at intervals. And he did try – at times with moving courage and determination. But he could not or would not make a consistent effort.

And so the stomach pains persisted intermittently. And he had other aches too; ever since his operation for the removal of several vertebrae from the top of his spine, he had suffered, periodically, the most excruciating pain.

I noticed that he had great difficulty in putting on his sweater or jacket. It was painful to watch him – eleven years my junior, but considerably less fit and healthy than I was. In fact, for years my brothers and sisters and I had had the distressing experience of watching him losing ground, of sitting helplessly on the sidelines as his health deteriorated.

Now, after the serious telephone conversation with his physician, I was in that familiar dilemma of wanting to continue the dialogue myself, but knowing I would risk being counter-productive if I did. As usual I said nothing; we reverted to our reading.

As for Sally and Brook, they seemed to be following the same rule: provide support, but do not try to control him.

Sally had many charming captivating qualities. I could see how they had come together, and felt that she could only do Richard good. She had certainly understood that he needed all her time and energy; that the relationship would be doomed if she made any attempt to develop a career or life of her own. He was a full time job all right.

I think one of Sally's problems was that her role was so ill-defined. During the holiday routine that I was witness to, she spent much of her time in the wings, waiting for her cue, and hoping she could cope when it came. One incident I remember well. I was the last up one evening, and, unusually for me, was in the mood to open a bottle of wine which happened to be around.

Next morning, I got up to find a very concerned Sally.

'He's started drinking again,' was her greeting. She was ashen-faced. 'He came down last night for wine.'

When I told her I was the one who had opened the bottle, her face broke into relief. 'Thank God,' she said.

I understood then the heaviness of the shadow hanging over her. Alcoholism must place an almost unbearable strain on any marriage. It was hard enough work for us as brothers and sisters, but we lived our own separate lives for most of the time. When we were with Richard he made such a terrific effort for us.

For Sally, this was her first experience of the melancholy that invariably descended when Richard was not working. The aware-ness that even she, his wife of six months or so, could not dispel the gloom must have been painful for her. Work, like drink, had long helped to meet Richard's escapist needs. And Sally had been around long enough to know that signs of boredom meant danger, but like all those close to him, she could do little or nothing about it except wait and hope.

With these faint shadows of unease about us, the first phase of my American holiday drew to a close. It was December, a clear Monday morning, and Richard, Sally, Brook and I were preparing to set off for New York. At six a.m. a large van arrived for our luggage. Mildly astonished, I presented my two modest suitcases. Then I understood. Through the imposing front porch, I could see one massive trunk after another being carefully deposited in the van. There were thirty-nine of them, followed by twelve large suitcases.

'Rather a heavy load,' I remarked with casual understatement to Richard who was standing nearby. 'That's nothing,' he said. 'When I was married to Elizabeth there was always twice as much.'

There was a practical reason for the vast amounts of luggage. A year beforehand, Richard had bought a house in Haiti. As is so often the case, the journalists and even one of his biographers got this wrong. They claimed he bought the house with the earnings he had salvaged from *Private Lives*, to prove to the world that he still had buying power despite another 'failed' production. That idea is neat and convenient, but untrue. He bought the house *before Private Lives*, specifically so that he and Sally would have somewhere which was free of all other associations; a place which they could look on as their own haven. Moreover, Richard felt the climate would be ideal for his back and his various other health problems – the temperature hovered between an accommodating seventy and eighty degrees all year round.

Sally, with bridal enthusiasm, had been eagerly buying linen, kitchenware and pictures, which of course would be unavailable in Haiti, and arranging for the transport of Richard's hundreds of books – including many new ones he had ordered – to the new hideaway. Hence the thirty-nine trunks.

First, though, we were going to New York for a brief stopover. Off we went to Los Angeles airport where we were shepherded like royalty to the VIP lounge. At New York the process was repeated until we found ourselves comfortably lodged in the Pierre Hotel on Fifth Avenue, overlooking Central Park. This is the style for a visit to New York, I thought. I was by now feeling increasingly like a VIP myself.

We had called at New York for two reasons. The first, and by far the more important, was to see Richard's daughter Kate. She had a leading part in the comedy *Doonesbury* which was being performed on Broadway. This was a real achievement for Kate, but I think Richard would have been almost as delighted to see her in any amateur production in a church hall. He was the epitome of the proud father, and was the more thankful for the health and lively alertness of his older daughter because of the tragic handicap of his younger, Jessica. Kate was the justification for his existence that no film or stage success could ever match. He was always fiercely adamant that she took after his own family – that she was a 'Jinks'. No one who knew him well would dare comment on her quite striking resemblance to Sybil. Kate was much more to Richard than a daughter. She was his link with the past and future, his hope (as I had observed in Rome) of immortality. When the two of them were together, the bond was strong and apparent to all.

Richard watched Kate's performance in *Doonesbury* with infectious pleasure. The rest of the audience, it seemed to me, watched Richard. His reaction to his daughter's performance was a strong rival to anything that was happening on stage.

Afterwards we went back-stage to meet all the cast and then to dinner at Sardi's restaurant just behind the theatre. Kate, as always, had to suffer the comment, 'You don't have your father's voice,' – but she was used to that. 'I'm a woman!' she would retort cheerfully. Her fiancé Michael Ritchie was there. He too had a 'voice' – deep, rich and cultured. And he had an aura of great warmth. Richard observed him shrewdly – they had not often met. 'Is he really the one?' he asked Kate at one point during that evening. She was unhesitating. It is just as well he stands out, I thought. With Richard's fierce pride in his daughter, any man who seemed even slightly imperfect would have a tough time.

The other purpose of the New York stay was for Richard to give an interview to Trevor Nunn, veteran producer of Shakespeare, who was arranging a series of television programmes on *Hamlet*, in which six actors explained their interpretations of the leading role.

I was pleased to be able to go along to the interview. Richard's extensive quotes transported me back to the 1950s and the Old Vic, where he had first made such an impact; where I had wept with pride. He spoke now without notes; *Hamlet* had always held a peculiar and extreme fascination for him. He claimed, by this time, to have moved on, identifying both in his advancing years and his Welshness with Lear; but in fact it was always Hamlet's dilemma that absorbed him. For an hour at least, with Trevor Nunn's quiet encouragement, he quoted and explained how he juggled with the punctuation for maximum effect, assuming the licence of familiarity. The result was a version which, for all its deviation from Shakespeare's intention (and who knows what that was? There have been endless debates on his punctuation.) was aggressively sincere. Here is one of Richard's 'alternatives' from Act II (His pauses are indicated by dashes):

I have of late but wherefore! – know not lost all my mirth forgone all – custom of exercises and indeed it – goes so heavily with my – disposition that this – goodly frame the earth seems to me a sterile promontory, this most excellent canopy the air look you this – brave o'erhanging firmament this – majestical roof fretted with golden fire why it appeareth nothing to me but a – foul and pestilent congregation of vapours – What a piece of work is a man how – noble in reason how infinite in faculty in form and moving how – express and admirable in action how like an angel in apprehension how like a god the beauty of the world the paragon of animals and yet to me what is this – quintessence of dust?

As this illustrates, Richard tended at times to add to controversy by skipping punctuation altogether, except for unorthodox pauses, and would literally plough through the lines with a technique that could only be justified by a conviction of his own depth of feeling as he spoke them. Of course, I speak with all the bias of an older brother.

I confess that I sat through the interview in rapt admiration. I had of course heard Richard quote extensively from *Hamlet* hundreds of times, but I was never tired or bored. I can draw an analogy with the most famous try scored by Gareth Edwards at Cardiff Arms Park when he played for the Barbarians. I could see that run a thousand times and still enjoy every step of it.

Our stay in New York, then, drew to a close without mishap; Richard was well content with his meeting with Kate and his interview, and there was no question of his having a drink.

Chapter Thirteen

Home-making in Haiti

On 8 December 1983, we left New York for the poorest country in the Western Hemisphere. Many of its five million inhabitants, mostly descended from African slaves sent to work the cotton and sugar plantations, were the victims of malnutrition, disease and illiteracy.

At the time of our visit, the 'Baby' Doc Duvalier regime still ruled, backed by the terrifying Tonton Macoute, the secret police recruited partly from the Voodoo underworld. Then there was the cult of the Voodoo itself, vying with Catholicism for supremacy and solace in the minds of the oppressed Haitians. Voodoo, as seen by the western white establishment, is a primitive cult of lurid superstition and black magic, and as such was clearly fostered by the Duvaliers as a tourist attraction. On the other hand, it can be viewed as a genuine religion, much more readily accessible than Catholicism, in which the people enlist the spirits of their ancestors for help, guidance and strength.

When we arrived, it was the acceptable face of Haiti that greeted us. We had left New York in a gale force wind, with all the signals of a long winter ahead; we reached Haiti in a welcoming blaze of sunlight, temperatures soaring into the nineties. Meeting us at Port-au-Prince airport was Shantal Wichert, wife of the manager of the El Rancho hotel which was to be our temporary home until Richard's house was ready for us. Fluent in English, French and Creole, Shantal was a native of Haiti who had been privately educated in New York. She was already a friend of Richard and Sally's, and clearly a person of some influence locally.

A colourful band of youngsters played traditional Haitian tunes to us as we walked from the plane. On the rooftops of the airport buildings were hundreds of people, mostly young, waving and smiling. The arrival of foreigners was always treated as something special; Richard's coming particularly so. He was by now a familiar figure in Haiti, having visited it two or three times before. There were cries of 'Hi, Mr Boorton! Hi, Mr Boorton!'

The truth behind the facade was as remote and invisible to us here as was, no doubt, the darker side of Richard's life to the masses of admirers lining our way. What *they* saw was a confident actor in complete control, living proof of the fusion of success, wealth and happiness. What *we* saw was an apparently peaceful and harmonious world where crime, at least *reported* crime, was virtually non-existent. (As a former police officer I was *very* interested in this!)

Perhaps there was more than a little irony in the fact that Richard and Sally had selected such a place for their first real home together. Richard would have laughed at the very mention of the idea, but I am not sure how easily he would have explained his contact with the Duvaliers. I confess I did not challenge him on that. He always claimed that they had chosen Haiti purely for its climate and the corresponding warmth of the people. He could be apolitical when it suited him.

As we passed through the streets, I was fascinated to see scores of young men and women carrying considerable loads on their heads with remarkable poise and ease. The men wore only shorts, the women short bright coloured dresses. Some had thin sandals, but mostly they went barefoot.

We were taken straight to the Hotel, and Richard, delighting in his surroundings, was in a very convivial holiday mood. He always showed an almost childlike pleasure when there was a change of scene. He enthused now about the land in Haiti – if we were, he said, to drop three pencils into this fertile soil, they would sprout the next day!

The new house, empty and ready to be furnished, was in Pensionville, the Hampstead of Port-au-Prince, further up the hillside from the hotel. Its last owner had been a French family who had named it 'Courvoisier'. Richard chuckled over his house being named after a make of brandy.

We spent a pleasant few days at the hotel basking at the poolside, serenaded on the terrace by strolling guitarists, and generally being very sociable.

I did a bit of exploring on my own and discovered the local minibus system, known as the 'Tap-tap', although each had a biblical name. You could stop a 'Tap-tap' anywhere by simply raising a finger, as if you were at an auction. There was no limit to the numbers allowed to cram on board at peak times. Motorists following behind would blow their horns furiously, but the Tap-tap carried on unconcerned, stopping every few hundred yards.

Although I had a car at my disposal, I liked to use this minibus system to get about, and to feel I was actually part of the life of the island. For Richard of course, such mingling was impossible. Most of the time he and Sally could not even have their dinner in the hotel dining-room, or sit at the poolside, unmolested. As soon as other guests got to know he was there they would walk up to him and simply stare, apparently content to behave so rudely. No wonder Richard was inclined to hide away. While we were at the hotel they had most of their meals in their suite.

While Sally worked hard at home-making, Richard began to withdraw into a cocoon, with his books. The behaviour was something I could cope with and had learnt to expect. Brook reacted in a similar way. For Sally it was another matter; when it is your partner of only a year who cuts himself off from a world which includes you, well, that is hard to take.

The days, as they had in Los Angeles, settled into a predictable pattern. Richard was not to be approached in the mornings, except by Sally. The rest of us only went up by invitation. Sally, though, he always liked to have around, or at least to know where she was. Once when we were still in Los Angeles, she had gone out somewhere without telling him. He woke and needed her for something – and the time until she eventually returned seemed interminable. After that he asked her always to leave a note when she went out. This she obediently did. It was characteristic of Richard that although he was very much the dominant one in this as in previous relationships (that with Elizabeth excepted – it was in a category of its own), he was also very dependent. And Sally needed his dependence. If he teased her by admiring other women, or by even mentioning Elizabeth, she was invariably unsettled.

As our time at the hotel wore on, Richard grew bored and restless. He read more and communicated less – and when he did talk he was inclined to be morose. Fortunately there was a diversion; the house was ready for us to move in. Not that there was much – if anything – for Richard to do. Sally and Shantal between them had arranged everything.

The carefully chosen furniture was installed; the books, over two hundred of them, were taken out of their trunks. Richard had bought them by the case-load in Los Angeles, with a fine disregard for the many duplicates he had in Switzerland.

His one contribution to this home-making was his impulsive decision to present Sally with a kitten. One morning shortly before Christmas, he hinted to Sally that he had a surprise present for her. A few days later Brook told me that a message had come for us to collect a half-starved stray kitten. I thought fleetingly of my father and the bedraggled greyhound. We managed, with some difficulty, to get the struggling frightened animal into the car. When we arrived at the house Richard and Sally were there. Sally looked at the kitten and it was immediately obvious from her expression that this was not her idea of a surprise present. Richard noted her reaction, but said nothing. Very quickly she covered up and made a great fuss of the kitten.

Richard saved his comments for dinner that evening. Sally, Brook and I were waiting at the table. Eventually Richard appeared looking hostile. We knew what to expect when he filled his wineglass. Sure enough, he burst in with no preamble.

'You ungrateful woman – you obviously didn't want the kitten. Typical of the *English*!' (He was always glad of an opportunity to malign the English.)

Sally was silent. She had learnt that there was little point in trying to reason with Richard when he was in this mood. Brook and I tried to smooth things over, but the hostile atmosphere remained. Eventually, Sally said hesitatingly to Richard:

'Shall I book a room in the Hotel Rancho for the night then?'

'Yes, by all means,' retorted Richard. 'Go when you bloody well like, and *stay there*.'

I felt like an eavesdropper. When Richard had left the room, Sally turned to me quietly. 'Do you think I should go down there?'

'You go,' I said, 'and that will be the end of you and Richard.'

Of course, I might have been wrong – such assertiveness might have been the right approach for Sally to take with Richard. But I spoke instinctively, and Sally stayed at the house.

Christmas was now very near. Sally again confided in me. She was clearly feeling increasingly unsure of herself, and admitted that she found Richard difficult to handle.

'Do you understand him, Dai?' she asked, somewhat helplessly. I could only commiserate with her: yes, he did have a strong personality; yes, he could be overpowering and very difficult, especially if he had been 'on the spree'. I in turn felt helpless and unable to do much for Sally. My position as an older brother on a rare, relatively short visit, was vastly different from hers – a wife of a few months who was suddenly, and (it seemed to me) somewhat unwillingly, thrust into the glare of publicity.

Then there was Elizabeth. There was always Elizabeth. And the *Private Lives* run, for all its mixed reviews, Elizabeth's notorious lateness, and Richard's back trouble, had heightened the emotions, strengthened the links between the old sparring partners. It seemed to me that Elizabeth was there, an unacknowledged presence, for all of us. There were times when she was more acknowledged than others. More than once Richard told me, in the confidential small hours, 'If I live to be a hundred, I'll always love that woman.'

He was always very anxious when Elizabeth was ill. In the pre-Christmas edition of the *New York Times*, which we had just received, there was an article on Elizabeth's somewhat precarious state of health (she was a heavy drinker, too) stating the possibility of her entering a Los Angeles Health Farm for a cure. Richard reacted by saying that if her condition got worse, he would like to visit her.

Shortly after this, I was making my daily visit to the Hotel Rancho for a swim, since there was no water yet at the pool attached to the house. A French woman journalist I had met several times at the hotel was there, waving a French magazine at me. It had just arrived from Paris, she announced, handing it over and studying me intently for my reaction. There on the front cover was a forlorn and distressed Elizabeth entering, not a health farm, but the Betty Ford Clinic in Los Angeles, for treatment and 'drying out'. Richard, of course, had done just the same thing many times.

I was noncommittal in my response to the article. I did, however, take the magazine back to the house with me, and called Sally to my own room to let her see it. As soon as her eyes touched the headline 'Elizabeth Taylor Enters Clinic for Treatment' she turned to me.

'For God's sake, *don't* show it to Richard or we shall be bloody flying out to see her.'

I had already decided privately that it might be unwise to pass the news on to Richard, if not for quite the same reasons.

As Christmas approached, the familiar stocking up of provisions was discussed. Richard decided to accompany Sally on a trip to the drinks market – the local equivalent of an off-licence. I groaned inwardly. No doubt Sally did too. But there was no point, indeed no hope, in attempting to dissuade him.

So back they came with festive supplies: large bottles of Drambuie, whisky, gin; crates of red and white wine (Richard was a great lover of red). The bottles were duly stored away; fortunately, none was opened.

A few days later, the owner of the Hotel Rancho, Albert Silvera, invited the four of us to visit his riding school which adjoined his luxurious home about four miles from the hotel. We drove up into the ripe mellow afternoon sunshine. I thought of the doubtless freezing conditions back home.

Our hosts, the Silveras, were on the step waiting for us, beaming with pride at having an international star among their guests. We were introduced to everyone; it was a small party, which suited Richard.

Soon we were sitting on a verandah with a grandstand view of the paddock. There was a loaded buffet and flowers everywhere. Haitian servants, the most charming and courteous I had seen anywhere, proffered glasses of wine. I looked at my watch: three o'clock. I cast a swift glance at Richard's chair. He was leaning over the balcony for a better view; it was impossible to tell whether he planned to drink or not. I walked over to him and said with studied casualness: 'Well, Rich, I am not going to drink at this hour of the day.'

I was, of course, highly apprehensive that he might overdo it, giving journalists a field day. He guessed my feelings at once and said, 'Don't you worry about me, Dai. I'm not going to drink at all, so you carry on.'

Knowing he meant it, I moved along to a group some distance away and joined them for two or three glasses of wine. Out of the corner of my eye I spotted Sally looking relieved; she had been watchful, as always. The event henceforth was relaxed and free of anxiety.

Then it was Christmas Day. Very early Christmas morning there was already a sign of impending trouble: Richard started what I call his 'negative reminiscing'. It seemed he could only do things in extremes. Either he thought and talked of the family in the most glowing terms, or he sank into gloom. Today it was gloom: certain Christmases past, not quite buried. Our brother Will, who had just been diagnosed as having cancer. 'He'll be the next,' said Richard uneasily, little dreaming that Will was to survive him by two years.

And gloom, we knew too well, led to a need to block off the pain stirred up by the recollections. And the unopened bottles were waiting, waiting, waiting. . . .

Christmas morning was uneventful enough. We exchanged presents and enjoyed the traditional lunch. But beforehand, Richard had hailed me: 'Get a bottle of wine, Dai.'

I disliked being a party to his drinking, but Brook had warned me (as I well knew from my own experience) that it was fatal to oppose him. The most likely thing was that I had been called upon because he had started drinking already and recognised that he was too unsteady to organise more drinks himself.

By mid-afternoon, Richard's appetite was whetted for more – and to help him along we had guests for tea – Shantal, Wilhelm and their two children of about three and five. They arrived dressed as for a banquet, especially Shantal, who looked stunning.

We sat convivially at the table; the children, of course, held the stage for a while. There was a fair amount of joking and laughter – and champagne. Suddenly, out of the blue, Richard announced:

'I think it would be a good idea to have a straight swap. I'll marry Shantal and Willie can have Sally.'

Everyone laughed except, predictably, Sally. Which, of course, was precisely why Richard baited her, again and again and again. Our anxiety grew after this. Because Richard had been sober so long, of course, the effect of this unrestrained Christmas drinking would be all the greater. And, as always, there was nothing we could do to stop him.

But we could at least stop him from being out of control in

public. At the riding school the focus had been on the horses and riders, so that drinking, or rather not drinking, could pass unnoticed. At a cocktail party it would be rather different – and it was a cocktail party that now awaited us given by American diplomats. My excitement was restrained by the thought that it would be difficult for Richard not to drink at such an event, and that if he did, it could be extremely embarrassing.

In the end, the whole thing was taken care of. The date of the cocktail gathering was 27 December. By the evening of Christmas Day it was obvious that Richard could not possibly go. Sally telephoned the American Embassy with our joint apologies. Little did the host know the real reason; it would have been the focal point of the party.

Richard's return to the bottle, and as I saw it, another period of decline, coincided eerily with the nightly beating of drums in the surrounding hills. At first I thought the drum-beats constituted some Christmas celebration, but Willy, the hotel manager, explained that it was nothing to do with Christmas: it was part of the Voodoo cult. On and on went the monotonous sound, right through the night, a sinister background to Richard's lonely nights of drinking and days of isolation. I began to feel a kind of despair, a sickening conviction that he would never shake this thing off.

There were times when he seemed to erupt, when he was totally unreachable. I remember one such night when Sally, like me unable to sleep, listened helplessly to the sound of glasses being knocked over and smashed again and again. There was something utterly pathetic in his being in such isolation, thwarted even in his attempts to get another drink.

In a way, once we had accepted that another drinking phase had begun, it was kinder both to Richard and to us to go along and drink with him, to accept and meet his almost childlike need for companionship and comfort.

One such occasion happened towards the end of the year, about seven o'clock in the evening. Richard casually invited Brook and myself to join him for a glass of wine. We exchanged glances, and accepted. He had a characteristically determined look on his face, and we knew there was little point in resisting.

Brook enjoyed wine so the three of us drank together. Sally hovered around uncertainly until I told her with assurance that we

211

could take care of Richard. She drank little herself, like a true daughter and wife of an alcoholic, and went off to her room, knowing quite well that he would get drunk but relieved of the responsibility of looking after him.

For once, Brook took the stage. He could be highly amusing when he started reminiscing, and now recounted an anecdote about himself and three well-known actors. The setting was London, many years ago, in the early hours: Brook was driving, sober and sensible, but his three companions were, as he put it, 'three sheets to the wind'. Suddenly, and predictably, a police car hailed them down. Brook was questioned on his movements and destination.

As if it had all been rehearsed, the three actors promptly jumped out of the car and stood rigidly to attention like grenadier guardsmen. With a precision which was rather remarkable in the circumstances, they saluted the police officer and awaited instructions from their superior. Brook, slipping naturally into the role, asked them to stand at ease. From the end of the line, he instructed them to number off as if they were on a parade ground and about to be inspected by the commanding officer. He brought them to attention with a snappy word of command, and for the second time they saluted smartly and clicked their heels, German style, as a mark of respect for the police officer. The officer duly went along the line, asking each actor in turn if he had been drinking.

The first declared emphatically: 'Most (hiccup) certainly (hiccup) *not*, Sir!'

The other two gave precisely the same answer. The police officer then turned to Brook and asked if he could tell him the truth. Brook looked grave.

'They're as pissed as newts, sir,' he declared with exaggerated solemnity, 'and I am as sober as a judge. Will you please forgive them?'

By this time the officer was helplessly convulsed with laughter. Richard and I, hearing the anecdote, were equally affected. Brook played the part of each actor with no small skill, reliving the event to Richard's great amusement. But being Richard, of course, he could not confine himself to listening for long. When I remarked to Brook. 'You often use this phrase when a man is drunk, that he is "pissed as a newt",' Richard intervened.

'Very well,' he declared in sonorous tones, 'I'll be judge and you shall cross examine the witness, Dai.' I turned to Brook. 'What evidence do you have to support the allegation that this small tailed amphibian has been drunk, or as you so colourfully put it, pissed?'

There was a pause. Brook, who had run out of steam after his centre-stage piece, searched for a witty reply.

Richard as judge came in gleefully.

'Come along now, the question is perfectly straightforward.'

No real answer.

Richard was persistent.

'I simply must hold an inquisition into this rather novel term.'

He took some delight in Brook's discomfort. The truth was that having performed his party piece, and very well at that, Brook now found himself unable to keep things going. Eventually it petered out, and Richard took the floor with some anecdotes of his own.

There was, inevitably, more drinking, but no nastiness, no unpleasant memories, no broken glasses. Fortunately Richard, as well as the rest of us, had eaten a hearty meal earlier that evening, cooked and served by the Haitian cook. She must have started her preparation especially early that day; she always took an age, though the food, when it eventually appeared, was superb.

Little did we know that during the whole of this episode Sally was not, after all, asleep but secretly enjoying a grandstand view of the proceedings from her balcony which overlooked us in the enormous lounge. Because she felt that Richard was safe, she could relax and allow herself to be entertained, something his drinking rarely permitted her. She told us next morning when we were all drinking coffee – no hangovers – that she had been in fits of laughter.

The final source of amusement for Sally came in the early hours, when the question arose of how we were to persuade Richard to go to bed without making it obvious that he had reached his limit. Eventually Brook hit on the right plan; he pretended to be extremely drunk – that is, even more drunk than he really was. Once again he took the stage and gave an exemplary performance of a man who did not have a leg under him. He convinced Richard that he was well and truly canned and therefore not in a fit state to continue with the spree. The ploy worked perfectly.

I quietly wound my rather unsteady way up to my bedroom while Brook lumbered down to the floor below with Richard's dubious assistance. If I had not been concentrating so hard on my own uneasy progress, I would have laughed out loud at the spectacle of the pair of them swaying on the stair-case. When Richard's mission of chaperoning Brook was completed, he called to me in confidential tones, 'He was drunk, you know, Dai.'

He realised then with some dismay that he had two spiral stairways to negotiate, to my one. 'Dai, come down and help me,' he pleaded. Of course, I could do no such thing. We must have got through seven or eight bottles of wine, and it took all my own energy and concentration to get myself to bed. Eventually Sally came to Richard's rescue. But the evening had, thank God, been harmonious. And by two a.m. we were all, I think, sound asleep.

But sadly, such light-hearted interludes were rare. The blackest, gloomiest period of my stay had begun. Now that Richard was drinking again, he was a recluse in his room. Sally took meals up, but he ate little. Occasionally, very occasionally, he would come down, looking fresh despite the underlying weariness, announcing that he was 'not touching a drop henceforth'. He always had a book in his hand. Then he would read, companionably, sitting in the lounge. But sooner or later (and usually sooner) he would return to the bottle, and to solitude.

One of the fleeting sober spells was, oddly enough, around New Year. This was a time when the whole world generally takes to the bottle, but for Richard it was important to be sober, to sustain a controlled image. He and Sally had been invited, along with Willy and Shantal, to the Presidential Palace for a New Year's Eve dinner with the Duvaliers and a banqueting hall full of guests.

The Wicherts came to collect them. Shantal was almost regal in her shimmering blue evening gown. Sally was erect and confident in a full-length strapless deep red dress, Richard's favourite colour. The men wore dinner jackets; Richard was dignified and sober, but also somewhat haggard – the effects of the Christmas drinking could not quite be concealed.

They were on a guest list of over a hundred and fifty. Richard said afterwards he would never go to the palace again. He was uncomfortable there on two counts: the uninspired conversation of Duvalier himself (his wife, Richard conceded, was at least intelligent) and the glaring contrast with the appalling poverty on most of the island.

To ease his conscience, perhaps, as well as to inject some life into the evening, Richard hit on the idea of making a film to raise funds for a hospital for the poor of Haiti. The President of course was delighted. What could be better for his image as a caring head of state than to co-operate in such a venture? And, more importantly, it would cost him nothing. Richard was full of the idea. He would use his influence and friendships to bring together a suitable cast.

While he enthusiastically expounded this new project over the high table dinner, Brook and I were preparing for some rather less elaborate New Year celebrations at the Hotel Rancho. We set off in Richard's Mitsubishi saloon with Brook at the wheel. Apart from the constant pounding of the tom-toms which were unconnected with our calendar, the atmosphere was calm and undistinguished.

During the short drive Brook informed me that he had invited two American ladies to join us for dinner. Both were known to me, I discovered: one, a frequent visitor to the hotel, was manager of the riding school we had already visited. The other was an American journalist who had interviewed Richard. I was surprised to find her included in Brook's New Year's Eve plans, but supposed that as a close friend of the stable-manager, she could not be left out.

I braced myself for the predictable onslaught. Sure enough as soon as we had started eating, the gentle probing into Richard's life and background began. I was prepared. I had my own manoeuvre ready and speedily changed the subject, my protective instincts towards Richard instantly roused. My assailant could hardly persist in the circumstances, so I relaxed and allowed myself to enjoy the food, the wine, the candle-lit setting alongside the swimming pool. It was one of those times when I just sat back and revelled in my good fortune and Richard's generosity.

We saw in the New Year. Brook decided to adjourn to the hotel's casino, which as always came to life just after midnight. I was slightly less at sea this time after my initiation a few nights earlier with Richard and Sally, but still felt something of a novice.

215

The regular croupiers and gamblers were already assembled, all seriousness, at the tables. I discovered they played such games as roulette, black jack, craps, *chemin de fer*, poker and so on.

Brook and I each bought twenty dollars worth of chips. Brook promptly lost all his money, whereas I won thirty dollars. I felt rich. With my customary caution I stopped playing and was about to exchange my chips for dollars when Brook looked at me briefly but pleadingly. I was in a charitable mood and cheerfully handed over the whole of my winnings, fully prepared not to see a dime of them again. Sure enough, Brook's luck was out.

When we finally made it home, I asked Richard about the party at the palace. 'I was extremely bored,' he said. 'That is the last time I accept an invitation to go there.'

Thus we began 1984, the last year of Richard's life.

Chapter Fourteen

The curtain falls

Early in 1984, I returned home to Wales. Shortly afterwards, as winter ended, Richard had a familiar bout of *hiraeth*. As always, he acted on impulse and telephoned Verdun. He sounded anxious.

'Can you come out straight away?'

'Do you want me on my own?' asked Verdun, wondering if his doctors would let him go – he was not too well himself.

'No,' said Richard. 'Bring Betty, Hilda and her Dai, [Cassie, newly married, was away] and tell your doctor I'll have a limousine waiting for you. Just get permission to fly.'

Verdun nervously approached his doctor, and was delighted by his response.

'That will be better than any dose of medicine I can give you.'

So they went, and were duly met at Geneva Airport by Richard and Sally in the limousine. Rich looked healthy and his guests were relieved. Only Verdun had the feeling from the first that all was not as well as it appeared. Still, Richard was sober: always good news.

The days fell immediately into a pattern, guided by Verdun who disliked sitting at the dinner-table long into the night. When the huge bowls of ice-cream – Richard had a passion for it – had been consumed, Verdun would look round briskly.

'Right. Come on Rich. Come on the rest of you. Torch at the front and back – we're going for a walk.'

Richard fell obediently into line like everyone else and they marched into the cool Swiss night.

'We must have made a strange procession,' Verdun recalls, 'tramping out with our little beacons of light, talking furiously in two languages with Richard Burton in the middle.'

He remembers that Richard asked endless questions about everybody back home; he went over old ground almost obsessively. For the first time, he talked to Verdun about Ivor's death.

At intervals Verdun, veteran comedian of the family, would 'crack a few jokes' as he recalls, to lift their spirits. There was side-splitting laughter; there was hilarity; there was camaraderie.

In fact, melancholy and *hiraeth* notwithstanding, it was, according to Sally, Richard's happiest fortnight since she had known him. They would stop at a café in the village of Léon, and return promptly to Céligny by 10.30pm.

One night there was a 'phone call from New York.

'Do you know, Verdun?' Richard confided. 'They want me to go out there and talk about the modernising of Shakespeare's language. Now tell me what you think!'

Verdun gave one of his looks.

'Now, Rich, it's no good you asking *me*,' he began with mock humility, 'but if you want my opinion, it doesn't work. Shakespeare needs to stay the way it is.'

'Exactly what I intended to tell them,' pronounced Rich with satisfaction.

It is sad to relate, however, that even during this happy visit, Richard seemed on occasions wilfully to start scenes in which Sally was hurt or embarrassed. They did not last long, and would end as soon as they began. But I wondered just why Richard seemed to take such fiendish delight in being so difficult with Sally. Still, discretion was not usually part of his nature. I remember him declaring that no man should ever keep a secret from his wife, because she would surely find out eventually. At times, you could not help feeling that Richard was being deliberately cruel.

One day, Richard surprised the family by asking them if they would like to visit Elizabeth's villa in Gstaad. They had been there before, of course. Sally did not seem upset by the idea. So – yes, they said, they would like to go.

They took two cars, Richard driving one and Sally the other, and arrived early on a Friday evening. After a short while Richard announced that they would all be spending the night there, and instructed the family to select their bedrooms. For his part, he declared, he would sleep in Elizabeth's room. He needed, it seemed, some private place to retreat to. Later, Richard appeared in the sitting-room and looked round engagingly singing a Welsh hymn to himself. Then he cheerfully whistled the same tune. Everyone including Sally exchanged relieved glances as they noticed the transformation in him. One could only speculate as to what had brought it about; but this time there was no more cruelty, no more dark moods.

They were back in Céligny. Suddenly it was the eve of their return home. Richard talked to Hilda about giving them keepsakes. 'You're clearing out, then?' she replied, not without a certain intuition. Welsh hymns, as always, were sung. Richard turned to Verdun and said with a curious blend of humour and solemnity. 'I hope you will still be alive when I'm gone. Don't forget that lovely hymn in my funeral – 'Os Efe Gaif Ei Le.'

That was to be their last night with Richard.

Richard continued working as 1984 wore on. Unexpectedly he was offered the part of O'Brien in the film of George Orwell's novel, *1984*. It was a sudden chance to do something worthwhile, and it fell to Richard because the first choice for the role, Paul Scofield, had broken a leg. When Richard accepted the part, the filming had been underway for some time. Still, this high calibre supporting role (to John Hurt's Winston) gave Richard the chance to try something new; a quiet, restrained performance. It was his film swansong.

On Saturday, 4 August 1984, I set off for a week's holiday in West Wales with my daughter and her family. Less than twenty-four hours after our arrival, I was reading in the hotel garden with my daughter when I was summoned to the telephone.

'I don't like the sound of this,' I said to her as I went in to take the call. Who would be telephoning me on holiday? My daughter followed me to the telephone. I heard my brother Verdun's voice as if from a great distance.

'Prepare yourself for a shock, Davy. I have some bad news for you. Our Rich has passed away. He died from a brain haemorrhage.'

'Never!' I said sharply, my voice harsh with shock. All these years later, I can still feel the sensations of that moment. Although we all knew his health was precarious and that he had been fighting against physical disintegration for years, we still thought, at some

219

irrational level, that he was immortal. And here I was in a seaside hotel, trying to digest the fact that Rich, twelve years my junior, was lying dead in Switzerland. A year ago it was my wife. Now Richard. It was hard to bear.

I shared the news with my family in a state of shock. The sunshine and the holiday atmosphere seemed all wrong; I could no longer relate to them. Then there was the curiously 'twilight' sensation of knowing privately what would certainly become international headlines in a matter of a few hours. At six o'clock we duly assembled in the television lounge with several of the other guests. Sure enough, the first dramatic burst of music playing in the BBC news was accompanied by a single photograph of Richard which filled the screen. Again I remember the intensity of the moment.

'The actor Richard Burton died early today of a brain haemorrhage at his home near Geneva.'

Eyebrows were raised. Jaws dropped. People began muttering. I felt, despite the comforting presence of my family, isolated in this impersonal, anonymous place where nobody yet knew of my connection, of my shock, of my grief.

The hours that followed were a blur of telephone calls and lengthy speculation and discussion about funeral arrangements. One thing was clear. Richard was going to be buried. He had made it known years beforehand that he did not want cremation.

Presumably, during these first few days of turmoil, Sally and Valerie Douglas were planning the funeral. We – his brothers and sisters – were not consulted. But my mind went back to six years earlier, when I was involved in correspondence with Richard's (then) lawyer, Aaron Frosch, over this very issue. At the time, of course, he was married to Susan Hunt.

On 4 October 1978, I had received a letter from Aaron Frosch asking if I would make enquiries of the secretary of Pontrhydyfen Cemetery to find out if there was room in my parents' grave for Richard and his wife Susan to be buried there. I was also asked if there was any other room in the cemetery or any new plots available for sale.

After some investigation, I was able to confirm there was indeed room for the couple in our grandparents' grave.

I duly wrote again to Aaron Frosch on 10 October 1978 telling him what I had found out. I gave Hilda a copy of my letter so that we would both have a record of Richard's wishes.

Richard's wish, in 1978 at least, had been to be buried in the family grave in Pontrhydyfen. But now? It was all I could do to deal with my own shock and grief and the gathering momentum of public reaction. Telephoning Sally and Valerie Douglas in Switzerland – to argue the case for Richard's body to be flown to Wales – that was unthinkable. We had to let them go ahead with whatever arrangements they cared to make.

Meanwhile I cut short my holiday and left the hotel thirty-six hours after my arrival. I drove back to Neath, feeling already incongruous in my holiday clothes. The first important call I wanted to make was to Hilda's house in Pontrhydyfen. As much as anything I needed to be with my family – my brothers and sisters especially – and to share my feelings and reactions with them, as well as give them moral and spiritual support.

I prepared myself for the fact that it would not be a quiet private meeting. There would be, I reckoned, a few dozen sympathisers calling in the course of a day. But nothing could prepare me for what I saw when I reached Pontrhydyfen. The whole of the side of the village that included Hilda's home in Penhydd Street was awash with hundreds of visiting cars packed with sightseers. Then there were television crews and dozens of journalists and photographers. I had to fight my way, almost literally, into my sister's house. The front room was packed; the middle room was occupied by the BBC television crew: the back room was full of neighbours. My two sisters and brother Verdun were in the process of being interviewed. Like me, they were clearly distressed and did not know what had hit them. I joined them in front of the cameras, vaguely aware of the contrast between the subdued tones of the interviewers and the jarring telephone which rang incessantly in the background. My niece Megan, who had been about to set off on holiday, had the job of dealing with the hundreds of phone calls.

In response to our interviewers, we again told the painful story of our reaction to the news. We knew by now that Valerie Douglas had tried repeatedly to contact us on the fateful Sunday – only yesterday, though it felt like years ago. My sisters, Hilda and

Cassie, had been in chapel at the time. In the end it was Verdun who received the news from Valerie and had the grim task of telling the rest of us.

I was surprised at my own show of emotion. Me? Cry on television? Not likely, I would have thought. But the sensitive questioning of the interviewers drew tears from my eyes as I described my last winter with Richard, and talked of his failing health. Another thought was also strongly in my mind.

'I only wish,' I said, 'that the present generation could have seen Richard on the stage in the 'Old Vic' in London when he played Hamlet, Othello and Coriolanus, and in Stratford when he played Prince Hal, and Henry V. He astounded all those who saw him,' I declared with pride. 'He dominated the stage. The tremendous power of his acting was something I shall never forget. I have never seen anything like it, before or since.'

A few days later, I noticed that Nigel Andrews of the *Financial Times* was making a similar point. 'When was there last,' he queried, 'a British film star whose death dominated the front page of almost every national newspaper?' He went on, 'Though I'm one of the unlucky many who never saw him act on the stage, I've never stopped hearing about him from the lucky few who did.'

On the whole, the media were kind to Richard. His photograph was everywhere. Vast amounts of copy were devoted to the details of his death, as well as those of his life, his work and (perhaps more importantly for sales) his loves and his problems. Again, Nigel Andrews summed it up in two apt sentences. 'What people loved about Richard Burton was that he graduated from playing tragic heroes to becoming one himself. There was surely never in the acting world such a paradigm of princely magnificence fallen from grace.'

We were all swept into the media whirlpool at this time; then there were the inevitable bursts of neighbourhood sympathy, interest and plain curiosity – not always sensitive to our need to have a little peace in which to grieve. Most of us had at least some privacy at home, but for Hilda, that was not to be: home became the most public place of all. Cassie was then living just along the road, and Hilda sometimes slipped out to her house, which was quieter; but mostly she was right in the thick of it. I really felt sorry for her and still marvel at the way she coped with it all. There were relatives, friends, neighbours, distant acquaintances, journalists, photographers . . . Some came to the front door, others to the back. Most dispensed with the formalities of knocking and waiting, and the place was like an open studio. And all the while the telephone kept ringing. Leave it off the hook, we suggested. But no – it might be one of the family trying to get through, or Sally, or Valerie Douglas. It was just as well that Hilda was constitutionally strong.

When we came up for air we pondered briefly on what might be happening in Céligny. I think we still hoped that Richard's body would be flown home for burial in Pontrhydyfen. But it became increasingly clear that that was not to be. The date and place of the funeral were fixed, Thursday 9 August, 1984 in Céligny, Switzerland. We were all to fly out.

I still had to collect my things from the seaside hotel. I travelled a day later than the rest, and Hilda recounted to me what had happened when she arrived in Switzerland. She went upstairs to find Sally, who at once confided that Richard had changed his will six weeks before he died and had declared that he wanted to be buried in Céligny. So *that* mystery was cleared up.

Sally was clearly distraught. If *we* had been exposed to the media glare, *she* must have experienced it a hundredfold. And there were times when the emotional pressure proved almost overwhelming. She confided to Graham that she feared Cis's grieving would be excessive if she came – too much for Sally, too much for Cis herself, now nearly eighty. But this was Cis, whose reaction to Richard's death was that of a mother for her treasured son.

Cis's predictable retort was that nothing would keep her away. If the funeral was to be held in Switzerland, to Switzerland she would go. And, she declared, she would be as strong as the occasion required.

By Wednesday, we were all installed in Céligny. We were glad to be there, for up until then we had had to rely on news bulletins for most of our information about the funeral arrangements: communication between Céligny and the Pontrhydyfen 'home base' had been minimal. Now at least we were on the spot, or as close to the spot as possible. Kate and others who had flown in from the States were staying at the villa. We had rooms at a nearby hotel.

223

We still did not yet fully understand *why* Richard was not being buried in Wales – it was hard to believe he had changed his will without telling a single member of his Welsh family. Moreover, Sally was becoming increasingly distressed. The press, always eager for gossip, were poised hungrily over the 'Elizabeth – Richard – Sally' triangle even now. If they discovered that anyone had made the slightest move towards contacting Elizabeth, if Elizabeth herself made a comment about her own grief, there was no knowing just how much of a meal they would try to make of it. I visualised a series of possible headlines – 'Which one is the real widow?' 'Rival claims to Burton's love' – each more disagreeable than the last, each causing distress to everyone, not least Elizabeth.

It was partly to avoid such a scenario that Elizabeth, after discussions with the family, decided to stay away from the funeral. Sally was visibly relieved. The headlines were still there, but were somewhat less inflammatory since reporters had so little to build on.

Sally's distress, however, continued to take the form of high agitation. It was hardly surprising, given that she had been plunged into a highly publicised widowhood just one year after her marriage. She was hard to reach on any real level, certainly resisted being comforted, and the slightest thing could make her jumpy.

The pressure of publicity, especially at the coming funeral, took on disproportionate significance – one of the first scenes my sisters encountered when they arrived was Sally, in her bedroom, giving instructions to her mother.

'You see that suit, mother,' she was saying. 'Get me shoes, a bag and gloves to go with it.'

Her mother duly arranged to go on a shopping expedition to Geneva next morning, Wednesday, the day before the funeral.

Mary Hay more than once took one or two of the family – usually Cassie and Hilda – to one side and confided apologetically, 'You'll have to excuse Sally. She is very distressed.' Once Sally overheard her and declared sharply, 'You've no need to apologise for me, mother.' Cassie and Hilda, and doubtless Mary herself, felt even more uncomfortable.

Another area of concern was security. The tight security

arrangements, essential of course in the circumstances, were terribly important to Sally and she clearly felt threatened by any relaxation of the rules.

An incident which highlighted her anxiety took place on the eve of the funeral. Arrangements had been made for us to be driven to the house for dinner, but the two expected cars were an hour late. While we waited at the hotel, a BBC friend of Graham's (who was also staying there, and had his own car) offered to help by making two journeys over to the house. We accepted willingly: Cis, Hilda, Cassie and Graham duly got into the car: I waited with the others for the second trip.

The car soon returned and we drove to the house, our emotional state by now punctuated by hunger pangs. We were glad to get there.

The television journalist was as discreet as the circumstances required. He dropped us off at the door and immediately drove off back to the hotel, making no attempt to take photographs or to ask any questions. I was all the more astonished, then, when Cis greeted me tearfully as I went through the door. 'What's the matter?' I asked worriedly.

We all felt especially protective towards Cis. She explained that Sally had been furious with Graham for allowing a BBC man to bring his car into the drive. She had apparently exploded, not only at Graham, but at my three sisters as well. Graham's assurance that the man was a trustworthy friend did little to relieve Sally's concern.

Anxious for Cis, I moved her away from the scene into the garden and quietly consoled her. We tried to understand and accept the fact that Sally's reactions were irrational, but it was difficult because we were all so vulnerable ourselves.

Somehow the incident was put to one side and we had our much delayed meal. We never did find out why the 'official' cars had never arrived, but it would have saved a lot of trouble if they had done.

There were other moments, to put it tactfully, of discord. On the very eve of the funeral Graham, who was in constant touch with Elizabeth anyway, impulsively invited her to come. Sally got to hear of it and – in the middle of dinner at the hotel – expressed her concern.

The situation was saved by a timely telephone call which Cassie made. Flanked by sisters Hilda and Cis, and Sally herself, she returned to the privacy of the house to make it. Elizabeth, who must have learnt to expect contradictory messages from our family, readily agreed to stick to the original plan and to stay away.

Thursday was the day of the funeral. The organist was an old friend of Richard's, David Robello, then living in France, and at his suggestion we, the brothers, got up early, and went over to the church. All was calm and quiet; it was hard to envisage the tumult which would undoubtedly follow that morning stillness.

David tried the organ, but it would not work. We looked at each other. Our zeal to get the hymn right had saved the dignity of the whole occasion.

'Broken-down organ at famous actor's funeral.' Some of the press would have relished that. A hasty phone call was made to arrange the repair, and we got on with our rehearsing, filling the small church with our enthusiastic tenor and bass voices.

The church was fourteenth-century, Protestant, and quite beautiful. For me it recalled the Welsh chapels – in fact Céligny itself had some of the characteristics of the Welsh village. This was all very ironic, as in our hearts we felt that the funeral should really be taking place in Pontrhydyfen.

We returned for the funeral around midday. The church could only hold a congregation of one hundred and thirty at the most. On that Thursday there were thousands who would have liked to squeeze in; only about twenty of us were officially permitted. The chief mourners were Sally, Kate and her fiancé, Liza (Elizabeth Taylor's daughter) and her husband, my three sisters Cis, Hilda, and Cassie, brothers Verdun, Graham and myself, Brook Williams, Valerie Douglas, and David Robello and his wife.

The thousands outside were not cut off completely from the service; it was relayed to them by loudspeaker. Inside we sat, our emotions barely controlled, facing Richard's coffin. This indeed was a fine sight: the church can never have witnessed anything like it before or since. It was adorned conventionally enough with white carnations, chrysanthemums and dahlias, in striking contrast to the bold red Welsh dragon flag beneath, the symbol of

226

Richard's beloved Wales and his much-publicised favourite colour. I have mentioned how he had always proudly boasted that he made a point of wearing at least one red garment, even if it was just a pair of socks or pants. Faithful to his own request, his body was dressed as he would have wanted: red sweater and red trousers.

Because of this, some of those closest to Richard broke with tradition and wore red at the funeral: his daughter Kate wore a simple red woollen cardigan; Maria his adopted daughter had on a red and black dress. Someone else was clutching a bunch of red roses. This favourite colour was more conspicuous in the sombre circle of mourners at the graveside than in the great mass of sightseers who seemed to be always above and around us, pressed against the thin shield of trees, avid for a closer glimpse of the coffin, the family, the intimacy of the burial.

The sermon was deeply personal, delivered in French and English. Passages from the gospels of St Paul and St John washed gently over us. The voice was that of pastor Arnold Mobbs, who had known Richard for many years and who had baptised both his daughters. Then there were some family contributions. Kate read with tenderness Dylan Thomas's lines 'Do not go gentle into that good night', the poet's powerful exhortation to his own father to die with anger, not humility. There is more than a little irony in Kate's choice: Thomas went to great lengths to conceal his poem from his own father who he said, 'doesn't know he is dying'.

Perhaps everyone close to Richard knew that he was dying – perhaps even he knew it himself. But we had all believed in some stubborn innermost part of us that he was immortal. Kate's moving reading encompassed all the ambiguities of the poem.

> And you my father, there on the sad height,
> Curse, bless me now with your fierce tears, I pray.

Graham read in Welsh from Corinthians, Chapter Thirteen, a passage familiar to Richard and to all of us, and with its own application to the man we were mourning.

> For now we see through a glass darkly; but then face to face. Now I shall know in part; but then shall I know even as also I am known.

Then there was the singing. For the Welsh, the singing is the emotional centre of any funeral. It has an immediate therapeutic

227

effect which can be quite remarkable; almost simultaneously there is a feeling of intense grief and loss, but also of healing and relief.

Richard had stipulated in his will that two of his favourite Welsh hymns should be sung at his funeral, and had also asked that the famous Welsh 'Sosban Fach' be sung by the family. This is very popular at all rugby international matches, and if it is sung at a slow tempo, it is surprising how effective it can be despite the mundanity of the lyrics.

There were only eight of us to sing the Welsh hymns, but we sang as we had never sung before. The Swiss, both in the congregation and those thronging in the streets outside, said they had never heard anything like it. Sally's mother said the same.

At the graveside, it was Hilda and I who cried the most. The others seemed to have quite a remarkable capacity for keeping their feelings under control. Cis was particularly determined not to be emotional, not to let anyone down. She was thinking of Sally's earlier disquiet, relayed to her by an embarrassed Graham.

Within herself, heaven knows what she was going through. The day she could not possibly have prepared herself for had come. Richard was dead. She still lived. And all the time I heard in my mind his words so recently spoken.

'You'll have to hold me down Dai, when Cis goes. . .'

Perhaps the hardest thing of all for Cis was to leave him there, so far from home, in a grave she would rarely, if ever, be able to visit. During the burial she remained composed but looked utterly disconsolate. Finally she burst out,

'Richard should never be buried here in Geneva. We must get him brought back home.'

We would have said anything that promised her a grain of comfort right then.

'We'll arrange it, Cis. We'll have him home.'

I think at the time we really believed it.   But we were still in the moment of Richard's burial. And our very last tribute to our brother was utterly spontaneous; had someone suggested it beforehand, I doubt if any of us would have agreed. But somehow at the time it felt right: the same eight of us who had sung so heartily and emotionally inside the church now broke into a rousing chorus of 'Sosban Fach'.

Sosban Fach

Mae bys Meri Ann wedi brifo,
A Dafydd y gwas ddim yn iach,
Mae'r baban yn a crud yn crio,
A'r gath wedi scrapo Joni bach,
Sosban fach yn berwi ar a y tan,
Sosban fawr yn berwi ar y llawr,
A'r gath wedi scrapo Joni bach.

Mae bys Meri Ann wedi gwella,
A Dafydd y Gwas yn eu fedd,
Mae'r baban yn y crud yn chwerthyn,
A'r gath wedi huno yn ei hedd.

Sosban fach yn berwi ar a tan,
Sosban fawr yn gollwng ar a y llawr,
A'r gath wedi huno yn ei hedd.

Dai bach y sowdiwr, Dai bach y sowdiwr,
Dai bach y Sowdiwr a chwt i grys e ma's.

Translation:

Mary Anne's little finger is aching,
And David the servant's feeling ill,
The baby's in the cradle crying,
And the cat has scratched Johnny, poor lad.

The large saucepan's boiling on the stove,
The large saucepan boiling on the floor,
And the cat has scratched Johnny, poor lad.

Mary Anne's finger is better,
Little Dai is a soldier,
And the tail of his shirt is hanging out.
And David the servant is in his grave,
The baby's in the cot laughing,
And the cat is sleeping peacefully.

Eventually we moved away from the graveside. The dozens of photographers and journalists who had monitored the whole event pressed after us; their appetite was insatiable. They even ran after the cars as they slowly gathered speed. But I think we had developed a certain immunity to all the publicity and the fuss.

229

Perhaps even we accepted it as something natural and inevitable, given Richard's fame. We felt proud. His curtain had, after all, come down for the last time, and the applause and acclaim resounded everywhere. At least, that was how we liked to think of it.

There was another angle on things, of course. The eternal success/failure debate over Richard's career, the drink, the sex appeal, the triangles, the women, Elizabeth.

Elizabeth, as I have said, had agreed to stay away from the funeral to avoid embarrassment and excess publicity. However, it was natural that she would want to visit Richard's grave. There was intense media speculation as to how and when she would make the trip.

Days went by. For Elizabeth, the prospect of her graveside reflection and grieving being accompanied by the whirring of cameras and the flashing of notepads must have proved too much. Finally she took the only sensible course of action: with her daughter Liza she made the journey one morning soon after dawn, and stood quietly sobbing by the fresh grave for fifteen minutes. The press had not organised a twenty-four hour vigil, so Elizabeth and Liza managed to make an exit which was almost as unmolested as their arrival. Journalists made as much of the graveside visit as they could, and linked it with their earlier story of the single red rose which had been placed on Richard's coffin at the time of the funeral. It was, naturally, attributed to Elizabeth.

Looking back, in the light of all our recent contact with Elizabeth, it seems strange that we were so separate at the time of the funeral. It was of course mutually accepted that we should be apart; more precisely that the two central women in Richard's life should not meet in the immediate aftermath of his death.

By the time the funeral was over and we were back at the house for the ritual food and drink, tensions seemed to have dissolved somewhat and everyone was more relaxed. One of the younger members of the family pointed out good-naturedly that there seemed to be fish and chips on the menu again and why did everyone think the Welsh only had a taste for fish and chips? (Though it was, of course, the best fresh fish.) It somehow happened that the men set off for the Café de la Gare and the women stayed at the house; the traditional roles prevailed in Switzerland as much as in Pontrhydyfen.

As I recall it, we arrived at the restaurant to find an impressive array of tables lavishly spread over the garden. The funeral congregation, apart from Sally, my sisters, Kate, Elizabeth's children and a few others, all seemed to be there. It was a far cry from the demure tea and cakes we were used to on these occasions, and the relentless August afternoon heat added to the sense of incongruity. It was unreal, but for today anyway our grief and other emotions were spent. We just needed to unwind.

Sally still went around with a glazed look and we could not really communicate with her. It was as if she moved on a separate wavelength, in a world apart; her way perhaps of dealing with the shock, with her loss.

We flew home together on the Friday, the following day. When we arrived at the airport, Graham went ahead to check that the single tickets he and Cis had travelled out on could be changed to returns. As soon as our identity was revealed, the airport manager appeared and made a great fuss of us, converting the single tickets at no extra cost, transferring tickets to executive class, and setting aside an entire VIP lounge. There we spent the hour before departure in exceptional comfort with food and drink, even bottles of spirits freely available. Again there was a feeling of unreality. It was reminiscent of those many occasions when Richard had feasted and treated us. And now in this celebratory atmosphere, we were still trying to absorb the fact that he was dead.

Chapter Fifteen

'It takes a precious stone to be flawed'

So we flew home in style. But it was not possible to pick up the threads of our anonymous unpublicised lives – not yet. Saturday, the following day, had been scheduled for the memorial service in Pontrhydyfen. The cameras would be thrust once more into Hilda's house; the streets would groan again with the volume of journalists, camera crews, sightseers. This time more of the family would be there – partners, children, more relatives, friends, neighbours.

Yet again there was speculation and rumour; would Elizabeth be there? She had planned to be. But in the end it was too soon and too risky – on many counts. She could wait for the next occasion. There was so much confusion however that even Melvyn Bragg, in his otherwise authentic biography, mistakenly reported that 'Elizabeth came to Wales where the singing in the chapel at Pontrhydyfen brought out the tears in everyone'.

It certainly brought out the tears in the family. This was the most personal and poignant of all the services for Richard, the one in his birthplace, the one where we were not eight lone voices singing in Welsh but hundreds, with thousands listening respectfully in the streets, thousands more at home glued to their radio and television sets.

Reaching Hilda's house that day was a major achievement in itself. The village was filled to capacity with crowds, just as it had been before the funeral – could it really have been only six days earlier? But this time there were even more people because of the chance of glimpsing at least some of the rich and famous.

The police had cordoned off Penhydd Street so that only the family and the invited could get through. Inside Hilda's home, pots of tea were constantly being made and the three rooms were packed. Hilda had risen at four in the morning to hoover and dust because she was so concerned that the house should be tidy enough for the occasion. Cassie kept a special eye on Cis and took her on frequent escape trips to her house, peaceful by comparison. Sally was there of course, Brook, Kate, virtually all our family. Even Edie's husband Ron came with their children and his second wife. He was so caught up in the nostalgia of the day that he called her Edie at least twice, to his own surprise and embarrassment.

While we tripped over each other at the house, an army of villagers, mostly chapel women, worked like beavers preparing the tea in the chapel vestry. Tray upon tray of sandwiches, Welsh cakes, *teisan-lap* and innumerable cups and saucers were set out on trestle tables in somewhat more cramped conditions than had prevailed at the Café de la Gare. These people were so busy that many of them missed the service altogether. The tea was an institution. It had to be ready and good at whatever cost.

Meanwhile it was time for us to set off for the chapel.

'Let's go the back way,' suggested Megan, Hilda's daughter, hopefully, 'through the lane straight to the back of the chapel.' But no: we had to troop round the road way in pairs, Sally at the head of the procession, in full glare of the awaiting cameras and hordes of onlookers – nothing new by this time, for most of us.

Inside the chapel places had been reserved for us at the front. The rest of the congregation must have queued for hours to get in. I doubt if they were disappointed. The occasion was highly charged with emotion.

Brook Williams was in the pulpit for the first reading from Dylan Thomas:

> Though they go mad they shall be sane,
> Though they sink through the sea they shall rise again,
> Though lovers be lost love shall not;
> And death shall have no dominion.

Next came a real preacher, Rhydwen Williams, one of the literary giants of our generation, who offered the main prayer, emphasising the closeness to God we feel more in sadness 'than in the self-sufficiency and over-confidence of our joy and happiness'. He went on, 'We thank you particularly this day for the abundant measure of genius you bestowed upon Richard of the family of this village. Oh Lord renew and revive our drooping faith this day.' It was a very moving prayer.

Stuart Burrows, the Welsh tenor, had flown in from the United States for the service. He gave an inspired rendering of the hymn, *'Mi Glywaf Dyner Lais'*.

Then it was Kate's turn for a repeat of 'Do not go gentle into that good night.' 'I just read it,' she said simply, later. And so she did; but it was the more effective for that.

The main address was given by the 'family' minister, Eric Williams: 'He was a man of colour – he was a colourful man,' he said in a manner worthy of the best sermons. The Richard of old would have imitated him with relish. More predictable epithets followed – 'a legendary institution' 'a man of genius' 'a superstar'. But Eric spoke the words with such naturalness and sincerity that we all welcomed hearing them again. He spoke warmly of Cis, who was looking steadfastly up at him.

'We owe a great deal of debt to Cis – and to the late Elfed – don't we? – for nurturing this young boy.' And he paid tribute to Richard's humility: 'He remembered the little things. And he never forgot his roots, the rock that he was hewn from.'

I was sitting next to Valerie Douglas. At this point she nudged me and whispered urgently: 'David, I think you ought to go up to the pulpit and tell the congregation that although Richard was buried in Switzerland, his heart and spirit will always be in Wales.'

I was taken aback. It was a nice thought, but I did not feel it was appropriate for me to jump up and make a statement of any kind. And now Eric was quoting a letter, one of the hundreds the family had received already since Richard's death.

Dear Burton Family,

You may have lost a brother and a famous actor but the Ibos of Biafra, Eastern Nigeria, have lost a god.

For these starving children, and all men and women whom Richard helped in their hour of need, will remember him for ever and ever. After all, man is God to man, and that's how we saw him.

May the Buddha and the mighty angels of the black man guide him to peace.

Love from an Ibo

Kent St George

234

Finally we sang the second hymn, the gentler, more thoughtful one '*Pwy sy'n dwyn a Brenin adref*?' and filed out again into the blaze of sun and camera lenses, through to the vestry where the scuttling village women were putting the final touches to the tea. They hovered about anxiously throughout the proceedings, making sure everyone was constantly supplied with a loaded plate and brimming cup. Again there was that feeling of unreality we had experienced in the very different setting of the Café de la Gare in Céligny.

Afterwards the front-seaters withdrew once more to Hilda's, which seemed to have an infinite capacity for absorption (though it must have reached saturation point by now). There were little bursts of humour and poignancy: a pair of neighbouring women created one by putting on their party piece by special request – a comic dialogue to which Richard had more than once given enthusiastic audience during his Pontrhydyfen visits. Kate was called to the middle room to watch. Everyone scanned her face anxiously for the response. But she was smiling and relaxed. It was all right.

Brook spent the time in the house looking slightly disorientated. For twenty-five years or more he had shadowed, shopped for, supported his own supporter. Now what? He wandered about hailing Kate from time to time with confidential cheeriness: 'Katie! Katie!' But beneath the bright front there was a chasm – a huge gaping hole in his life.

For Sally that chasm was there as well, of course, and it must have been more intense, though she had spent a relatively short time with Richard. She and Brook leant on each other for support.

It was a long day, that funeral-without-a-body, and as the August afternoon wore on the polite clusters fragmented and began to splinter. We men looked and felt restless; the women, most of them, were exhausted. The traditional division took place; the men set off for the Pontrhydyfen Rugby Club, and the women, in a burst of reaction to the dainty cakes and sandwiches, made themselves chip butties and put their feet up at last. Edie's children made a little pilgrimage to the family grave. The photographers, who had spent the afternoon hunched in shrinking puddles of sunlight in the street, sprang briefly into activity when the last of the rich and famous left Hilda's house. Megan took up her host position in the terraced doorway and thanked them all for coming. One more memorial gathering was over. I drove home through the now deserted streets and at once wrote to the chief constable and my former colleagues – to thank them for their part in the smooth organisation of the day. They had cordoned off the streets and cleared the traffic so much more efficiently than their Swiss counterparts, I informed them.

But even in the saddest times, there is humour. Elizabeth, saddened by the cause of this particular visit, nonetheless thoroughly enjoyed staying at Hilda's house in Pontrhydyfen later that month. The bathroom and toilet however were situated downstairs adjoining the kitchen – not really convenient for the bedrooms upstairs, so chamber pots were placed underneath each bed. The next morning Elizabeth came downstairs, chamberpot in hand. 'Oh,' said Hilda when she saw Elizabeth emerging with her burden. 'Oh, for goodness sake, don't throw it away. I shall bottle it and sell it.' Elizabeth laughed heartily.

There was time to breathe, at least, between the Pontrhydyfen memorial service and the Thanksgiving Service, as it was called, at the London church of St Martin-in-the-Fields. This was an occasion: a time to be wholeheartedly proud of Richard. And all my brothers and sisters were to go – even Will, dying slowly of cancer up in Edinburgh. We doubted until the last minute that he would make the journey. But when the day arrived – it was Thursday, 30 August, 1984 – there he was, grimly determined, proudly climbing out of the taxi into the maelstrom of people, cameras, notebooks, microphones thrust at you at every turn.

There was something majestic about this event. In Céligny we had been shocked and numbed by comparison, in Pontrhydyfen nostalgic and tearful. Now we held our heads high with pride as we marched up the imposing steps of the great church. We knew very well that a good proportion of the thronging crowd outside had come to catch a glimpse of Richard's three wives, Sally, Elizabeth and Susan, coming to the service. There was even a rumour that Sybil was to be among the guests. (She did not in fact come.) But we also knew that the majority of the congregation and a substantial number of onlookers had come to pay tribute to a great actor, a universal entertainer – our brother.

I politely moved away from the microphone and its human attendant which had jointly monitored my progress through the foyer, brought yet another interview to a close, and followed my family up to the front of the church, past the packed rows of ticket holders. My nieces Siân and Megan, who lived in London, were helping the ushers with the seating arrangements. Siân was looking just a shade anxious about the forthcoming reading – she was to be one of the participants in the service. We sat close to the front, on the right side of the aisle. Shortly after our arrival there was a flurry of excitement and Elizabeth appeared, an impassive exterior concealing great anxiety (but not from those who knew her), her hair drawn back severely in a black turban. Coming in alone, she was welcomed by the family and shown to a seat near Siân and Cis. She tapped Kate, sitting just in front of her, on the shoulder and they embraced warmly.

Meanwhile, Sally had come up closely flanked by Brook Williams. They moved straight to the front and took their seats just to the left of the aisle. Susan Hunt was already in her place a little further back. Nothing untoward about this seating arrangement, or so we all thought. Sally cast several swift sidelong glances at Elizabeth, who looked steadfastly to the front.

The service began. Although we were in the heart of the English capital, the Welsh atmosphere was quickly established with the familiar and beautiful harp solo – 'Dafydd-y-Garreg Wen' (David of the White Rock) – played by Sioned Williams. The hymns throughout the service were a blend of English and Welsh – 'Guide me O Thou Great Jehovah', to the tune of *Cwm Rhondda*; 'Jerusalem', the family favourite; '*O Iesu Mawr*' sung lustily by the Rhos Cwm Tawe Choir, with our enthusiastic support.

The readings were impressive – Siân and Kate were in the illustrious company of Sir John Gielgud and Paul Scofield.

Stuart Burrows was with us again, singing a Bizet aria. But the true tone of the occasion was irrevocably and somewhat irreverently set by Emlyn Williams, who gave the main address. I still remember the feeling of relief almost as soon as he got started, and it was clear he was not going to be heavy.

After the inevitable solemnity of the funeral and memorial service, it was refreshing to hear Richard being talked about with such affectionate humour. I was so taken with Emlyn's speech that I quote it here in full:

Richard Burton by Emlyn Williams

Our dear Richard . . . Or, the way I used to start a letter to you – *Annwyl* Richard . . . Our dear Richard, here we all are, joining Sally and Kate and all your family in thinking about you, and talking about you. Yes, I can see the old twinkle in the eye, as if to say – 'Well, now that the smoke's clearing away . . . what are you going to say about me? Not going to be easy, is it?' How often, in the past three weeks, have my thoughts gone back to the first time you and I met, forty-one years ago next month! We spoke of that first meeting, you remember, at our last meeting, in New York a year ago . . .

It was one evening in Cardiff, in 1943, the Sandringham Hotel, where I was interviewing possible Welsh-speaking actors for a new play. After a dismal procession of no-goods, an older man introduced himself as the schoolmaster who had written about a pupil, apparently a promising amateur. He beckoned, and the pupil stepped forward: a boy of seventeen, of startling beauty, and quiet intelligence. He looked – as very special human beings tend to look at that age – he looked imperishable.

I asked young Jenkins what was the last part he had played, at school. The answer came clear as a bell, 'Professor Higgins in *Pygmalion*.' I was later to realise the added incongruity of that: the schoolmaster – the unique Phil Burton – was, at the time, playing a real-life Higgins to a markedly male Eliza.

At rehearsals in London, it was interesting to watch the boy work, for he did something very rare: he drew attention by not claiming it. He played his part with the perfect simplicity needed, and offstage was quietly pleasant – not shy, just . . . reserved – except for the sudden smile, which – there is no other word for it – glowed. He didn't talk much. I think he was a bit self-conscious about his accent, and the need to work on it – it's a phase actors sometimes go through. But inside there, there was humour. A twinkle in the eye, no doubt about it. One evening, as he and I walked away from a late rehearsal, I asked what was the book he was carrying. 'Dylan Thomas'. I just knew the name. 'He is a great poet.' Then he suddenly stopped, and recited. The words resounded through the blackout of the deserted street: Upper St Martin's Lane, just up the road. 'They shall have stars at elbow and foot . . .'

I did not say to myself, in a flash, 'This lad will be famous!' But it did occur to me that here was more than a well-graced adolescent who could speak lines naturally, this was a 'voice'. And behind the 'voice' a mind which, like my own, was in love with the English language.

Then I asked him, in an avuncular manner – I was thirty-seven – if his digs were all right, and was he behaving himself in London? He said he was. Even then I doubted it.

Oh, the English language – let me touch, in passing, on something which – up till now – has only been known by those closest to him. His devotion to spoken English has over the last years, extended to words on paper. Steadily, unobtrusively, he has been writing. Diaries? Autobiography? Time will tell, and may surprise. Anyway . . .

Back to spoken English. After the war, five years of invaluable stage experience, with in between, several films. Then in the early fifties, the young actor's life was taken over by Shakespeare, at 'Stratford' and the 'Old Vic'. They were salaries you couldn't save on, but gruelling hard work built up to triumph.

My former school-teacher, Miss Cooke, was curious about this second Welsh peasant who had been seduced into the theatre and I presented him to her. Richard was on his best behaviour. But she did say afterwards, 'He's going to do well, what's more he's go the devil in him. You haven't.' I felt commonplace.

Then – America! The Movies, Capital 'M', and – and even bigger capital M – the money! The dollars poured in.

Then – 1962. Which means we have to touch lightly – no names mentioned – on a certain Roman – Egyptian epic. (I nearly said 'a Roman-Elizabethan Epic') . . . Gossip blossomed into sensation. Mind you, it is my duty here to emphasise that, at the time, nobody could have guessed that what looked like an irresponsible escapade, was to mature into a long, deep, important relationship.

But at the time all the public knew was that – as a romantic novelist might have put it – Cupid's dart had hit both targets. And set the Nile on fire. And the Tiber. Even the Thames sizzled, a bit. I have an idea that the South-Wales River Tawe kept its cool.

Well, as the scandal grew and grew, I – oh, Richard, you and I have talked of this so often since, and it's so long ago it can come out now – I remembered that I had introduced you to Sybil, and that I was godfather to little Kate: I flew to Rome. Once again the heavy uncle, but this time on a mission. A romance-puncturing mission. Sitting in the plane, I did remind myself that I was playing a very bad part, was miscast, and had to pay my own fare.

I was met by our delinquent friend, and as he drove me to the studios, we talked of this and that, but not of it. Then, bump – he stopped the car and looked at me. I was about to embark on my lecture, carefully prepared, when he said – I shall never forget it – he said, very calmly, 'Dwi am briodi'r eneth 'ma.' Which is Welsh for 'I am going to marry this girl.' Dwi am briodi'r eneth 'ma.

There was, in the green eyes, the twinkle – but a mischievous devilish twinkle, Miss Cooke had been right. And the fact that he'd said it in Welsh proved, to my Celtic instinct, that he was going to marry this girl. Though even a Celtic instinct could hardly foresee that he was going to do it *twice*.

After Rome, the dollars no longer poured. They cascaded. Up to the waist he was. Having started life as a simple child of the valleys – the smallest luxuries out of his reach – Richard Burton 'Super-Star' found himself, like an orphan with a sweet tooth, let loose in the biggest candy-store in the world – Hollywood!

He spent lavishly. And the more he spent, the more he earned. And the Media – 'media', what a useful word, the plural of 'medium', however did we manage without it, covers everything – the Media began to mutter. As they donned the unsuitable mantles of the old Welsh-Calvinist preachers, they hinted at Mammon, and the Mess of Pottage, and the golden calf: omitting to note that while the 'Super-Star' enjoyed getting rich – who wouldn't have, who wasn't a hermit? – it was a joy he shared with a beloved family, with his friends and with countless acquaintances and causes in need of help. He was bountiful.

I remember, in Manhattan, a glimmering party, where I sat next to the elder sister who brought Richard up. He had taken Cis out shopping, and she looked stunning; she could have been a film beauty who had retired into New York society. I complimented her on her dress. She looked round – the stars were hanging from the chandeliers, Danny Kay, Gina Lollobrigida, Sinatra, fabulous. Cis looked round and said, 'Well, Emlyn, I thought I'd put on my Sunday-best for them all.'

No need to go into the rest of an eventful saga, with its ups and downs. Many downs, because the man had a passion for life, and where there is passion, there has to be – sooner or later – trouble. Side by side with the light, the dark; behind exaltation. . . . melancholy. No need to go into all that, because the Media was there, keeping the world up to date on every detail, true or false.

(To be fair to them, Richard, you sure did supply them with copy! You with the cheerfully cynical attitude of the quick-witted public figure trapped in limelight – 'If they want something quotable, here goes, with salt and pepper.' And out would shoot some outrageous quip, often to our detriment. But quotable.)

The ups and downs. . . . Permit me to administer a reproach. Concerning the recent obituaries and commentaries.

They're funny things, obituaries. When something like this happens, a bolt from the blue, within a couple of hours the newspapers are swarming with meticulously detailed judgments; and we all think – 'How uncannily quick – brilliant!'

The fact is that most of the Obits, for months or even years, have been lurking in cold storage along shelves in Fleet Street, at the ready for. . . . I was going to say 'starting gun' but what I mean, of course, is the opposite. . . . For any of us who have done anything public, the posthumous verdicts, signed and sealed, lie in wait. Long before curtain is down. We can only hope the notices won't be too bad. And at least we have the comforting thought that we ourselves won't be tempted to rush out and buy all the papers. Richard's notices have been. . . . mixed. Oh, much emotional affection, some of it touching, some toppling over into the maudlin. But when it came to the career. . . . not much emphasis on the ups, concentration on the downs. So I'd like, quickly, to set the record a bit straighter, credits versus debits.

For instance – while there has been harping on physical indulgence, has there been any mention of the crippling illness which cut short a distinguished stage appearance in *Camelot*? What of the days and nights of pain, endured with stubborn fortitude?

His mistakes. Of course he made mistakes – he has said so – we all make mistakes, unless at the age of ten we retire into a retreat, for life! Of course some of the films were trash, again he said so – but has there been – apart from a couple of serious articles – has there been any appreciation of such pictures as. . . .

Look Back In Anger; *The Taming Of The Shrew*; *The Night Of The Iguana*; *Under Milk Wood*; *The Comedians*; *The Spy Who Came In From The Cold*; *Becket*; *Anne Of The Thousand Days*; *Equus*; *Who's Afraid of Virginia Woolf?*, and quite recently, the immensely bold *Wagner* with Olivier, Gielgud and Richardson – trash?

Moreover, while the film only just completed has been mentioned by name, well it has to be – has anybody remarked that *1984*, with a subject infinitely disturbing – is patently a venture worthy of respect? And is it not heartening to reflect that all these performances are permanent? Which leaves. . . . the accusation that he turned his back on the serious theatre, in order to worship that wicked old mammon. No salute to three returns to the same 'serious theatre'. First, at the Playhouse Oxford, *Doctor Faustus*. No slouch Chris Marlowe. Or Neville Coghill. . . .

Then two theatre gambles, which he won. First, his appearance in that fine play *Equus*, on Broadway, where two stars had already been successful in the same part. Second again on Broadway, at the height of the super-star combo. . . . *Hamlet*, directed by Gielgud, a run which broke John Barrymore's record.

Finally, no mention of the fact that when this sadness hit us, the man was in fine shape. Richard was himself again. Which meant there was a good chance that he might, in a year or two, fulfil a dream, of his and of others: a return to the English poetry which he cherished with all his Welsh heart. As Prospero. As Lear.

After that, I don't much like going back to his 'notices', but – two brisk quotes, and I have done. Very brisk, they are one word each. At least two journalists had the cheek to tap out, on their typewriters the word 'failure'. Well,. . . . if a man is a failure who, on leaving this planet, monopolizes the front page of every national newspaper throughout the Western World – then quite a few mortals would give anything to be such a failure.

And what of the other word, which has recurred so often that it has become a cliché – the word 'flawed', f-l-a-w-e-d, – 'a flawed

242

career' and so on. But this word happens to imply a compliment. Because it takes a precious stone to be flawed. And we have here. . . . a precious stone.

We thank you, *ein annwyl* Richard, for your shining gifts, for your love of your devoted wife, of your family, of your friends, of your country, and of life. And thank you for. . . . that twinkle in the eye. I can only think at this moment, of Upper St Martin's Lane. A boy of seventeen, standing in the black-out, spouting poetry. Imperishable. And death. . . . shall have no dominion.

* * * * *

As Emlyn was talking, warming to his theme, pausing theatrically for effect, I looked around me. Not to gauge the response of the congregation at large; it was obvious from their appreciative laughter that they were enjoying it all. No, it was Sally I was wondering about – and Elizabeth and Cis and the rest of the family. Elizabeth and Cis, to my relief, were smiling when I looked at them. Sally, sitting next to Emlyn's son, Brook, looked impassive. No doubt she would give her reaction later.

Perhaps the most emotional moment in the whole service occurred when the vast auditorium of the church was suddenly filled with Richard's unmistakable voice. We all knew his recording of Donne's 'Death be not proud' was included in the programme. But an audible gasp rippled through the congregation as the first words reached us. Elizabeth was almost overcome and turned to Siân at her side for support. Like everyone else, I was immensely moved. It was a fitting climax to the thanksgiving service, and whatever our individual beliefs concerning the eternity of the spirit, it was a forceful reminder that Richard's interpretive gifts were going to be much more than just a memory.

After the joy and serenity and laughter of the service, it was back to the bedlam of traffic, crowds, journalists and cameras. We were in some confusion because originally we had expected to go to the Dorchester, Richard's long-time London home, for the upmarket equivalent of tea and cakes in the vestry. But it seemed all plans were changed when Elizabeth turned up at the Dorchester, which had of course been her London 'corner' as well. Sally promptly moved herself and the reception venue to the

243

Savoy. Elizabeth and Susan were also invited and both came. Luckily no journalists were present to witness the unusual gathering of ex-wives and widow eyeing each other uneasily over the cocktails and canapés. Susan Hunt seemed the most relaxed of the three. But Elizabeth looked taut and nervous and smoked almost continuously – 'ten for each lung,' she joked. Sally seemed both inaccessible and dreamy.

After I had warmly congratulated Emlyn Williams on his speech, Sally came up to me and asked me what I thought of it. 'Brilliant,' I said, deciding that honesty was the best policy in the circumstances.

Sally was clearly not so enthusiastic. I later discovered that the 'Elizabethan' references had not gone down too well with some others in the family either. Susan was discreetly silent. But there were a number of confidential mutterings beneath the surface affability of the festive atmosphere, where glasses were refilled well before they were empty. Aware of Sally's fragility, we were all careful to be tactful, and not to spend too much time with Elizabeth during the Savoy reception.

Everyone floated sociably about in an atmosphere of conviviality that convinced most people. Sally warmed to her theme as she talked of the visits she had made already as Richard's widow. 'I've just left Philip Burton in Key West, Florida,' she said. 'It was great to talk to him; he was so welcoming . . .'

From somewhere among us, the brothers and sisters, a feeling of hollowness began to emerge. This would surely be the last of the big gatherings, the final link with the great warm ebullient nostalgic reunions Richard loved to regale us with. The last link with Richard himself, in a sense. Even his grave was too far away to visit.

People began to drift away from the reception. There had been no speeches, no official beginnings or endings. Sally, still in a world apart, was one of the drifters.

But we had reckoned without Elizabeth.

Back at our hotel, the Cumberland, later in the day, we had a telephone call inviting us to join her at the Dorchester for dinner. This was a wonderful reunion, a feast in all senses. We celebrated Richard's memory and Elizabeth's generosity with storytelling, nostalgia and song. With an enthusiasm we thought was lost a few hours before, we sang all Richard's favourite Welsh hymns. Elizabeth joined in. She sang, with impeccable pronunciation, the lovely song '*Ar Lan y Mor*' (At the sea-shore red roses grow) which Richard had taught her in that quiet Rome villa in 1966. We were all moved. It seemed Elizabeth understood and shared our need to gather in this way, this curious mingling of mourning and celebration. We were invited again by Elizabeth the next night. And impulsively she thought of another idea: would we all join her at the Dorchester for the weekend of St David's Day, 1 March, the following year, 1985? We returned to Wales, feeling decidedly less hollow, back to the normality of our everyday lives.

As the months passed and Elizabeth's invitation was not confirmed, we put it out of our minds to avoid disappointment. But she had not forgotten. In early February a letter was sent out to each of us from Marjorie Lee at the Dorchester and long-time friend of both Richard and Elizabeth. We were all invited to spend the weekend of St David's Day at the Dorchester, with our families, as Elizabeth's guests. The first big gathering was for dinner on the Friday evening. Elizabeth, true to her reputation, was late. But when she did eventually appear, all was warmth and cheer and singing and nostalgia. No expense was spared.

A bond between us and Elizabeth was now firmly established. At Christmas in 1985 she sent us each a beautiful white wool 'throw' embossed with our names. At each subsequent Christmas a magnificent sumptuous Fortnum and Mason hamper has been delivered to our doors.

Elizabeth's gestures to us of generosity and support were not purely altruistic – it seemed she got as much out of the contact as we did. Sally, of course, was Richard's widow, and everyone including Elizabeth respected that fact. But with Elizabeth there was a shared history which fell into a special category of its own. It was as if her bond with us enabled her to maintain and strengthen her link with Richard after his death.

At times she was overcome by powerful waves of nostalgia. One such time occurred in September 1989. Elizabeth telephoned us from her villa in Gstaad, Switzerland. She had just visited Richard's grave in Celigny and was filled with melancholy. Could she come and visit us in Pontrhydyfen? Hilda's home, as always, was assumed to be the base, and Elizabeth was given a warm welcome. Once again she came up with an idea for another London reunion: lunch at Claridge's the following month.

October 1989 witnessed the gathering of the Jenkins family at yet another elegant and luxurious venue. We were a slightly reduced crowd. Will had died in 1985; Cis was not feeling strong enough to attend; Graham was absent. The publication of his book about Richard had upset us and had caused a temporary rift in the family.

We were suitably impressed by Claridge's, with its palatial entrance and door. The staff, immaculate in tails and black dresses, led us to the French salon. We were there promptly at 12.30 for lunch at one o'clock, though of course we had no expectation of Elizabeth herself appearing until much later. She had not changed. She eventually made her entrance about an hour late. Strangely enough, although I am a great one for punctuality myself and highly intolerant of lateness, especially persistent lateness in others, I never feel irritated by Elizabeth. Even Richard who was also, as he put it, ferociously over-punctual, was remarkably tolerant of this particular trait of hers.

Sitting in exquisite comfort at Claridge's, we were plied with champagne and indulged in a customary bout of Welsh song while we waited. Finally in she came with all the grace and elegance of a queen. She greeted us individually with great warmth and genuine delight at being with us again.

Predictably, we enjoyed an excellent lunch. I had decided in advance to make a special contribution myself this time. Many tributes had been paid to Elizabeth over the years and it was high time, I thought, that we added a little something of our own. So, taking Elizabeth for once completely by surprise, I delivered a little speech to her on behalf of the family. In it I pointed out her beauty, generosity (especially to little Maria, the child she adopted) and kindness to us, Richard's kin.

Elizabeth was clearly moved. Hilda and Cassie told me later that the tears were running down her face as I spoke. The bond was, and is, very strong between us. We are, as she has often declared, Richard's history and living heritage. Through us, in a sense, she

246

has access to a part of him – and through her of course we have the same thing. But she also responds to us, and we to her, in our own right.

Perhaps here would be the place to thank Richard, too. Richard brought so many good things into the lives of his brothers and sisters, indeed of all those he cared for. He gave unstintingly to life in a thousand ways.

Let Shakespeare have the last word:

They say best men are moulded out of faults,
And, for the most, become much more the better,
For being a little bad.

Epilogue

The family had shared moments of great joy and happiness with Richard; then there had been those sad, commemorative occasions which brought us together again in his name – the funeral, the memorial services. It is fitting, however, that the very last occasion on which some of us gathered in his name was a moment of pride and remembered affection.

On 22 November 1990 Hilda, Cassie and I were invited to the première of the television adaptation of Richard's book *A Christmas Story*, held at the Aberystwyth Film Festival. Verdun was too ill to go and for Cis, eighty-five by then, the journey would have been exhausting. So the three of us represented the family.

It was a moment for nostalgia and proud reflection. The film brought back vivid and poignant memories, both of Richard's childhood with Cis, and of our own motherless plight.

The reason this particular Christmas was stamped indelibly on Richard's memory is that it was disconcertingly different from others in his early years. And the real subject of the book is not Christmas, not the secrecy surrounding Rhianon's birth. Scarcely mentioned, but always present, is the relationship between Richard and Cis. When she, for the first Christmas in his life, became unavailable to him, however briefly, no one and nothing could fill the gap. He was not only 'immensely proud of her'; he loved her with a fierce passion that determined the course of his emotional life.

'It wasn't until thirty years later,' he says in the book, 'when I saw her in another woman, that I realised I had been searching for her all my life.' This was a reference to Elizabeth; the book had been written in 1964, when his relationship with her was at its highest point.

All this and much more came back to us as we watched the film – a moving tribute to both Richard and Cis, the woman who in a real sense launched his life.

Index

251

252